LONDON AND THE ENGLISH ECONOMY,

1500-1700

F.J. FISHER

LONDON AND THE
ENGLISH ECONOMY, 1500-1700

F.J. FISHER

EDITED BY

P.J. CORFIELD

AND N.B. HARTE

THE HAMBLEDON PRESS

LONDON   AND   RONCEVERTE

Published by The Hambledon Press, 1990

102 Gloucester Avenue, London NW1 8HX (U.K.)

309 Greenbrier Avenue, Ronceverte WV 24970 (U.S.A.)

ISBN 1 85285 025 X

British Library Cataloguing in Publication Data

Fisher, F.J. (Frederick Jack), *1908-1988*
    London and the English economy, 1500-1700
    1. England. Economic conditions, 1500-1700
    I. Title II. Corfield, Penelope, *1944-*
    III. Harte, Negley, *1943-   330.942'05*

Library of Congress Cataloging-in-Publication Data

Fisher, F.J. (Frederick Jack), 1908-1988.
    London and the English economy, 1500-1700/
    F.J. Fisher; edited by P.J. Corfield and N.B. Harte.
    Includes bibliographical references and index.
    1. London (England) – Economic conditions.
    2. England – Economic conditions.
    3. England – Economic conditions – 17th century.
    I. Corfield, P.J.   II. Harte, N.B. III. Title
    HC258. L6F57   1990
    330.9421 – dc20   90-39162 CIP

Printed on acid-free paper and bound in Great
Britain by W.B.C. Ltd., Maesteg

Contents

Preface

F.J. Fisher (1908-88) was an economic historian of remarkably powerful influence. This book brings together his major essays with new assessments of his impact as a scholar and teacher.

Part I contains an analysis of F.J. Fisher as an economic historian by P.J. Corfield, and a collection of tributes to his memory, edited by N.B. Harte, who has also compiled the list of Professor Fisher's published writings.

Part II reprints ten essays by Professor Fisher, which are collected together and presented here with kind permission from Mrs. Barbara Fisher. We are most grateful for her approval and help, as well as that of Matthew Fisher and Mrs. Theresa Rickett.

For permission to reprint these essays we are grateful to the editors of the *Economic History Review* (for essays 3, 4, 5, 7 and 10), to the Royal Historical Society (for essay 6), to the editor of *Economica* and Basil Blackwell Ltd (for essay 8), to the Cambridge University Press (for essay 9), to Edward Arnold Ltd (for essay 11) and to Kluwer Academic Publishers of Dordrecht (for essay 12).

The photograph of Professor Fisher was taken at the Economic History Society's conference at the University of Hull in 1977 by Professor Barry Supple, and we are grateful to him for his permission to reproduce it here.

P.J.C.
N.B.H.

The Published Writings of F.J. Fisher

Essays reprinted here are indicated by an asterisk

'Some Experiments in Company Organisation in the Early Seventeenth Century', *Econ. Hist. Rev.*, 4 (1933), pp. 177-94.*

'The Development of the London Food Market, 1540-1640', *Econ. Hist. Rev.*, 5 (1935), pp. 46-64. Reprinted in E.M. Carus-Wilson, (ed.), *Essays in Economic History*, I (London: Edward Arnold 1954), pp. 135-51.*

A Short History of the Worshipful Company of Horners (London: George Becker, for private circulation, 1936), 138 pp.

(with Amabel Williams-Ellis) *A History of English Life: Political and Social*, 4 vols, 124 pp., 136 pp., 169 pp., 165 pp. (London: Methuen 1936). 2nd ed., 1939; 3rd ed. (revised), 1953; 2nd ed. (sic) (revised), 1962.

(ed.) *The State of England Anno Dom. 1600 By Sir Thomas Wilson* in Camden Society 3rd ser., 52, *Camden Miscellany*, 16 (1936), vii + 47 pp.

'List of Sources for the History of the Existing London Companies' in George Unwin, *The Gilds and Companies of London*, 3rd ed. (London: Allen & Unwin 1938), pp. 372-89.

(with Amabel Williams-Ellis) *A First History of English Life*, 4 vols., 563 pp. (London: Methuen 1940, vols I and II; 1949, vols III and IV). 2nd ed. (revised), 1962.

'The Economic Background of Eighteenth-Century Literature' in H.V.D. Dyson and J. Butt (eds.), *Augustans and Romantics, 1689-1830* (London: Cresset Press 1940), pp. 139-53. 2nd ed., 1950; 3rd ed., 1961.

'Commercial Trends and Policy in Sixteenth-Century England', *Econ. Hist. Rev.*, 10 (1940), pp. 95-117. Reprinted in Carus-Wilson (ed.), op. cit., pp. 152-72.*

'The Development of London as a Centre of Conspicuous Consumption in the Sixteenth and Seventeenth Centuries', *Trans. R. Hist. Soc.*, 4th ser., 30 (1948), pp. 37-50. Reprinted in E.M. Carus-Wilson (ed.), *Essays in Economic History*, II (London: Edward Arnold 1962), pp. 197-207 and in I.R. Christie (ed.), *Essays in Modern History* (London: Macmillan 1968), pp. 75-90.*

'Economic Systems Past and Present' in W. Arthur Lewis *et al.*, *Economics: Man and his Material Resources* (London: Odhams Press 1949), pp. 117-42.

'London's Export Trade in the Early Seventeenth Century', *Econ. Hist.*

Rev., 2nd ser., 3 (1950), pp. 151-61. Reprinted in W.E. Minchinton (ed.), *The Growth of English Overseas Trade in the Seventeenth and Eighteenth Centuries* (London: Methuen 1969), pp. 64-77.*

'The Sixteenth and Seventeenth Centuries: The Dark Ages in English Economic History?', *Economica*, new ser., 24 (1957), pp. 2-18. Reprinted in N.B. Harte (ed.), *The Study of Economic History: Collected Inaugural Lectures, 1893-1970* (London: Frank Cass 1971), pp. 181-200.*

(with R. Firth and D.G. MacRae) 'Social Implications of Technological Change as regards Patterns and Models' in C. Balandier, (ed.), *Social, Economic and Technological Change: A Theoretical Approach* (Paris: International Social Science Council 1958), pp. 261-93.

(with J.R. Williams and R.M. Titmuss) *R.H. Tawney: A Portrait by Several Hands* (London: Shenval Press 1960), 35 pp.

(ed.), *Essays in the Economic and Social History of Tudor and Stuart England in Honour of R.H. Tawney* (Cambridge University Press 1961), 235 pp.

'Tawney's Century' in ibid., pp. 1-14. Reprinted in M.E. Falkus (ed.), *Readings in the History of Economic Growth* (Nairobi: Oxford University Press 1968), pp. 51-61.*

'Influenza and Inflation in Tudor England', *Econ. Hist. Rev.*, 2nd ser., 18 (1965), pp. 120-9.*

(ed.), *Calendar of the Manuscripts of the Rt. Hon. Lord Sackville of Knole, Sevenoaks, Kent: II, Letters Relating to Lionel Cranfield's Business Overseas, 1597-1612*. Historical Manuscripts Commission, LXXX (London: HMSO 1966), 267 pp.

'The Growth of London' in E.W. Ives (ed.), *The English Revolution, 1600-1660* (London: Edward Arnold 1968), pp. 76-86.*

'Rejoinder' (to J.D. Gould's 'F.J. Fisher on Influenza and Inflation in Tudor England'), *Econ. Hist. Rev.*, 2nd ser., 21 (1968), pp. 368-70.

'London as an "Engine of Economic Growth"' in J.S. Bromley and E.H. Kossman (eds.), *Britain and the Netherlands, IV: Metropolis, Dominion and Province* (The Hague: Martinus Nijhoff 1971), pp. 3-16.*

PART ONE

1

F.J. Fisher and the Dialectic of Economic History

P.J. Corfield

F.J. Fisher's work as an economic and social historian began as a student at the London School of Economics in the later 1920s, when the subject was just gaining momentum as a separate field of study.[1] He often recalled it as an exciting era. Everything was yet to be pioneered and all discoveries seemed fresh and important. His own first degree was in history, which he always praised as an excellent grounding, but the vitality and scope of the new specialism made it an irresistible field for research.

While certainly not a Marxist, he shared a Marxist awareness of the significance of economic and social factors. He viewed economic history not as a hermetic discipline but as a key element that needed to be integrated into wider interpretations.[2] Indeed, throughout his career, his lectures and conversation displayed a scintillating breadth of information; and he was very quick to absorb new concepts from related fields of study.

Influential among tutors at the LSE was Eileen Power,[3] whose

Note: Personal tributes to Jack Fisher are recorded in Chapter 2. These comments therefore concentrate on his approach to economic history, with thanks especially to Donald Coleman, Walter Elkan, Barbara Fisher, Negley Harte, Barry Supple and Jay Winter for references and comments on these comments.

Fisher's essays are cited in numerical sequence as printed in Part II, pp.43-198; full publication details are listed separately in the Bibliography, pp.ix-x.

All works cited in the footnotes that follow are published in Britain, unless otherwise specified.

[1] In 1926 he went as an undergraduate to the London School of Economics, where the Economic History Society held its inaugural meeting that same year. Publication of the *Economic History Review* followed in 1927: see T.C. Barker, 'The Beginnings of the Economic History Society', *Economic History Review*, 2nd ser. 30 (1977), pp. 12-14; and N.B. Harte, 'Trends in Publications on the Economic and Social History of Great Britain and Ireland, 1925-74', ibid., pp. 40-41.

[2] This meant that he also shared the later disappointment when economic history became more introverted and technical in the 1970s. For a full critique by Fisher's close friend and former pupil, see D.C. Coleman, *History and the Economic Past: An Account of the Rise and Decline of Economic History in Britain* (1987); earlier prefigured in Coleman's *What has Happened to Economic History?: An Inaugural Lecture* (1972).

[3] Eileen Power (1889-1940), Lecturer (1921) and later Professor of Economic History (1931) at the LSE, was author of *Medieval People* (1924) and *Medieval Women* (ed. M.M. Postan, 1975); she also edited with R.H. Tawney the staple *Tudor Economic Documents*, 3 vols. (1924).

magnetic and elegant lectures were much admired. But, above all, his mentor was R.H. Tawney, some thirty years his senior, to whom he always remained deeply devoted. When Fisher was subsequently appointed as a Lecturer at the School, Tawney and he worked harmoniously together. They shared a common intellectual unorthodoxy as well as common research interests in Tudor and Stuart economic history. For example, Tawney's celebrated 1941 article on 'The Rise of the Gentry, 1558-1640' acknowledged Fisher's help in counting the sales of gentry manors – in what proved to be a much-contested technique for assessing English social mobility before the Civil Wars.[4]

Nonetheless, there was a very marked intellectual divergence between the two scholars. Tawney was a social philosopher – a theorist of Christian socialism – as well as an economic historian: the author not only of *The Agrarian Problem in the Sixteenth Century* (1912) and *Religion and the Rise of Capitalism* (1926) but also of *The Acquisitive Society* (1921) and *Equality* (1931).[5] It was an unusual multiple role, and one that few among his contemporaries or his successors have sought to emulate, as the academic world has become relentlessly more specialised. Among later historians, only E.P. Thompson has shown the same scope, as man of letters, as

---

[4] R.H. Tawney, 'The Rise of the Gentry, 1558-1640', *Economic History Review*, 11 (1941); reprinted in E.M. Carus-Wilson (ed.), *Essays in Economic History*, I (1954), pp. 173-206. F.J. Fisher supplied the case histories of some 2,500 gentry manors from seven counties between 1561 and 1640, as extracted from the relevant volumes of the *Victoria County History* (see Carus-Wilson, *Essays*, p. 192 fn. 59 and p. 202 fn. 90), while Tawney used a further 800 examples from another three counties for his final tabulation (*ibid.*, p. 174 fn. 3 and p. 204 fn. 97). Tawney's robust defence of his methods and conclusions was presented in 'A Postscript', *Economic History Review*, 2nd ser. 7 (1954), pp. 91-97, also reprinted in Carus-Wilson, *Essays*, pp. 206-14, including a recalculation of the data from Fisher's seven counties (*ibid.*, p. 210). For criticisms of this approach, see H.R. Trevor-Roper, 'The Gentry, 1540-1640', *Economic History Review*, Supplement I (1953), esp. pp. 4-8; and, with greater lethality, J.P. Cooper, 'The Counting of Manors', *Economic History Review*, 2nd ser. 8 (1956), pp. 377-89, reprinted in J.P. Cooper, *Land, Men and Beliefs: Studies in Early-Modern History* (ed. G.E Aylmer and J.S. Morrill, 1983), pp. 1-16: a note (*ibid.*, p. 7 fn. 18) indicates that Cooper had corresponded with Fisher about the composition of Tawney's data.

[5] R.H. Tawney (1880-1962), who was appointed to a personal chair in economic history at the LSE in 1931, had an extremely wide-ranging influence, in adult education, politics and civic philosophy, as well as in his subject specialism. For fruitful studies, see: J.R. Williams, R.M. Titmuss and F.J. Fisher, *R.H. Tawney: A Portrait by Several Hands* (1960), pp. 33; R. Terrill, *R.H. Tawney and his Times: Socialism as Fellowship* (1974); D. Reisman, *State and Welfare: Tawney, Galbraith and Adam Smith* (1982), pp. 19-130; A. Wright, *R.H. Tawney* (1987); and N. Dennis and A.H. Halsey, *English Ethical Socialism: Thomas More to R.H. Tawney* (1988), pp. 149-69, 184-98. Tawney's impact upon social policy is noted in R.M. Titmuss, 'Introduction' to R.H. Tawney, *Equality* (5th edn. 1964), pp. 9-24; and his historical essays sympathetically analysed by J.M. Winter, 'Introduction: Tawney as Historian' in J.M. Winter (ed.), *History and Society: Essays by R.H. Tawney* (1978), pp. 1-40; and in *idem*, 'Introduction: Tawney on Labour and Labour Movements' in J.M. Winter (ed.), *R.H. Tawney: The American Labour Movement and Other Essays* (1979), pp. ix-xxiv.

participant in the theoretical debates within the broad tradition of European Marxism, and as campaigner for nuclear disarmament.[6]

By contrast, Jack Fisher had no interest in contributing to civic philosophy, and was sceptical of ideology in any form, hence endorsing neither Christianity nor socialism. He was influenced by the left in the 1930s, but then and thereafter he kept his own political views very much to himself. He also enjoyed demolishing any uncritical slogans that were rashly uttered in his hearing. In the 1960s, for example, he frequently challenged the more euphoric nostrums of the revivified left. Naive Marxists, especially those who stressed 'the economic factor' without knowing any economics, found him a tough critic. But he remained ecumenical in his unorthodoxy. If he was not a stereotypic man of the left, nor was he a standard right-winger, either of old or new vintage.

Indeed, he willingly tendered his own trenchant analysis to historians of very different intellectual persuasions. To take three examples: as a young man in 1932 he acted as a vigilant proof-reader of J.U. Nef's classic study of capitalist industrial growth in sixteenth-century England, *The Rise of the British Coal Industry* (1932);[7] in the later 1930s, he gave detailed briefing on seventeenth-century social history and criticised the text of David Petegorsky's Left Book Club book on agrarian communism, *Left-Wing Democracy in the English Civil War: A Study of the Social Philosophy of Gerrard Winstanley* (1940);[8] and in 1962 F.J. Fisher and Olive Coleman were jointly thanked for 'much stimulus and invaluable criticism of the typescript' by their colleague, A.R. Bridbury, whose revisionist *Economic Growth: England in the Later Middle Ages* (1962) argued the case for economic expansion rather than decline or a 'crisis of feudalism' in the fifteenth century.[9]

In other words, Fisher was not by any means a straightforward Tawney 'disciple' but the Tawney legacy that he did enthusiastically accept was a dedication to the study of English economic and social history at the LSE;

[6] For a preliminary survey of Thompson's fusion of history, theory, and praxis, see B.D. Palmer, *The Making of E.P. Thompson: Marxism, Humanism and History* (Toronto, 1981). Thompson, a heterodox Marxist, is sometimes bizarrely caricatured by his critics as a crude economic determinist, but his own historical and theoretical writings have explicitly insisted upon the active role of social consciousness, as well as upon the pluralism of modern Marxism, stressing the bifurcation between the Stalinist and anti-Stalinist traditions: see esp. E.P. Thompson, 'The Poverty of Theory: Or, an Orrery of Errors' (1978) in *idem*, *The Poverty of Theory and Other Essays* (1978), pp. 380-84.

[7] Nef paid generous tribute to many helpers, especially to R.H. Tawney, and thanked his young proof-reader, F.J. Fisher, for his zeal, patience and 'valuable suggestions': J.U. Nef, *The Rise of the British Coal Industry* (1932), Vol. I, p. xiv.

[8] Petegorsky recorded warm thanks to Harold Laski, plus F.J. Fisher's assistance with 'scholarship and good nature in lengthy and frequent discussion': see D.W. Petegorsky, *Left-Wing Democracy in the English Civil War: A Study of the Social Philosophy of Gerrard Winstanley* (1940), p. 7.

[9] A.R. Bridbury, *Economic Growth: England in the Later Middle Ages* (1962), p. 8.

and it was there, as a researcher and teacher, rather than as an administrator or departmental empire-builder, that he exerted his immense influence.

With others of his generation, he contributed to the process whereby the new subject specialism was consolidated, professionalised, and advanced. That was not achieved by a single person or a single academic institution. But from the mid-1940s onwards, when he returned to the LSE after active war service, Jack Fisher was undoubtedly one of the most challenging figures in what was widely accepted as one of the key departments of economic history, staffed by eminent figures such as T.S. Ashton (who succeeded Power and preceded Fisher in the established chair in economic history), Eleanora Carus-Wilson, and Lance Beales. There was an atmosphere of excitement and expansion. Fisher's work as teacher, writer, and critic helped to give new rigour and new direction to the developing subject. His formidable intellect was undoubtedly feared by some as well as admired by many. But his analytical sharpness, in combination with his lack of pomposity and willingness to treat everyone on equal terms, made his style uniquely challenging.

The major intellectual influences upon him in turn came from the ferment of ideas – from both left and right – at the London School of Economics,[10] supplemented by his own wide reading, particularly in development economics, sociology, and social anthropology. His interests were eclectic. He was, for example, well versed in classical economic theory, which he thought essential training for economic historians; but he viewed economics as an analytical tool rather than as a satisfactory interpretation of human behaviour, being equally firm that economists should study the complexities of economic history. Instead he was particularly attracted by debates in the developing social sciences. Among LSE colleagues from those disciplines with whom he enjoyed friendly disputation were the anthropologist, Lucy Mair,[11] and the demographer,

[10] The London School of Economics – always more left-wing by reputation than in actuality – enjoyed considerable intellectual vitality in the post-war era, when a variety of subjects and approaches cross-fertilised each other: including the sceptical philosophy of Karl Popper, the economic liberalism of Friedrich von Hayek, the evolving traditions of welfarist Fabianism, the new insights of development economics, and the cultural pluralism of social anthropology. For the early years, see F. von Hayek, 'The London School of Economics, 1895-1945', *Economica*, new ser. 23 (1946), pp. 1-31. And for some flavour of the immediate post-war era, see J. Abse (ed.), *My LSE* (1977), esp. pp. 64-103 for essays by J.W.N. Watkins and Robert McKenzie, both subsequently Professors at the School; and pp. 104-62 for essays by R. Moody, J. Wheldon and B. Crick.

[11] L.P. Mair, whose mother had been Secretary of the School in the 1930s, was LSE Professor of Anthropology (1963) and author of *Studies in Applied Anthropology* (1957), *An Introduction to Social Anthropology* (1965), *Witchcraft* (1969) and *Marriage* (1971). For an appreciation, see J. Davis (ed.), *Choice and Change: Essays in Honour of Lucy Mair* (1974), pp. 1-6.

David Glass.[12] In general, however, it was notable that Fisher referred only very infrequently to his own intellectual sources and development, remarking that scaffolding was to be pulled down once it had served its purpose. Nonetheless, his essays and his conversation between them have, in retrospect, supplied a number of clues.

Not surprisingly, he was attracted to iconoclasts. For example, among the early sociologists, he was impressed by Thorstein Veblen's acerbic analysis of conspicuous consumption in later nineteenth-century America,[13] which provided the spur for his own perceptive discussion of the role of consumption in the growth of sixteenth-century London.[14]

Among economists, he was particularly interested in those studying the new and topical subject of Third World experience of underdevelopment, or colonial history as it was termed before decolonisation. He enjoyed, for example, the spare logic of Hla Myint, another colleague at the LSE, whose analysis of development economics in 1964 highlighted the diversity of 'backwardness' and the problems involved in state planning for growth.[15] Here, theory was augmented by practice. During the Second World War, Jack Fisher – then in his mid-thirties – had been seconded from the RAF to the post of deputy economic and financial adviser to the Minister of State in Egypt. It was an experience he greatly enjoyed but also one that sharpened his awareness of social, cultural, and economic constraints upon growth. That subsequently became one of the themes of his stimulating lectures, both at the post-war LSE and at the Institute of Commonwealth Studies, on comparative colonial economic development.

On that subject, one of the few economic historians to win his unqualified praise was Alexander Gershenkron, especially for his magisterial 1952 essay on 'Economic Backwardness in Comparative Perspective'.[16] There, universal models of growth were explicitly rejected. 'The iron necessity of historical processes has been discarded', wrote

[12] D.V. Glass, a friend of Fisher from their postgraduate days, became Professor of Sociology at the LSE in 1948 and pioneered the study of both modern and historical demography. *Inter alia*, he wrote *The Town and a Changing Civilisation* (1935); edited *London Inhabitants within the Walls, 1695*, London Record Society, 2 (1966); and co-edited with D.E.C. Eversley, *Population in History: Essays in Historical Demography* (1965), which reprinted Glass's two important articles on Gregory King as demographer.

[13] See T. Veblen, *The Theory of the Leisure Class: An Economic Study of Institutions* (New York, 1899) and for Veblen's own conspicuous unorthodoxy in ideas and life-style, see C. Wright Mills, 'Introduction' to New American Library edition (New York, 1953), pp. vi-xix.

[14] See Chapter 6, pp. 105-18.

[15] H. Myint, *The Economics of the Developing Countries* (1st pub. 1964 and many later editions).

[16] A. Gershenkron, 'Economic Backwardness in Historical Perspective', first published in B. Hoselitz (ed.), *The Progress of Underdeveloped Countries* (Chicago, 1952); reprinted in A. Gershenkron, *Economic Backwardness in Historical Perspective: A Book of Essays* (New York, 1962), pp. 5-30.

Gershenkron. Earlier generations had enjoyed an untroubled intellectual
confidence about the links between past and future. But 'modern
historical relativism moves gingerly'.[17] Gershenkron's viewpoint was
certainly revisionist, in denying the inevitability of either a Whiggish
linear progress or a Marxist sequence of revolutions in the mode of
production. But it was neither anti-growth nor anti-change. If
unromantic and cautious in comparison with the great ideologies of the
nineteenth century, it was still optimistic that even the complex past could
be unravelled. This approach was equally characteristic of Fisher, who
also adopted the concept of economic backwardness in his own
reinterpretation of sixteenth- and seventeenth-century England as a pre-
industrial economy.[18]

Furthermore, his astringent style of analysis and distrust of 'grand
theory' had found theoretical sanction in the sceptical philosophy of Karl
Popper. In responding to that, of course, Jack Fisher was far from alone.
Popper's study in political theory, entitled *The Open Society and its Enemies*
(1945), and – especially – his critique of universal models of historical
change in *The Poverty of Historicism* (published as essays in 1944-45; as a
book in 1957) have proved seminal contributions to twentieth-century
intellectual life.[19] The impact of this passionate and liberal scepticism was
particularly heady in the aftermath of the Second World War, when
totalising ideologies were at a discount. And at that time, Popper was
himself appointed first as Reader (1945-49) and then as Professor of Logic
and Scientific Method (1949-69) at the LSE, which he later was to term a
'marvellous institution'.[20]

Although Fisher was not interested in philosophical detail, he found the
general thrust of Popperian 'critical rationalism' intensely congenial.[21] It
certainly encouraged his readiness to challenge historians who based their
proof upon no more than assertion, or even upon assertion plus a
Gilbertian profusion of corroborative detail for artistic verisimilitude.

[17] *Ibid.*, p. 5.

[18] See Chapters 8 and 9, pp. 131-62.

[19] See K.R. Popper, *The Open Society and its Enemies, Vol. I: The Spell of Plato* and *Vol. II: The
High Tide of Prophecy – Hegel, Marx and the Aftermath* (1945); and *idem*, 'The Poverty of
Historicism', 3 pts. in *Economica*, new ser. 11 (1944), pp. 86-103, 119-37; and 12 (1945),
pp. 69-89; later published as *The Poverty of Historicism* (1957). B. Magee, *Popper* (1973),
pp. 9-10, stresses the extent of Popper's impact in political and academic circles as well as
among professional philosophers.

[20] K.R. Popper, *Unended Quest: An Intellectual Autobiography* (1974; in 1976 edn.), p. 121;
and, for a comment on Popper's lectures at the LSE, see Watkins in *My LSE*, pp. 76-7.

[21] A passage in Popper's 'Knowledge without Authority' (1960) in D. Miller (ed.), *A
Pocket Popper* (1983), p. 52, gave the following definition:

> The proper answer to my question 'How can we hope to detect and eliminate error?' is, I believe,
> 'By *criticizing* the theories or guesses of others and – if we can train ourselves to do so – by *criticizing*
> our own theories or guesses . . . This answer sums up a position which I propose to call "critical
> rationalism".'

After Popper's invitation to trial by 'falsification', he remarked, such a procedure was inadmissible.

If the past could not, by definition, be submitted to experimental scrutiny, at very least arguments about the past could be critically tested by evidence, logic, and opposition: the ancient Greek art of dialectic, or critical examination by contradiction. It was important to know and refute the case against, as well as to make the points for any given proposition. Fisher's own capacity to assess the overall strengths and weaknesses of an argument and to pounce upon the vulnerable points was one of his most formidable powers as a critic.[22] Indeed, but for a few trifling obstacles — such as an aversion to argument based upon accumulative precedent — he would have made a daunting forensic lawyer.

All these influences crystallised in Jack Fisher's problem-solving approach to history. He did not either seek or supply a grand theory or general synthesis. That was for weaker brethren, for whose needs he remarked that religion had been invented. Economic history was, however, ideal terrain for sceptical but earnest enquiry, where historical data and economic theories jostled in constant dialectical tension. For, although wary of ideology, he was certainly no mere empiricist. He welcomed the use of theoretical models, but models were to be tested rather than embalmed. The more elaborate the methodology — as in the new econometric history — the more crucial it was to contest the basic assumptions built into the exercise. Conversely, he enjoyed the quest for new historical data, but the sources were to be probed rather than revered. Borrowing a sardonic joke from Popper, he once defined as *mystics* those historians who claimed that they were interested only in getting 'all the facts'.[23] Instead, the important thing was to test theory against evidence and vice-versa; and to pose the most interesting and not merely the most readily answerable questions.

---

[22] It is difficult to write about someone as a critic wthout conveying a negative impression; and undoubtedly some people had negative experiences, especially if they found that criticisms had come too close to home. But many found that Jack Fisher's analysis of their work was exhilarating in its clarity and objectivity, as he identified the internal logic of an argument and the explicit or (usually) implicit assumptions upon which it was based, reviewed the strengths and weaknesses of the presentation, and finally suggested ways of improving the whole.

[23] Popper, *Historicism*, pp. 76-78, argued that all knowledge, whether intuitive or discursive, had to be selective; and (p. 78 fn. 3) he specifically criticised the search for both 'reality' and/or holistic knowledge: 'The doctrine that we may obtain a kind of concrete knowledge of "reality itself" is well known as part of what can be technically described as *mysticism*; and so is the clamour for "wholes".' Similar criticisms of pure fact-seekers were voiced by M.M. Postan, iconoclast among medieval economic historians: see his 'Fact and Relevance in Historical Study' (1968) in *idem, Fact and Relevance: Essays on Historical Method* (1971), pp. 48-49. In return, some of P stan's more conventional Cambridge colleagues regarded him as charlatan, as reported in Coleman, *Economic Past*, p. 91.

Reprinted here are ten essays by F.J. Fisher, written over some forty years between 1933 and 1971. Although not designed as a collection, they display a common focus upon the social and economic history of London and England from 1500 to 1700. They are remarkable essays, not only for their past contribution but also for their topicality. The issues they address are still very 'live' ones. Indeed, the history of London is only now getting the detailed research scrutiny it requires.

Certainly, the essays fulfil Fisher's first requirement by being interesting. He enjoyed the abbreviated format, which suited his wry, concise style. His prose is pellucid and has dated very little. Indeed, he always urged that historical writing should be accessible as well as logical and learned. He avoided hyperbole, and, although not averse to confident assertion, he also enjoyed the English art of meiosis, or emphasis by understatement. The analytical tone throughout is positive. Unlike some essayists, he was not inspired to write in order to refute a heresy or to condemn a heretic. References in his text to the work of other historians are relatively rare (and then usually friendly), and in his footnotes are informative rather than combative, although when his work did generate controversy his published response to challenge was tersely dismissive. In general, he followed the tenets of critical rationalism in being his own best critic, which may have inhibited his pen but fortified him against external criticism.

These essays have proved highly influential. Although not all of equal weight, collectively their analysis has had major resonance, directly for their insights into Tudor and Stuart England, and indirectly for the questions they raised and the stimulus they gave to new research. Two contrasting themes recur: prospects for growth; and constraints upon growth. As he noted, both features co-existed in uneasy tension: 'The late sixteenth and early seventeenth centuries constitute perhaps the last period in English history in which economic appetites were remarkably vigorous but in which economic expansion was still slow'.[24] These interlinked themes were then explored in greater detail, with a focus upon trade, demographic history, the role of London, and the general economic context.

Trade was important not only for its commercial dynamic but also for its influence upon government policy-making. The latter theme was a subject of one of Fisher's earliest essays, published in 1940. Penning a reassessment of 'Commercial Trends and Policy in Sixteenth-Century England',[25] he was concerned to establish the political importance not of economic ideology *in vacuo* but of economic contingency in practice.

It was a topical theme, written in the disputatious 1930s, and still with

[24] See below, p. 150.
[25] See Chapter 5, pp. 81-103.

pointed relevance some sixty years later. In detail, he provided a succinct and now standard chronology of Tudor overseas trade, as it changed from early expansion based on the Antwerp connection; to depression in the 1550s and 1560s; and to cautious recovery and diversification in the later decades. To that, he matched the phases of policy-making, from early liberalism; to defensive mid-century regulation; and to renewed calls for 'free trade' in the Parliament of 1604. Here was no abstract debate about 'mercantilism' at work,[26] but a plethora of worried politicians, merchants, and pamphleteers, grappling with the recalcitrance of economic realities.

A matching essay extended the investigation of commercial trends to look at 'London's Export Trade in the Early Seventeenth Century'.[27] This discussion was terse but highly informative. It revealed Fisher's pioneering construction of statistical indices and his skill at making sense of the incomplete Customs Accounts and metropolitan Port Books. Their scrappy records were probed with caution. For example, in one case he noted, in a characteristic turn of phrase, that the Port Book evidence was 'suggestive rather than conclusive'. But, by testing the statistics in the light both of contemporary testimony and of economic plausibility, a convincing picture of London's – and thence a large section of the nation's – overseas trade was established. He found not an unfettered expansion but a hesitant growth amidst much uncertainty, with some diversification into new products and some expansion into new markets. The conclusions to these studies in trade were rapidly accepted, and, although there may perhaps be scope for an upwards revision to the scale of trade from provincial ports, the general tenor of the analysis has been strikingly upheld by subsequent research and analysis.[28]

Demographic history was another key topic, where uncertainty and doubtful statistics reigned. In his 'Influenza and Inflation in Tudor England',[29] Fisher returned to the troubled mid-sixteenth century, when there were complex economic problems and a distinct 'pause' in the

[26] The concept of systematic 'mercantilism' has proved resilient, despite much criticism, including Fisher's demonstration of the empirical context of Tudor policy-making. For a careful overview of the debate and reprint of key essays, see D.C. Coleman (ed.), *Revisions in Mercantilism* (1969); and for a close examination of political, diplomatic and economic factors at mid-century, see G. D. Ramsay, *The City of London in International Politics at the Accession of Elizabeth Tudor* (1975).

[27] See Chapter 7, pp. 119-29; and quotation on p. 127.

[28] The *locus classicus* for the trading context is B.E. Supple, *Commercial Crisis and Change in England, 1600-42: A Study in the Instability of a Mercantile Economy* (1964). In addition, see W.E. Minchinton's 'Introduction' in *idem* (ed.), *The Growth of English Overseas Trade in the Seventeenth and Eighteenth Centuries* (1969), pp. 1-57, and esp. p. 9, n. 1, for comment on the scale of outport trade; and B. Dietz, 'Overseas Trade and Metropolitan Growth' in A.L. Beier and R. Finlay (eds.), *London, 1500-1700: The Making of the Metropolis* (1986), pp. 115-40, for London's foreign trade.

[29] See Chapter 10, pp. 163-72.

secular rise of both food prices and wages. For the latter, Y.S. Brenner had suggested a demographic explanation, in the form of Malthusian checks (delayed marriage and falling birth rates), indicating that a fast-growing population was responding instinctively to fast-growing pressures upon scarce resources.[30] Fisher, however, doubted that there had been a communal 'epidemic of chastity'.[31]

Instead, he found a grimmer Malthusian check at work. Using a variety of sources – including literary evidence and the number of wills proved in diocesan courts – he pointed to exceptionally high mortality from a virulent influenza epidemic in the years 1556-58. This analysis provoked some critical debate, particularly with reference to the interpretation of fluctuations in grain prices.[32] Yet the adverse impact of the epidemic has now been generally accepted, even if the scale of the net population loss may not have been quite as great as he suggested.[33] In all, it was a probing and speculative intervention, notable for its cross-matching of a diversity of sources to illuminate the crisis. Since then, however, developments within demographic history have tended to shift the subject into a different style of analysis, with a rather more austere statistical modelling of long-term trends.[34]

Meanwhile, throughout his work, Fisher was preoccupied by another major feature of the sixteenth- and seventeenth-century English economy. That was the growth of London, the 'great wen'. Although he did not write his projected big book on this massive and multifaceted subject, five of his essays,[35] including some of the earliest and the last, analysed the ramifications of metropolitan growth, and another one dealt with city

[30] Y.S. Brenner, 'The Inflation of Prices in England, 1551-1650', *ibid.*, 2nd ser. 15 (1962), p. 284.

[31] See below, p. 168.

[32] See J.D. Gould, 'F.J. Fisher on Inflation and Influenza in Tudor England', *Economic History Review*, 2nd ser. 21 (1968), pp. 361-68. In a 'Rejoinder', *ibid.*, pp. 368-70, Fisher reaffirmed his use of the grain figures, while stressing that demographic change could not properly be deduced from that evidence alone.

[33] For example, L.A. Clarkson, *Death, Disease and Famine in Pre-Industrial England* (1972), pp. 12, 48-49, accepts 'a mortality crisis of serious proportions' in the later 1550s, with cases of influenza and perhaps typhus as well. E.A. Wrigley and R.S. Schofield, *The Population History of England, 1541-1871: A Reconstruction* (1981), p. 212 and fn. 28, also confirm that in the later 1550s there was 'a surge in deaths and a sharp drop in births', leading to a sizeable, if temporary, decline in population numbers; but their recalculations of long-term trends suggest that the epidemic probably had a smaller overall impact than Fisher had proposed.

[34] This development, which is also not without controversy, has been led by the work of the Cambridge Group for the History of Population and Social Structure, culminating in Wrigley and Schofield's compendious *magnum opus* (see above, fn. 33) and their reconstruction of earlier demographic profiles by 'back projection' from nineteenth-century data.

[35] See Chapters 4, 6, 7, 11 and 12, pp. 61-79, 105-29, 173-98.

guilds.[36] He was thus an 'urban historian' well before the term came into vogue in the 1960s,[37] albeit not one who accepted the constraints of the specialist label.

One exploratory early study was concerned with the regulatory guilds, both in London and the provincial towns. Published in 1933 as 'Some Experiments in Company Organisation in the Early Seventeenth Century',[38] it developed material from his MA thesis, which investigated the variety of constitutional bodies that had attempted to control industry in Stuart England.[39] He found not a uniform progress from regulation to *laissez-faire*, but a series of expedients, often framed to meet immediate needs (both fiscal and economic) and usually failing on both counts. Fisher therefore argued that it was practical disillusionment rather than theoretical principle which led eventually to the lapsing of many controls. This essay usefully extended a theme that was dear to the heart of George Unwin,[40] who had been Tawney's own synoptic mentor; but analysis of the guilds since then has lain curiously dormant.[41]

Consumption rather than regulation has, however, proved of enduring interest. Jack Fisher here contributed two key essays that remain essential reading. In 'The Development of the London Food Market, 1540-1640',[42]

[36] See Chapter 3, pp. 43-60.

[37] 'Urban history' was successfully promoted and coordinated as a specialist theme by the enthusiasm of H.J. Dyos, himself another LSE graduate who had been greatly influenced by Fisher. Jim Dyos edited *The Study of Urban History* (1968) and produced a regular *Urban History Newsletter* (begun in December 1963), which was later converted into the annual *Urban History Yearbook* (1974 onwards). Fisher took a benign view as the specialism flourished in the 1970s but warned its practitioners not to become divorced from the rest of social and economic history.

[38] See Chapter 3, pp. 43-60.

[39] F.J. Fisher, 'The Influence and Development of the Industrial Guilds in the larger Provincial Towns under James I and Charles I, with Special Reference to the Formation of New Corporations for the Control of Industry' (unpublished MA thesis, University of London, 1931).

[40] See variously G. Unwin, *Industrial Organisation in the Sixteenth and Seventeenth Centuries* (1904); *idem, The Gilds and Companies of London* (1908), esp. pp. 243-351, to the third edition of which F.J. Fisher contributed a 'List of Sources for the History of the Existing London Companies', *ibid.* (1938 edn.), pp. 372-89; and Unwin's essay on 'The Merchant Adventurers' Company in the Reign of Elizabeth' in R.H. Tawney (ed.), *Studies in Economic History: The Collected Papers of George Unwin* (1927; reprinted 1958), pp. 133-220.

[41] There have been studies of individual London Companies, including F.J. Fisher's *A Short History of the Worshipful Company of Horners* (1936), pp. 1-138; and helpful provincial surveys, such as D. Palliser, 'The Trade Gilds of Tudor York' in P. Clark and P. Slack (eds.), *Crisis and Order in English Towns, 1500-1700* (1972); but relatively little general debate. Exceptions are J.R. Kellett, 'The Breakdown of Gild and Corporation Control over the Handicraft and Retail Trade in London', *Economic History Review*, 2nd ser. 10 (1957/8); and, for renewed enquiry into medieval guilds, H. Swanson, 'The Illusion of Economic Structure: The Craft Guilds in Later Medieval English Towns', *Past and Present*, 121 (1988).

[42] See Chapter 4, pp. 61-79.

he surveyed the expansion and commercialisation of English agriculture to feed the growth of the huge and hungry metropolis. This analysis used literary evidence, combined with statistics on coastal trade from the Port Books and references to inland trade in the State Papers. Much important detail was fused into a convincing overall picture that has again been broadly upheld by later research into the growth of agrarian specialisation and traffic in food.[43]

Similarly, in 'The Development of London as a Centre of Conspicuous Consumption in the Sixteenth and Seventeenth Centuries',[44] Fisher gave a sparkling *tour d'horizon* of the metropolitan bright lights. London was not only the hub of trade, industry, finance and government, it was also a social capital. For the landowning gentry in particular, it became a great magnet. Whether flocking to town for the winter 'season' in order to spend their rising rents or to escape from impoverished country estates, they established a distinctive two-fold migrational pattern that greatly boosted the urban economy.[45] Hence the growth of clubs, parks, theatres, smart town housing, professional services and all the other Veblenesque indicators of conspicuous consumption. This pioneering analysis of the metropolis as social focus was instantly accepted and remains unchallenged; indeed, it has been reinforced by later studies that have identified the same feature in regional capitals such as Bristol and Norwich, and in provincial urban culture more generally.[46]

After publishing his detailed research in the 1930s and 1940s, Fisher in the 1950s and 1960s – in his own forties and fifties – became more interested in putting his work into the wider economic context. He edited the important Cranfield papers and in 1965 published his study of the influenza epidemic, but his later essays were chiefly concerned with the

[43] But the detailed picture, not surprisingly, has proved more complex: see *inter alia*, P.V. McGrath, 'The Marketing of Food, Fodder and Livestock in the London Area in the Seventeenth Century' (unpublished MA thesis, University of London, 1948); A. Everitt, 'The Marketing of Agricultural Produce' in J. Thirsk (ed.), *The Agrarian History of England and Wales, Vol. IV: 1500-1640* (1967), esp. pp. 507-16 for the metropolitan market; J. Chartres, *Internal Trade in England, 1500-1700* (1977), esp. pp. 13-31; and *idem*, 'Food Consumption and Internal Trade' in Beier and Finlay (eds.), *London*, pp. 168-96.

[44] See Chapter 6, pp. 105-18.

[45] Interestingly, in a study of townward migration among the Kentish populace in the same period, Peter Clark later identified a similar duality of motivation, some seeking 'betterment' and others despairingly hoping for 'subsistence': compare P. Clark, 'The Migrant in Kentish Towns, 1580-1640' in Clark and Slack (eds.), *Crisis and Order*, pp. 117-63.

[46] See comments in W. Minchinton, 'Bristol: Metropolis of the West in the Eighteenth Century', *Transactions of the Royal Historical Society*, 5th ser. 4 (1954), pp. 69-89, esp. pp. 86-87; and P.J. Corfield, 'A Provincial Capital in the Late Seventeenth Century: The Case of Norwich' in Clark and Slack (eds.), *Crisis and Order*, pp. 263-310, esp. pp. 290-93. For provincial urbanism more generally, see also P. Borsay, *The English Urban Renaissance: Culture and Society in the Provincial Town, 1660-1770* (1989).

general characteristics of the English economy. Here historic tensions between growth and constraints upon growth were made particularly clear. That was appropriate, for both themes had emerged repeatedly in his work.

Two essays were concerned with growth and they concentrated upon the remarkable impact of the great metropolis. Indignant royalists in the 1640s had blamed the king's problems upon the 'proud, unthankful, schismatical, rebellious, bloody City of London'.[47] Fisher disagreed with this stark vision, and warned against projecting civil war passions back onto pre-war society. Nonetheless, in his brisk sketch of 'The Growth of London',[48] he agreed that the metropolis did constitute a major force for change. The civil war was, for him, no 'bourgeois revolution'. It was 'the result less of a major social conflict than of the break-down of a clumsy political machine in the hands of a remarkably inefficient operator'. But these short-term events occurred within a wider context. Hence, insofar as long-term developments had rendered both the theory and practice of prerogative kingship more difficult, the growth of an assertive metropolis was to be accounted 'among the most important of those changes'.[49]

Economically, as well as politically, a massive urban centre of almost 400,000 inhabitants by 1650 was not a negligible phenomenon. Nor was it brief in duration. From the 1520s onwards, London had experienced a long-term expansion in population that showed no sign of abating in the course of the seventeenth century or afterwards. Even if not uniquely rebellious and schismatical,[50] the metropolis was different from the rest of England, and, eventually, an accumulating difference in degree became a difference in kind.

Dubbing London as an 'Engine of Economic Growth',[51] Fisher proceeded to analyse its wider impact. That operated both via its own role in production, distribution and consumption, and via its stimulus to change elsewhere in the economy. The metaphor of the engine was a deliberate one: London was not sole cause or location of growth, but it provided vital motor power. If regional specialisation eventually promoted the growth of many specialist provincial towns, it did not

[47] *Somers Tracts* (1810), Vol. IV, p. 598, cited below, p. 174.

[48] See Chapter 11, pp. 174-83. This essay was based on a talk originally given in 1966 for a BBC series on the theme of 'The English Revolution'.

[49] See below p. 183.

[50] Debates about London's seventeenth-century political role have not, of course, concluded: compare V. Pearl, *London and the Outbreak of the Puritan Revolution: City Government and National Politics, 1625-43* (1961) and R. Ashton, *The City and the Court, 1603-43* (1979) – the latter dedicated to F.J. Fisher and acknowledging his 'devastating but enormously fertile criticism' (p. x). In addition, *The London Journal: A Review of Metropolitan Society Past and Present* (1975-) provides a forum for discussion of these and related themes in metropolitan development.

[51] See Chapter 12, pp. 185-98.

preclude a key role for the one capital city, particularly in the seventeenth century when its relative predominance was at its height. In sum, this essay presented a lucid and persuasive discussion. It has remained relatively little known, partly because it was published in a recondite volume of conference papers, and partly because its general thesis was not surprising to urban historians; but it deserves fresh attention, as a constructive contribution to continuing debates about both the chronology and the implication of metropolitan expansion.[52]

There was a yet more important reason why Fisher on growth had less resonance and attention than Fisher on constraints upon growth. That was his own earlier success in fostering a powerful new interpretation of the overall economic context of Tudor and Stuart England. He had jettisoned the old view that the sixteenth and early seventeenth centuries were years of emergent 'capitalism', a term he notably avoided.[53] Rather, he suggested that England then exhibited many of the characteristic signs of economic backwardness. Therefore, the relevant concept was not 'capitalism' but 'underdevelopment'.

That case had been made in two bravura essays in interpretation. One was based on his 1956 inaugural lecture at the LSE, which was recalled by many as one of the most amusing inaugurals ever given. It was pruned for publication as 'The Sixteenth and Seventeenth Centuries: The Dark Ages in English Economic History?'.[54] He defined the period between 1450 and 1750 as one of statistical and analytical nescience. But the intellectual darkness was not impenetrable. Reviewing the countervailing evidence of growth and constraint, he developed the argument that the Tudor and Stuart era, especially before the 1640s, was one of relative economic underdevelopment. The Third World provided instructive parallels, citing here R.H. Tawney not on early agrarian capitalism but on twentieth-century *Land and Labour in China*.[55]

---

[52] A key discussion of London's role, which *inter alia* drew upon Fisher's work on food supply, was published by E.A. Wrigley in 1967 as 'A Simple Model of London's Importance in Changing English Society and Economy, 1650-1750', *Past and Present*, 37 (1967), pp. 44-70; reprinted in *idem, People, Cities and Wealth: The Transformation of Traditional Society* (1987), pp. 133-56. Later discussion has broadly agreed with its main argument, albeit suggesting that a complex rather than simple model is required: see essays in Beier and Finlay (eds.), *London*. A parallel study has confirmed that the seventeenth century in Europe as a whole was a period when urban growth was predominantly metropolitan: see J. de Vries, *European Urbanization, 1500-1800* (1984), esp. pp. 68-71.

[53] A few references to 'capitalists' can be found in his early essays, but even that term disappeared in his later writings and conversation.

[54] See Chapter 8, pp. 131-47.

[55] See below, p. 147. Tawney's study, published in 1932, had itself pointed to the parallels between twentieth-century China and sixteenth-century England. For the evolution of Tawney's own historical analysis, see Winter, 'Introduction' in *idem* (ed.), *History and Society*, pp. 25-29.

Returning to the discussion in 1961, Jack Fisher renewed the case, in perhaps his single most elegant formulation. Entitled 'Tawney's Century' and appearing in the *Festschrift* for Tawney's eightieth birthday,[56] this essay confirmed Fisher's dissent from Tawney's classic interpretation of a burgeoning capitalism, spear-headed by a rising landed gentry.[57] Not that the rupture was at all polemical. The essay contained a felicitous tribute to Tawney's inspirational role as teacher and scholar, and the difference in their views was never stressed by Fisher, either then or subsequently. Yet in his analysis, relative backwardness was again the keynote. Hence, the busy sixteenth-century land market was taken to indicate not the rapidity of growth but its sluggishness, which left capital without investment outlets in manufacturing or trade. Similarly, the flourishing London theatre and professions were nurtured by the entrepreneurial talents of thwarted businessmen, although Fisher noted wryly that 'it would be ludicrous to dismiss the works of Shakespeare as products of the mis-allocation of economic resources.'[58]

Collectively these essays succeeded because, with their panache and lucidity, they combined much accumulated research in economic history with new theoretical perspectives from development economics. In particular, they opened up new directions for enquiry by cutting through older assumptions, often implicitly held rather than explicitly substantiated, about the basic chronology of English economic growth.

Karl Marx had synthesised classical economics with Hegelian dialectic into a majestic dynamic of historical change through socio-economic conflict. In application to Engand, that postulated a decaying fifteenth-century feudalism, which was increasingly undermined by a nascent sixteenth-century capitalism, whose contradictions finally culminated in

[56] See Chapter 9, pp. 149-62. It was reading this essay as an undergraduate that decided the author of these comments to apply for postgraduate study with Fisher at the LSE.

[57] Tawney in *The Agrarian Problem in the Sixteenth Century* (1912), pp. 404-9, had identified an 'agrarian revolution' in sixteenth-century England, while still finding many elements of continuity; and in *Religion and the Rise of Capitalism* (1926), pp. 225-26, 270, 280-81, had analysed Stuart England's intensification of an age-old capitalist spirit. To that he added a new social interpretation of the civil wars in 'The Rise of the Gentry' (see above, fn. 4) and in 'Harrington's Interpretation of his Age' (1941), both reprinted in Winter (ed.), *History and Society*, pp. 68-128. Tawney, who was not a Marxist, hoped to avoid both the under- and over-valuation of economic factors, seeking instead *l'histoire intégrale:* see R.H. Tawney, 'The Study of Economic History' in Harte (ed.), *Economic History*, p. 106. Incidentally, Tawney's own mentor, George Unwin, used the term 'industrial capital' but in application to developments in the later eighteenth century, following the earlier 'domestic system': see Unwin, *Industrial Organisation*, 3-9, 225-6.

[58] See below, p. 159.

a mid-seventeenth-century 'bourgeois revolution'.[59] This was a bold interpretation, which had considerable impact in setting the general chronology, particularly in the case of English economic history.[60] It was by no means universally adopted but its influence spread well beyond the ranks of declared Marxists, and, although some non-Marxists preferred to shed the distinctive Marxist vocabulary,[61] others found it possible to use the concept of 'capitalism', while rejecting the political philosophy of communism.[62]

Increased research, however, generated increasing doubts about this general chronology. Evidence for Tudor economic growth in *per capita* terms was hard to come by, while the undoubted quickening of economic activity in post-medieval England could be explained logically enough as no more than the corollary of renewed population expansion. More specifically, it was difficult to perceive a new capitalist 'mode of production' in the sixteenth century, or yet a triumphant urban bourgeoisie on the scale required for revolution in the seventeenth. On that point, Tawney had already provided a heterodox alternative,

[59] Marx did not, of course, set out to write an economic history of England but his general analysis drew considerably upon the English experience and had interesting implications for the study of English history. See, for example, K. Marx and F. Engels, *Manifesto of the Communist Party* (1848) in *Karl Marx and Frederick Engels: Selected Works* (Lawrence and Wishart edn., 1962), Vol. I, p. 35: after the discovery of America, the growth of world-wide trade and new industry created an emergent bourgeoisie, which pushed aside the 'tottering feudal society' and made political advances to match its economic power. See also K. Marx, *The Eighteenth Brumaire of Louis Bonaparte* (1852) in *Selected Works*, Vol. I, p. 248, for a direct reference to England's 'bourgeois revolution' of the 1640s.

[60] Its influence proved less overwhelming in studies of Stuart political history, where a Whig/constitutionalist interpretation has survived alongside Marxist views: contrast J.R. Tanner's Whiggish *English Constitutional Conflicts of the Seventeenth Century, 1603-89* (1928) with C. Hill's modern Marxism in *The Century of Revolution, 1603-1714* (1961). In the 1970s and 1980s, Whigs and Marxists have together come under challenge from a neo-conservative 'revisionism' that stresses instead the survival of traditionalism: see B. Coward, *The Stuart Age: A History of England, 1603-1714* (1980). But these new debates also remain focused upon Stuart political and social life rather than upon its economic history.

[61] A liberal-progressive alternative was to discuss late medieval England as a manorial system whose use was 'exhausted', making way for the Tudor and Stuart 'growth of trade, manufacture and colonization' that was necessary for modern 'power, liberty and progress': see G.M. Trevelyan's influential *History of England* (1926; in 1960 illustrated edn.), pp. 6-7, 242-43. 'Feudal' and 'capitalist', however, recur not infrequently as adjectives: see for example *ibid.*, pp. 236, 285.

[62] Non-Marxist studies of 'capitalism' published in the 1970s and 1980s include J.E. Vaizey, *Capitalism* (1971); R.H. Preston, *Religion and the Persistence of Capitalism* (1979); M. Beaud, *Histoire du Capitalisme* (Paris, 1981), transl. as *A History of Capitalism, 1500-1980* (1984); I.S. Michelman, *The Roots of Capitalism in Western Civilisation* (New York, 1983); E. Preteceille, *Capitalism, Consumption and Needs* (1985). There are also economic guides, such as P. Jalee, *How Capitalism Works* (1977); I.D.S. Ward, *An Introduction to Market Capitalism* (1977); or R. Lekachman, *Capitalism for Beginners* (1981).

substituting a rising gentry for the rising middle class,[63] but, even with that adjustment, there were still problems. Not only was the timetable for the advent of capitalism uncertain,[64] but it was also difficult to match with the late eighteenth-century advent of industrialism.[65] One solution was by sub-division. 'Merchant' or 'commercial' capitalism could be seen as the necessary prelude to a subsequent 'industrial' capitalism, as the eminent Russian Marxist historian, Mikhail Pokrovskii, had argued in the 1910s.[66] But that was subsequently denounced as revisionism, as it diluted the coherence of what was held to be one basic 'mode of production', matching with one key stage in the revolutionary dynamics of historical development.

Fisher, impatient with the whole Marxist problematic, simply by-passed it. His stance was sceptical and ultimately revisionist, but was not presented as a polemic. There were plenty of others who waged outright war against Marxism, sometimes very bitterly. Their battles were,

[63] Tawney, 'Rise of the Gentry' (above fn. 4). Most modern Marxist historians of England have followed Tawney in interpreting the events of 1640-60 as a successful gentry revolution, and the terminology of the 'bourgeois revolution' in the seventeenth century has gradually withered away.

[64] If English feudalism was decaying in the fifteenth century, was the Tudor state and society capitalist? And, if so, how did that tally with a bourgeois revolution in the 1640s? Conversely, if capitalism did not break through until the mid-seventeenth century, was the Tudor state feudal? And, if so, how did that tally with the decay of feudalism in the fifteenth century? For explicit discussion of these and related questions by historians and economists within the Marxist tradition, see especially M.H. Dobb, *Studies in the Development of Capitalism* (1946); R.H. Hilton, 'Capitalism: What's in a Name?', *Past and Present*, 1 (1952), pp. 32-43; E.J. Hobsbawm, 'The Crisis of the Seventeenth Century', *ibid.*, 5 and 6 (1954), reprinted with postscript in T. Aston (ed.), *Crisis in Europe, 1560-1660: Essays from Past and Present* (1965), pp. 5-58; and essays in P.M. Sweezy *et al.*, *The Transition from Feudalism to Capitalism* (1976).

[65] One answer was to postulate a discrete phase of 'proto-industrialisation' before full factory production, but that has been sceptically received, both within and outside the Marxist tradition: see overview in L.A. Clarkson, *Proto-Industrialization: The First Phase of Industrialization?* (1985), pp. 9-67. A later permutation has been to revive another old controversy by a wholesale rejection of the concept of Industrial Revolution: see for a vigorous attack, M. Fores, 'The Myth of a British Industrial Revolution', *History*, 66 (1981), pp. 181-98. That proposal certainly resolves any debate about the relationship between capitalism and industrialism, but the wholesale slaughter of old concepts without recourse to new ones leaves the historian with a distinctly weak analytical repertoire for interpreting development over time.

[66] M.N. Pokrovskii, an associate of Buhkarin, had postulated a stage of 'commercial capitalism' in sixteenth-century Russia, but he was denounced by Stalinists in the 1930s for revisionism and, under pressure, recanted his view that commercial capitalism was a specific economic formation in its own right: see M.N. Pokrovskii, *History of Russia from the Earliest Times to the Rise of Commercial Capitalism* (Moscow, 1910-14; in Eng. transl., New York, 1931), 5 vol; and G.M. Enteen, *The Soviet Scholar-Bureaucrat: M.N. Pokrovskii and the Society of Marxist Historians* (1978), pp. 37-42, 48-49, 161-64, 179-84, 195-96. It was to this dispute that Fisher alluded in his inaugural lecture with a cryptic reference to 'the Pokrovsky-bog of merchant capitalism': see below, p. 135.

however, fought on rather different terrain. For example, Eric Kerridge, the most explicit anti-Marxist among the economic historians of Tudor England, was a leading exponent of the case for economic growth. He analysed the 'agricultural revolution' of the sixteenth and early seventeenth centuries, and fully accepted the terminology and chronology of 'capitalism'. His fierce disagreement with Marxism focused instead upon the social implications of these economic changes. Kerridge denied that growth was harmful and denounced Tawney's 'socialist dogma' that gave a 'wholly untrue picture of early capitalism as cruel and greedy'.[67]

Many, however, sympathised with Fisher in seeking critical distance from all debates that appeared to assume concepts of built-in growth, whether via revolutionary dialectics or by progressive evolution. He did not create this new approach single-handedly, but his essays helped to crystallise a trend. Gradually therefore, and without much direct controversy, the alternative interpretation became quite widely adopted, stressing instead England's relative underdevelopment in the sixteenth and seventeenth centuries.[68] By the 1970s, 'pre-industrial', an adjective borrowed from comparative economics and already with some circulation among historians, became popular to describe the economy of Tudor and Stuart England,[69] while 'capitalist', although not disappearing, was much less pervasive. It cannot be said that the new viewpoint became settled into a formal orthodoxy, still less that it ousted all the old ones. Marxist economic historians continued to study agrarian capitalism,[70] and endorsed the revolutionary, although not specifically 'bourgeois', nature of seventeenth-century change. At the same time, the expanding fields of

---

[67] See E. Kerridge, *Agrarian Problems in the Sixteenth Century and After* (1969), p. 15; and *idem, The Agricultural Revolution* (1967).

[68] For judicious discussion of this thesis and its problems, see D.C. Coleman, *The Economy of England, 1450-1750* (1977), dedicated 'For F.J.F.'

[69] See, for example, L.A. Clarkson, *The Pre-Industrial Economy of England, 1550-1750* (1971) and B.A. Holderness, *Pre-Industrial England: Economy and Society from 1500 to 1750* (1976), although Coleman, *Economy of England*, p. 1, preferred 'pre-industrialized'. An earlier application to urban history was proposed in G. Sjoberg, *The Pre-Industrial City* (New York, 1960), prompting an effective critique from O.C. Cox, 'The Preindustrial City Reconsidered' in P. Meadows and E.H. Mizruchi (eds.), *Urbanism, Urbanization and Change: Comparative Perspectives* (Reading, Mass., 1969), pp. 19-29. The dichotomy between pre-industrial and industrial has parallels with other dualisms, including 'pre-modern' and 'modern', and the celebrated distinction, made in 1887 by the German sociologist Ferdinand Tönnies, between *Gemeinschaft* (traditional community) and *Gesellschaft* (contractual society). But, while often suggestive, all these binary pairings have analytical weaknesses, particularly in presenting a very monochrome vision of the long centuries before 'industrialism', 'modernism' and/or 'mass society' are finally deemed to have arrived.

[70] The works of I. Wallerstein offer one example among many: see *The Modern World-System: Capitalist Agriculture and the Origins of the European World-Economy of the Sixteenth Century* (1974) and *idem, Historical Capitalism* (1983).

social and urban history set their own agendas, unworried by the problems of economic nomenclature. Yet the 'underdevelopment' thesis proved successful in fostering fresh perspectives and research – as well as highlighting still-unresolved questions about concepts and chronologies of change.

One historian does not, of course, make a subject. As already noted, Jack Fisher did not propound his own conceptual synthesis, become a departmental empire-builder, or found a new subject specialism or school of thought. He was not without his critics, for these and doubtless other errors. Furthermore, he did not make any claims for his own work, and would almost certainly have found this retrospective overview to have detected too orderly and coherent an intellectual pattern among life's contingencies and contradictions.

None of that can obscure Fisher's pervasive influence. He exerted sway as a scintillating teacher and as mentor to other teachers, for in the post-war years a remarkable number of his LSE graduates went on themselves to become eminent economic historians.[71] He also influenced others by the challenging style and content of his essays. Specifically, therefore, he helped to bring about a fundamental reconsideration of the nature of the Tudor and Stuart economy as well as the role of the metropolis. More generally, he jolted people into thought as meta-critic at conferences and seminars, where he was one of the generation of scholars that followed the early pioneers in economic history and brought the subject to its 'high noon'.[72] Yet more broadly still, he can be seen as one of many exponents of mid-twentieth-century relativistic scepticism before 'grand theory', particularly as mediated through the ferment of ideas from left and right at the London School of Economics.

Meanwhile, history and its debates move on. The current plethora of concepts and chronologies certainly needs critical re-examination. After the thematic diversification and analytical eclecticism of economic and social history in its 'boom years', there have come increasing calls for

---

[71] In 1976, thirteen colleagues and former pupils contributed to an aptly-entitled *Festschrift*: see D.C. Coleman and A.H. John (eds.), *Trade, Government and Economy in Pre-Industrial England: Essays Presented to F.J. Fisher* (1976). But the full number of teachers in economic history, whom he taught or influenced, was many times greater than that.

[72] In the immediate post-war years, the subject experienced an 'astonishing surge' in popularity: Coleman, *History and the Economic Past*, p. 94. Its impetus was sustained by the appointment of many economic and social historians to 'orthodox' history departments in British Universities and Polytechnics and further institutionalised by the multiplication of specialist economic and social history departments in the Universities. By the early 1970s, there were 'some fifteen' such departments (old and new): *ibid.*, p. 106. Since then, a variety of changes – in University finances, in patterns of student demand, in the bifurcation of economic from social history – have put the subject and its institutional arrangements under acute pressure; so that the 'high-noon' of economic history in separation from history has proved unexpectedly brief.

resynthesis of the myriad of approaches within the subject, and its reintegration into a broader history. Fisher was cheerfully sardonic: more holism, more *mysticism*, more triumph-of-hope-over-experience. But he relished the continuing dialectic of economic history, in which he had himself proved no mean practitioner.

2

In Memory of F.J. Fisher

Edited by N.B. Harte

Some academics have a profound influence on their subject, and on generations of students, without impinging much on the general reading public. Professor F.J. Fisher was an eminent example.[1] Writing and publishing came unfortunately low among his priorities. He wrote very little, and claimed to have written less. He was fond of quoting the advice given to him when young by a continental scholar to the effect that it is too risky to publish anything before becoming a professor, and unnecessary afterwards. He rarely referred to the history of the Horners Company that he wrote in 1936, nor to the two series of four-volume school textbooks he wrote with Amabel Williams-Ellis. Neither the economic history of early modern London on which he embarked before the war, nor the great work on the English economy in the sixteenth and seventeenth centuries on which he worked, on and off, for thirty years were ever completed. Nevertheless, his ten important articles, originally published between 1933 and 1971, have proved seminal. Two of them in particular – his famous inaugural lecture at the London School of Economics on 'The Sixteenth and Seventeenth Centuries: The Dark Ages in English Economic History?' and his contribution on 'Tawney's Century' in the *Festschrift* which he edited for R.H. Tawney – constitute what is still the most stimulating starting-point for the study of the pre-industrial economy in England. These articles are gathered together for the first time in this volume.

Fisher's articles, however, only partly explain the remarkable influence which he exerted on economic history in the period of its drive to maturity as a subject. He was a teacher for over forty years at the London School of Economics – he joined the staff as an Assistant in 1930, and occupied the chair of economic history there from 1954 until his retirement in 1975 – and it is above all for his power as a great teacher that he will be best remembered. In addition, he long served as a member of the Council of

---

[1] Obituaries of F.J. Fisher appeared in the *Independent*, 13 January 1988 (by Negley Harte), in *The Times*, 14 January 1988, and in the *Economic History Review*, 2nd ser., XLI, 3 (1988) (by D.C. Coleman). The notable address which Professor D.C. Coleman gave at his funeral service was printed in the *LSE Magazine*, 75 (June 1988).

the Economic History Society, and was its President in 1974-77. But he did not seek honours, or public recognition (though he valued the honorary D.Litt. he was awarded by the University of Exeter in 1983). He gave the Wiles lectures at the Queen's University of Belfast in 1973 and the Creighton lecture at the University of London in 1974, but no publications resulted. The first chapter in this book and the ten essays themselves go some way to explaining Fisher's influence on economic history, but the power of his personality needs to be captured too.

A memorial meeting was held at the London School of Economics on 17th June 1988, and a number of revealing personal tributes were paid to the memory of Professor Fisher. For publication they have been edited somewhat to remove unnecessary repetition, though some inevitably remains. The tribute by Professor Michael Wise has been added to commemorate Jack Fisher's place in the history of the London School of Economics. At the conclusion of the meeting, Professor Donald Coleman summarised the tributes and elaborated upon them, but he spoke extempore and has kept no notes of his remarks. He pointed out that Jack Fisher always disliked eulogy and would not have wanted to be represented as aspiring to faultlessness. Those present recall Donald Coleman saying that if Jack Fisher had had to wear a halo, he would have worn it at a raffish angle.

i

Dr Peter Earle

Reader in Economic History, LSE

I have been asked to set the scene for the other speakers by briefly outlining Jack's career. He was born on 22 July 1908 and was brought up partly in Southend where he attended the High School and partly in Newmarket where he acquired his wonderful fund of racing stories. After Southend, he came to LSE where he took his BA in History in 1928 and his MA in 1931. In the previous year, he had joined the staff as an Assistant in History and was to become successively Assistant Lecturer in 1935 and Lecturer in 1939. During this early period of his career Jack published amongst other things three important articles in the *Economic History Review* in 1933, 1935 and 1940 – the last two, on the London food market and on commercial trends and policy, still being on the reading lists of anyone who teaches the early modern period.

Jack gave two short courses of lectures related to his research interests but most of his teaching during the thirties, as far as one can tell from the LSE *Calendar*, was of a far more general nature. In the session 1939-40, for instance, he gave twenty-four lectures on the growth of English industry after 1760, shared in a big lecture course with Tawney and Beales on the economic history of Britain and the Great Powers from 1815, shared in another course with Beales on the Industrial Revolution, gave an eight-lecture course on the Historical Background to Contemporary Economic Problems, as well as teaching classes in English and European economic history and presiding with Tawney and Judges in a research seminar on 'the economic problems of the early capitalist age', a range of teaching which helps us to understand the breadth of his reading and knowlege.

Then came the war, a crucial break in Jack's career as in that of so many of his generation, a period which included his marriage to Barbara in 1943 and service in the RAF from 1941 to 1946 in East Africa and the Middle East, the latter not only providing him with a fund of entertaining stories but also giving him a first-hand insight into the reality of a pre-industrial society. This experience was quickly put to academic use when he returned to the School after the war, when he shared with Vera Anstey in a course on economic development of the British Empire, Jack's contribution being the dominions and the tropical colonies, an interest which was to be sustained through the rest of his career.

Jack became Reader in 1947 and then in the 1949-50 session, following the departure of first Judges and then Tawney, he began to concentrate more on teaching the period of his own research interests, though he continued to lecture on colonial history and more generally on the history of economic development. It was in 1949 that he took over the early modern lectures and developed his special subject on Tudor and early Stuart England. During the late forties and early fifties, Jack published two more of his path-breaking articles, 'London as a Centre of Conspicuous Consumption' in 1948 and 'London's Export Trade in the Early Seventeenth Century' in 1950. In 1954 he succeeded T.S. Ashton as Professor of Economic History, an occasion which was later to be celebrated by his famous inaugural on 'The Dark Ages in English Economic History'.

The period which followed, when Jack was professor and head of department, will I am sure be well covered by other speakers. I will therefore conclude by saying that Jack retired in 1975, the year after he became President of the Economic History Society. Retirement by no means meant the end of his influence on the world of economic history. He continued to supervise research students and, until the last few years, presided over the research seminar on early modern economic and social history at the Institute of Historical Research.

I remember Jack with affection for some ten years spent as his colleague at the School, in which I was able to share in the teaching of courses devised by him, as he had in the 1930s with Tawney, Eileen Power and Beales. I think perhaps that I remember Jack best as the most stimulating seminar chairman that I have ever encountered and, of course, as a wonderful man to spend the evening with afterwards.

ii

Dr Penelope J. Corfield

Senior Lecturer in History, Royal Holloway and Bedford New College

'I know nothing about this BUT . . .' I can't resist starting with one of Jack's most famous opening gambits, at which strong academics blenched. For, with characteristic understatement, it was the prelude to a comment or critique that invariably proved to be at once combative, wittily iconoclastic, and deeply incisive. Any of those qualities alone would be pretty powerful; but, in combination, they were devastating. But devastating in a positive way: opening up new areas of the subject for analysis and debate. Indeed it is a real loss to economic history that Jack never found his academic Boswell – for many of his throw-away remarks could in themselves have launched a thousand research projects.

These qualities made Jack not only a brilliant *extempore* debater but also a most exhilarating and remarkable teacher. He liked to use shock tactics to startle people into thought – and he was merciless with loose generalisations and sloppy remarks. It must be admitted that this pedagogic style was not to everyone's taste. But for those who enjoyed his training course in intellectual analysis and combat, there was really nothing quite like it. Jack was a man for whom, in other words, the dialectic might have been invented. He loved a 'thesis', which gave him a proposition to analyse and challenge. He was equally at home – if not more so – with 'antithesis', the more iconoclastic the better. And he was prepared to contemplate the possibility of 'synthesis' – well, as he used to say in characteristic phrasing, *one* half of that could be fun.

But this intellectual rigour and combativeness was not bad tempered, mean, or hostile. On the contrary, it was accompanied by a great personal kindliness and leavened by a stream of constant, unforced wit. The flow of laughter was a constant element in his teaching and company. He often stressed that history had to remain part of the entertainments industry – and he hated pretension and jargon as much as he tilted against conventionality and stuffiness. His own lucid essays were exemplary in their clarity and power of communication, and his wit was similarly designed to startle and stimulate people enjoyably into thought. It was said, in the early nineteenth century, that 'laughter is an involuntary action of various muscles, developed in the human species by the progress of civilisation'. That was based on the proposition that 'the savage never laughs.' It was meant jestingly; but, by the laughter criterion, Jack Fisher was a very civilised historian indeed.

Above all, he had a brilliantly critical and analytical mind, allied to great erudition, bringing concepts from development economics and sociology to bear on the study of economic history. That led him to break from the conceptual framework of his own mentor, R.H. Tawney, whom none the less – of course – he deeply revered and admired personally. By the same token, Jack himself as a teacher followed the same policy. He did not seek to impose his own views upon his students, but rather to encourage them to identify, develop, clarify, and criticise their own. A supervision session with Jack was therefore an exhilarating experience: starting with morning coffee, sometimes continuing literally all day. And he was equally generous with time and attention to those, at all levels in the profession, who sought his assessment of their work. No wonder that his colleagues sometimes complained that his administration was in arrears: they were right, as it often was.

Yet for Jack, the intellectual quest for historical understanding was the really important thing; and none of us – variously and alternately teased, challenged, refuted, goaded, stimulated, and provoked by Jack into joining that quest – none of us can ever forget.

iii

Negley Harte

Senior Lecturer in Economic History, University College London

Jack Fisher was the first professor I ever met. I met him in Houghton Street at the opening of the 1963 session. The first thing new LSE undergraduates had to do was to get into a coach to be taken to a freshers' conference at an establishment in Hoddesdon. As we nervously assembled in the coach, Jack appeared – anything but nervously; and though he wore the same sort of aged tweed jacket that some of my schoolmasters had, and wielded the same sort of pipe, and had something odd about his shoelaces, it was immediately evident that he was very different from the teachers I had previously known. His powerful directness of manner, his total lack of self-importance, his delight in iconoclasm, his willingness to take anybody on in conversation, his ready mastery of the sort of paradox that later came to be called lateral thinking – a technique he had made his own long before the term was coined: these characteristics were contagiously apparent at that Hoddesdon weekend, not just in the keynote address, as I suppose it was, that he delivered.

I was fortunate enough, like Penelope Corfield, later to have him as one of the supervisors of my graduate study, but I was also among the many who were privileged to be taught by him as an undergraduate. The teachers of economic history at LSE were then a remarkably brilliant group in their different ways, but it was impossible not to feel that Jack's influence was on a wholly different plane. His lectures were captivating: they were scintillating performances, and they made you think. In classes, his offhand dismissal – carefully contrived, as one later came to realise – of all the established authorities made us read them with enhanced critical powers. Why should we believe 'these chaps', 'these boys', just because they had been misguided enough to have their writings published? For some meek souls this attitude was perhaps counter-productive; but for many of us it was a breath of fresh air which blew the dust off whole areas of history.

It is true that Jack sometimes put obstacles in our path. I can recall the strenuous efforts one of my contemporaries made to get a reading-list out of him. Arthur John, she kept pointing out, had circulated a reading-list for those doing his nineteenth-century special subject; couldn't those of us doing the late sixteenth and early seventeenth century have one too? Eventually Jack managed to silence her: 'If you really want to understand the period, go away and read the Bible'. It was the sort of advice that has seemed more relevant in the long-term than it did at the time.

Jack once described one leading historian, in a devastating phrase, as the sort of man who published everything he wrote. Jack himself had no such failing. He published all too little. One reason for this was because he put so much effort into composing his lectures. He scorned to repeat a lecture already delivered. Another reason has only recently become clear to me as I have been helping Barbara Fisher sort out his chaotic collection of books and papers. He compiled elaborate notes on much that he read. One series of files contained his own transcripts of the standard printed sources – the *Calendar of State Papers*, the volumes of the Historical Manuscripts Commission, the diaries – all in separate files for each year between the 1490s and the 1710s. A large number of box-files, labelled by subject (often the wrong subject), contained the *précis* which he carefully made of masses of books and articles. I use the word *précis* deliberately, since they were not notes: he used few abbreviations, and everything was summarised in prose, in his own handwriting up to the early 1950s, and thereafter in his more legible typewriting.

It is the effort that he put into mastering the sources and the writings of others in this way that explains why he was so knowledgeable. He combined his brilliance and wit to a quite unusual degree with knowledge, knowledge of all sorts of out of the way things as well as things more obviously central to the very broad-based discipline he believed economic history to be. It was this combination of quick-wittedness and knowledge that made him so devastating at seminars.

I don't fully know why he was disinclined to continue Tawney's once-famous graduate seminar. But when Peter Earle, Penelope Corfield and I revived the seminar at the Institute of Historical Research for him in 1974, shortly before his retirement from the LSE – and we began it on the basis that we would do all the organising and corresponding, chores which he notoriously found boring – he shone as chairman. It was an exciting seminar. There were those who drew back from reading papers because they could not face his criticism. 'I don't know anything about this, but . . .' he characteristically began. Or, even more alarmingly, 'the trouble with people like you is . . .' 'The trouble with you,' he said to me after I had been bold enough to read a paper at the seminar, 'is that you are just like Clapham.' Pause. 'If you can't think, you start counting.' But Jack's irreverence and cynicism was always tempered by that gleam in his eye.

Jack is no longer with us, alas, in his most evident form, but he will always be with us for the rest of our lives. The keynote address he gave to that LSE freshers' conference twenty-five years ago has been and will be, for me, the keynote address of my life.

iv

Professor Lord McGregor of Durris

Chairman of the Advertising Standards Authority and
Emeritus Professor of Social Institutions, Bedford College

I came to LSE in 1939 after a year at Aberdeen where Henry Hamilton told me to go to LSE if I wanted to read economic history. That session – the first of the School's evacuation to Cambridge – began with eight months of phoney war and ended with the fall of France. Indeed, we came out of the B Sc(Econ) intermediate examination into King's Parade and bought the *Evening Standard* with a headline announcing the evacuation of Dunkirk. Those were not the days of wine and roses, but neither had we been stricken by terrified suspense over the prospect of air raids, parachute landings and, by the end of the summer term, the certainty (as most of us thought) of invasion. Academic life and work continued, perhaps more ardently and strenuously than in ordinary times. Maybe the pubs were full but so were the libraries. Such was the period when I first encountered Jack Fisher, by then a well-established teacher in the economic history department.

The School had acquired for its fewer students an admirable house and garden, Grove Lodge, next to the Fitzwilliam Museum. Place and circumstances created a closely acquainted academic community which, so we newcomers were told, had not existed in Houghton Street. Jack, then still a young man, gregarious, unshockable and a willing listener as well as a witty talker, was marvellously endowed to befriend and teach students in that early war-time environment. He became pastor to many students. He was always ready to talk and help and advise until he took his own departure to Cairo looking forlorn and uncomfortable in his Air Force uniform. In that role he played a key part in the very difficult but successful transfer of the School to Cambridge.

Intermediate students went to a course of lectures on the economic history of England from the middle ages onwards, given most elegantly by Eileen Power in what turned out sadly to be the last year of her life, and we also attended classes concurrently given by Jack. He was the very best teacher of the first-year students that I sat under. Spare and succinct in utterance, he insisted upon a precise definition of the question to be answered and always put the subject being discussed into an exciting context of the experience of different countries or other periods. He possessed a formidable power of analysis that penetrated through the verbiage to the central issue and taught us that economic historians were engaged in solving problems not in constructing narratives.

I was especially fortunate in that, after the war, he used me as an assistant examiner on the external degree. Characteristically, he devoted many hours of scrupulous care in training me how to tackle that most burdensome of all academic tasks. Like many of my generation at the School, I owe much to Jack Fisher and I remember him across half a century with affection and respect.

v

Professor Walter Elkan

Professor of Economics, Brunel University

I would like to recall Jack's lecture course to first-year students in the early post-war years. We all went to that course – not just the economic history specialists. And it is remembered by everyone.

Most of us were ex-servicemen on further education and training grants. We were predominantly in our mid-20s, and many of us, like Cyril Ehrlich and myself, had recently returned from service in the Middle East or Africa or the Far East. So had Jack, and that shared experience made a great bond. Although he was ten to fifteen years older, he seemed like one of us. We were, I suppose, a slightly bolshy lot – probably quite different in that respect from students before the war. But we were there because we wanted to learn.

Jack helped us to learn some economic history, and a great deal more besides. He opened up for us new ways of looking at the world. Let me try to explain. Most of us had arrived at the School imbued to a greater or lesser degree with the received wisdom of the '30s and '40s – a mixture of Noddy Marxism (to use John Rex's engaging term) and, I suppose, the Hammonds and G.D.H. Cole, mostly at second-hand. One of the things we soon learnt from Jack was the dire inadequacy of that received wisdom. Not that he ever said so. Wonderfully combative though Jack was in arguing his way through a lecture, it was not his custom to knock the views of others, unless it could be done with wit. But his way of putting things made so much better sense than the received wisdom that one could not afterwards think why one had never thought of it oneself. It was a devastatingly effective way to deal with widely held misconceptions and to help our generation to a new understanding of how things came about.

Those of us who had been overseas also found that Jack's approach helped to make sense, for the first time, of some of our recent experiences, by treating English economic history not as an isolated, unique, episode, but as an example of a response or adaptation to problems faced by all societies at some time or another.

Take the organisation and practices of medieval agriculture – a more puzzling topic it would be hard to find. But all becomes clear when it is pointed out that farmers must restore nitrogen to the soil if they want to grow crops on the same land in future years. I would not wish to vouch for the accuracy of Jack's soil chemistry. But by taking an apparently 'universal truth' as the starting point of his lecture, this deceptively obvious observation instantly made sense of strange agricultural practices not only in medieval England, but also in contemporary Egypt, India or Kenya. It made it sound ludicrously simple – and was overwhelmingly profound. My own introduction to development economics was Jack's introductory course to English economic history. It was a far better introduction than most economists have had.

And yet, given Jack's way of lecturing – straightforward and without hint of pomp or ostentation – I am ashamed to say that it never occurred to me at the time that I might be listening to the person who in the event most influenced my own way of thinking; or that we might be listening to a most uncommonly gifted teacher. When I told Cyril Ehrlich the other day what I was going to talk about, he said, 'Well, of course: Jack was simply the greatest teacher we had'. I was taken aback. I had never thought of Jack in those terms. But Cyril is, of course, absolutely right.

vi

Professor Cyril Ehrlich

Emeritus Professor of Economic and Social History, Queen's University of Belfast

We all remember Jack's superb lectures. The stance: very upright, with a characteristic tilt of the head. The lucid flow of words, forming a perfectly wrought argument. The assertive turn of phrase – 'it is a commonplace . . .' The total lack of pomp. The marvellous coherence and confidence of every performance. An infectious confidence which persuaded us that economic history was something we could understand; perhaps even *do*.

Some of us were also privileged to know him as a research supervisor or adviser. And here the same qualities – lucidity, coherence, confidence – were especially appropriate and productive. One presented him with half-baked ideas for a thesis or book: a jumble of incoherence, with self-doubt masquerading as dogma. One suffered the attack of that gleaming intelligence; the insistence on clear thinking; the edge of that tongue, often funny, never malevolent. One emerged, slightly shaken, thoroughly stirred, and confident that the thing could be written, and might even be shaped.

All this is familiar – a commonplace. I want to add an idiosyncratic footnote. A tribute to Jack's way with the maverick. It's an awkward word for an awkward type. The Oxford dictionary defines maverick as 'one who is roving and casual', an irrevocable put-down among pedants. Webster advances the more equivocal, one who 'bolts at will and sets up an independent course'. Jack welcomed mavericks. Quirky changes of theme and scope for a thesis, outlandish proposals for books, were greeted with that rare and fruitful reponse: sceptical interest, careful reading, probing, relentless argument. Not for Jack the arrogance and indifference of discrete knowledge, the 'keep out' notices around a subject. Like Tawney, he also rejected those who 'create a desert and call it research'. He was, by contrast, a cultivator, a teacher: the best I ever met.

vii

Professor Barry Supple

Master of St. Catherine's College and
Professor of Economic History, University of Cambridge

I first met – or, rather, listened to – Jack in the academic year 1949-50, when I came to LSE as an undergraduate to specialise in Economics. It didn't take me very long to decide that Economic History would be an altogether more congenial field of study than Economic Theory. In part, perhaps, this decision was rooted in my own mathematical inadequacies. But looking back, I now realise how enormously I must have been influenced by the remarkable series of survey lectures in English Economic History offered by Eleanora Carus-Wilson, Jack Fisher, Arthur John, Cliffe Ashton, and Lance Beales. And to my eyes, even among this galaxy, Jack's star shone with the most attractive scintillation.

There may have been those who took his superficial cynicism at its amusing face value; but his undergraduate audience soon came to learn that that mode of discourse was a powerful device to attain an extraordinarily stimulating intellectual penetration. For his students, Jack was capable of opening a remarkable window into the past – insisting on its strangeness and its resistance to easy generalisation; yet at the same time illuminating, with those familiar shafts of lateral thinking and devastating logic, the workings of exotic economic and social systems. It was inescapable, then, that I should not only decide to change my field, but also take Jack's special subject in the sixteenth century.

The attraction was, of course, personal as well as intellectual. And just as Jack's own easy and engaging, yet never lax, magnetism was such a profound incentive for many of us, so he was also able to create coherent and persuasive vision of the subject-matter. To this day – having wandered very far from sixteenth-century England – I still feel guilty at the desertion, because I still recall Jack's dictum that the only 'real' history was that of pre-industrial society, since its practitioners could be under no illusion about its differences from the modern world, whereas modernists were constantly misled into believing that they understood what was going on because of the spuriously familiar terminology used to describe, say, nineteenth-century economic and social institutions.

Jack's weekly class was a delightful mixture of scholarly dedication, energetic inquisitiveness, and (largely one-sided) repartee. He never affected a sentimentalism; but his care for and loyalty to his students and their work, his ability to treat youngsters as equals, his engaging way of taking you into his confidence in matters of personal judgement as well as academic exploration – were characteristics which have had an enduring effect on all who worked with him. Looking back, I find abundant memories of serious scholarship embedded in the most congenial company, or work inextricably mingled with pleasure. Jack was, of course, great *fun* to be with.

The fun as well as the work lasted. The day I had my degree results, I went to Jack's room, with the immodest intention of receiving congratulations – only to find pinned to the door a sobering note, conveying the unsober injunction: 'those of my students who did well will find me in the saloon bar of the White Horse.'

Naturally enough, I saw Jack very frequently in the years after I left LSE. He visited Cambridge when I was a graduate student there and reassured an unsuspecting seminar audience that the evidence for his talk was to be found in the *Calendar of State Papers Domestic* – and then added, in his inimitable throwaway style, 'and for all I know, in the State Papers themselves!'

He was also the person I wrote to when, after a year in the United States, I decided I should like to return to England – an opinion which elicited a characteristic mock-exasperated reply. I suffered and benefited from his powerfully sharp comments on manuscripts when I was editor of the *Economic History Review*. Like all great teachers he was a rock and a comfort to his students' subsequent academic careers. I have never written a research outline without recalling his comment on my original callow proposal for a Ph.D. topic: 'you obviously read too much Hemingway!' I have never written an article or a book without pondering his possible reaction.

I venture to think that all Jack's former students share this keen sense of deriving their work from him, and working continuously for him, and for his approbation. I can think of no stronger demonstration of the quality and rarity of the man. Like so many others, I shall miss him, and the twinkling discipline of his friendship.

vii

Dr H.E.S. Fisher

Senior Lecturer in Economic History, University of Exeter

Professor Jack Fisher was, without question, one of the most impressive university teachers I have ever met; a stimulating tutor, a fine scholar, an engaging man of great wit and warmth of spirit. Indeed, in his wit and learning he reminded me increasingly of Dr Johnson.

I count myself as very fortunate to have been a student of Jack's during my undergraduate and postgraduate years at the School. His lectures were lucidity itself, beautifully prepared, always pointed. His conduct of his special subject seminars was forthright yet urbane. Invigorating discourse would continue in the Three Tuns and other nearby taverns, where he was always willing to talk and argue, showing great tolerance of our innocent ignorance of the world and its ways. His discreet concern, as I now see it, was that we should go to the root of any matter: of all tutors he best exemplified the LSE motto '*Rerum cognoscere causas*'. His invariably modest approach before expressing a telling opinion was, puffing at his pipe all the while, 'Well, my impression is . . .' He had concern for our welfare too, as, for instance, turning up at the examination rooms to invite his special subject group for a post-examination drink.

In later years as one got to know him better, through visits to the School as an examiner, or at Institute seminars, my respect for him continued to grow. For me, he combined a formidably sharp mind with a friendly, generous nature, always welcoming when one knocked on his door, always encouraging of one's achievements. For a time I acted as his second marker for the external 1485-1760 paper: his acuity of judgement was remarkable, his views of candidates' efforts epigrammatic, as after an overdrawn and uncertain exposition of the nature and effects of Tudor price inflation, he added to the mark, 'gloomy as well as murky'. Institute seminars with him in the chair were occasions, his comments searching and frequently edged with humour: following one talk touching on how seventeenth-century occupational titles disguised the practice of other occupations, he said it reminded him of how the title 'actress' similarly could confuse. Post-seminar dinners were both enjoyable and instructive. At one he was quizzed on life peerages, and why he would not be unwelcoming should one be offered: 'Why was that?' – 'Well, the House of Lords has a very good library'; we then pressed him on where he would wish to sit: 'On the cross benches, of course, where there is most room'.

Any meeting with Jack Fisher was a pleasure and a challenge. One generally felt one had to offer something in return to be worthy of his time and attention, perhaps some gem of observation acquired through reading or travelling, or the latest news in academe. He was always ready for a discussion on any topic. Of all academics I have known he most clearly demonstrated: 'Wisdom is the principal thing; therefore get wisdom; and with all thy getting get understanding'.

ix

Peter Holwell

Principal of the University of London

I am absolutely sure that one thing that Jack Fisher would not have wanted would be anything that savoured of an eulogy. I knew at once which two anecdotes I should use to illustrate one aspect of his unique contribution to teaching at the School, namely the way in which his originality and strength of character impressed itself on his students.

I was one such in 1955 when he took up his Chair in succession to R.H. Tawney. As a would-be economic historian I had of course taken the trouble to attend Jack's inaugural and was therefore well seized of what was to come in the next three years. You can therefore imagine the scene at the first of Jack's lectures to that year's general BSc (Econ) intake. The Old Theatre was packed with fresh eager students clutching brand new notepads and freshly sharpened pencils – the age of the ubiquitous ballpoint had arrived but not burgeoned. You may therefore equally conceive the consternation of that tightly-packed multitude when that soon-to-be familiar figure ambled on to the stage and proceeded to treat us to fifty-five minutes of an unrelieved and deadly monotone, unenlivened by any characteristic witticisms, or, indeed, so far as I can recall, anything of great historical moment. The crowd dispersed, discomfited, with most wondering how so illustrious a figure as Tawney could have been succeeded in this fashion.

As you can guess the numbers turning up for the following week were rather more modest – about thirty-five devotees and, after a brief prologue on the lines of – but more robustly put – 'Well that's got rid of the passengers, I cannot bear to lecture to a huge audience of uncomprehending note-takers', the faithful were treated to one of Jack's most sparkling orations with that characteristic self-deprecating humour, that masterly exposition of subject, that unique way of making sixteenth- and seventeenth-century England come to life, and that art of drawing all the threads of his discourse together to provide new and coherent insights into whatever aspect of history he addressed, which we were soon to take for granted. We were quite rightly enthralled – and not a little smug at our foresight. I often think of that episode in the context of today's unthinking dedication to performance indicators.

My second and equally characteristic account of Jack's behaviour concerns the more intimate atmosphere of his classes. These took place in his room in Clare Market and it was not long before we students became aware of Jack's evidently idiosyncratic approach to correspondence. The system, if such it could be called, was this: he had a table in the corner of the room and as each new letter or package arrived it was tossed in that direction. Eventually there arose a rough pyramid of these various materials and the theory was that items were looked at – and possibly answered – when they dropped off the edge of the table.

There was something awe-inspiring about someone who could pursue such a system and in later years I received independent corroboration of his practice from distraught colleagues in the Senate House. The mere mention of the name Professor Fisher in the Examinations Department was enough to induce acute hysteria. Subsequently, I have learnt from bitter experience that there was a good deal of common sense and logic in his system.

I use these two first-hand observations mercly to remind us this afternoon of what a remarkable and altogether unique figure Jack Fisher was. His students, that is his real students not the note-takers, were immediately aware that they were in the presence of a master of his subject; his personal approach and sheer strength of character provided an experience for those lucky enough to enjoy it that matched the very best that Houghton Street has offered.

x

Professor M.J. Wise

Emeritus Professor of Geography and formerly Pro-Director,
London School of Economics

I came to LSE in 1951 from a university of a quite different kind, large, multi-faculty, highly departmentalised. I had had no previous experience of LSE, or of the University of London, and I was told that it would take me some time to settle down in this rather special place. In the event, it did not take long. There was an immediately perceptible general purpose and spirit in the place, a collegiate atmosphere, common themes and questions running in teaching and research in the different, but related, disciplines. At the personal level contacts were easy to make, thanks to the friendly, totally unforced, way in which a number of colleagues, of whom Jack was one, took me in to the School and into their talk about its past, its current tasks and problems and, of course, about its personalities. Very clearly, Jack knew what was going on, and equally clearly he was a moving spirit.

By that time, Jack was a Reader in Economic History and a very well-established figure. He had already in the 1930s been a member of the Library Committee: he gathered books to himself and, the story went, lent them readily to his students believing that books were meant to be read and to mark steps in academic progress, a faith that may have caused him occasionally to fall foul of official dates for return. Early in the war the School was moved to Cambridge and Jack became for a time the Warden of Grove Lodge, a social centre for LSE students. Thanking him for this work at the end of the 1939-40 session, the Director wrote 'all your spare time during the present session has been given to the School'. When the war ended, the Middle East office wanted him to stay on, but LSE insisted on his release and he came back for the 1945-46 session to what was then called a 'major' lectureship.

Jack succeeded T.S. Ashton in the Chair of Economic History in 1954. Others have written of his contributions to economic history; I wish to comment on the extent and quality of his service to the School community. He was, for a start, an ever present, never an applicant for sabbatical leave or leave to teach elsewhere. The School was truly his academic home. He was among those willing to give up time and to forego opportunities to ensure that the institution itself was in a healthy condition and offering the best possible opportunities and advice to its students.

A glance at the School's *Calendar* for the session 1958-59 bears this out. He was at that time a representative of the Academic Board on the Court of Governors and a member of the Library Committee, General Purposes Committee, Graduate School Committee among others. The School at that time taught undergraduates both in the day and in the evening and Jack and his fellow economic historians were never unwilling to take on part-time as well as full-time students, whether undergraduate or graduate.

Donald Coleman has written of the 'characteristic wit and verve' which enlivened Jack Fisher's teaching. The same could be said of his contributions to the morning gatherings over coffee in the Senior Common Room at which the events of the time were put under scrutiny. He was a realist, a man with cold water for the over-ambitious scheme or policy; to quote Coleman again, 'no friend to pomposity', with the ability when the occasion demanded it to deliver a deflating parting shaft and to get back to his waiting class. He set high standards and he was, I am sure, a critical teacher and supervisor, but for students his acute criticism was not meant to deflate, not I think did it often do so, for his intention in setting standards and in communicating his own critical spirit of enquiry was patently clear.

In 1965 he became Chairman of the Library Committee, the first academic to assume this post. Previously, the Director had been Chairman but, as the Director's *Report* for 1964-65 shows, the new intention was 'to ensure that the Library Committee acts more effectively as a close link between the needs of the academic staff and the library administration'. Jack was clearly seen as the man best fitted to bring the British Library and the School closer together in policy and practice. He held this post until his retirement in 1975. For a time, in the early 1970s, he was Vice-Chairman of the Academic Board and his election to this post tells us of the respect and trust in which he was held by his colleagues. The creation of this post had not really arisen from the need to have a deputy who would chair the Board in the Director's absence, for Directors were hardly, if ever, absent from Academic Board meetings. Much more important was the need for a person who would gather opinion in the School and use his judgement wisely in support of the School as an institution and community. And there was no doubt at all on the evidence of Jack's attitude and behaviour during the 'troubles' how greatly he cared for the School – not just for the words of the Articles of Association which embody its aims, important as those words are, but for the living body of students, research workers, teachers and administrators committed to the critical study of problems presented by changes in economy, technology and social life.

Jack was indeed a central figure in the School until he retired in 1975 and indeed beyond that time, for he continued as a part-time teacher for many years. Central, that is, to all aspects of the School's life. His election as an Honorary Fellow in 1980 reflected the breadth of his interests, the size of his contribution over half a century and the strength of feeling among his colleagues.

Those who know the LSE porters and maintenance staff are aware that invitations to their Annual Christmas Party (the Porters' Party) are very selectively issued and that those invited count themselves privileged. Jack was there every year and I recall one evening at about the time of his retirement when a special presentation was made to him by the Porters and Maintenance Staff Social Club. It was a significant event. All who served the School were equal in Jack's eyes: he was a man who bound others to him, who represented an institution in which they could feel a part and be at home. Jack was an embodiment of the spirit of the place. He was a part of the tradition as well as very much a part of the present. It was hoped at one time that he would write the history of the School. Alas, he never did so, but he did become a memorable figure in its history.

PART TWO

3

Some Experiments in Company Organisation in the Early Seventeenth Century

TO the student of the history of industrial gilds and companies the early seventeenth century is a period of peculiar interest. By that time, the social, financial, territorial and political foundations of the old gild system had been seriously undermined. It had been the product of a society strikingly homogeneous in texture; by the seventeenth century the divisions between entrepreneur and artisan, between industrial and commercial capitalist, were deep. It had been built up when industry was predominantly financed by those directly engaged in the technical processes of manufacture and distribution; by the seventeenth century the capital of the non-working investor was of considerable and growing importance. Traditionally the jurisdiction of a gild was coterminous with that of the town within which it functioned; yet the failure of economic and municipal boundaries to coincide was yearly becoming more marked. And whereas the gild had been in the past an instrument used by the local authorities for regulating economic activity, the integration of national life, the widening of markets, and the development of mercantilist thought were all making industrial policy a matter more for the central than for the local government, a matter more of development and promotion than of simple regulation.

Inevitably, therefore, the problem arose whether the old forms of corporate organization, based on the theory that " noe trade, ffacoulty or occupation can fflourish, prosper or continue in any good order without men of civill government, knowledge and understanding to rule and direct them noe more than a kingdome or a commonwealth without a ruler or a citty without a magistrate,"[1] could be adapted to the new circumstances. The desire of the public authorities to control industry did not pass away with mediæval industrial conditions; the problem was whether it could still best be served by the mediæval device of " an unitinge of a Societe usinge one trade, misterie or occupacion into one bodie by the Prince or Soveraigne, havinge aucthoritie to make lawes and ordinances tochinge suche trade, misterie or occupacion, whereunto every member of the same is subiect."[2] In other words, could the gild system be refashioned and given a new lease of

[1] Ferguson and Nanson, *Some Municipal Records of the City of Carlisle*, p. 211.
[2] Tawney and Power, *Tudor Economic Documents*, vol. iii., p. 265.

life ? The final answer to that question is, of course, among the commonplaces of economic history. It was a decided negative; English industry sloughed off the gild system as it grew to maturity. But it would be a mistake to suppose that such a reply, although ultimately so uncompromising, was either immediate or unanimous. Faith in corporate organization died hard, alternative administrative machinery was lacking, and in reality a negative was arrived at only after a series of attempts had been made to answer the problem in the opposite sense. The significance of the early seventeenth century in gild history is precisely that most of these attempts occurred within that period, and their failure made it in some degree a turning-point.

Apart from the sweeping reorganizations carried out by some provincial towns, the experiments of this period fall into two broad groups which, although they overlap slightly, are best considered apart. Those in the first were designed to bring within the company system classes—in some cases the landed gentry with capital to invest, in others the rural producers—which hitherto had remained outside, but which were becoming of increasing economic importance. Those in the second proposed to change the whole purpose of corporate organization. That attempts should have been made to adapt the gild system to meet the needs of the outside capitalist is scarcely surprising. For, except in certain branches, industry, as distinct from commerce, was not highly attractive to the investor under the early Stuarts. Although sleeping partnerships, such as that which Jeffrey Duppa, courtier and diplomatic agent, enjoyed in one of the largest London breweries,[1] were to be found in some of the larger towns, its general structure did not facilitate the entrance of large blocks of capital. And, except in mining, draining, and the supplying of water, large-scale production did not, in the pre-machine age, carry with it any very great reduction of costs. As a consequence, when the investor looked to industry for profits comparable to those to be obtained in trade, finance or land speculation, he demanded both some form of guaranteed market, and a *modus vivendi* with the established producers wherever they were too numerous or powerful to be ignored or suppressed. The first he found in a patent of monopoly;[2] the second, at least in the soap, salt, and starch manufactures and in certain London trades, in a chartered company, within which the new and old

[1] For details of Duppa's activities see Add. MSS., vol. 38,170, ff. 137, 144 and 180; Lansd. MSS., vol. 162, ff. 170-2.

[2] Cf. Gretton, writing of the corporate monopolies: " The practical explanation of the existence of all these monopolies is, of course, that the venturing of capital had become necessary, while the idea of speculation was still so far undeveloped that the owners of capital would not risk it in open competition, but demanded the closed market of a privileged association " (*The English Middle Class*, p. 162).

interests might arrange and enforce some measure of co-operation, and by means of which they might together exploit the consumer.

Obviously, associations such as these, however closely their constitutions and powers may have been modelled on the orthodox gild pattern, embodied, in fact, a new concept of corporate organization; had they been successful they would have opened a new and not unimportant chapter in company history. But for success it was essential that the interests of the new investors and the established producers should be reconciled. Failure in this respect simply meant a price-cutting war in which the new-comers, hampered by technical ignorance, the expense and difficulty of enforcing monopolistic rights, and, in most cases, the necessity of paying taxes on their output, could hope for no permanent victory, and upon which no permanent organization could be built. In theory, such a reconciliation seemed possible, for most investors brought with them monopolies and embargoes upon imports which might be used to obtain sufficient profits for both parties. In practice, all such hopes soon proved illusory. The terms of co-operation varied widely from case to case. In that of the first South Shields salt company, for example, the association was very loose, the existing pan-owners merely being offered the choice of leasing their pans to the new patentees or of undertaking not to sell below a certain price.[1] The Westminster soapmakers favoured a system of individual quotas.[2] The starchmakers' company of 1638 went to the opposite extreme, and restricted all manufacture to a single joint stock, to which both the new patentees and the established London manufacturers were to subscribe.[3] The favourite solution, however, appears to have been for the new investors to concentrate upon marketing and to take from the existing producers all their output at fixed prices.[4]

---

[1] Privy Council Register, vol. xliv., p. 437; vol. xlv., p. 384; S.P.D. Chas. I., vol. cccxli., no. 92. They were repeatedly urged to choose the former course.

[2] The manufacture of soap was divided into 40 shares, each carrying a responsibility for 125 of the 5,000 tons which the company undertook to produce annually. If less than 5,000 tons were sold, the output per share was to be reduced proportionately (Chanc. Procs., Ser. I., Chas. I., G. 36/8 and P. 53/54). It does not seem, however, that any of these shares were taken up by established soapmakers in London. A further 600 tons were distributed among the Bristol manufacturers (S.P.D. Chas. I., vol. cclxxxviii., no. 49).

[3] Patent Roll, 14 Chas. I., pt. 10, no. 12.

[4] As, for example, in the second Shields salt company (Privy Seal Docquet, December, 1638) and the pinmakers' company (Unwin, *Industrial Organization*, p. 167). A separate marketing stock, subscribed by the courtier investors and employing some of the old makers as agents, was also part of the Westminster soap company (Chanc. Procs. cited above; S.P.D. Chas. I., vol. ccxliv., no. 24). Cf. the selling organization set up by the gold and silver thread monopolists (Abrams, " English Gold and Silver Thread Monopolies, 1611-21," in *Jnl. of Bus. and Econ. History*, vol. iii., pp. 400-1).

The proposed terms of co-operation varied widely in detail, but they were all alike in their failure satisfactorily to establish the desired reconciliation, partly because the interests concerned had too little in common to make co-operation easy, partly because of the selfish policy of the new investors. The rapidity of their failure depended very largely upon the existing organization of the industry concerned. In the soap, salt and starch industries, where production was already in the hands of capitalists, opposition to the new régime was immediate and bitter. The established manufacturers had nothing to gain from the proposals laid before them, and, refusing to collaborate, they maintained a competition in which no privileges could bring success to the intruders. The refusal of the London soapboilers to come to terms and their struggle with and overthrow of the Westminster courtier investors have become a commonplace of the textbooks.[1] In the case of the first of the Shields salt companies the struggle was only less acute. After many exhortations from the Privy Council on their behalf the patentees obtained control over but 157 of the 240 Shields pans, and were never able to prevent a minority of the old makers from creaming the market by cutting prices.[2] And the same story was repeated in the case of the starch company, where the competition of recalcitrant individuals prevented the payment of any dividends upon the central joint stock.[3] When the industry was in the hands of smaller artisans the opposition was usually deferred. It seemed that co-operation with outside capitalists might prove less onerous than domination by the existing entrepreneurs, and neither the beaver-makers, the pinmakers, nor the tobacco-pipe makers seem to have objected at first, while the feltmakers actually took the initiative in seeking such collaboration.[4] But even in these cases harmony, if ever obtained, was but short-lived. The artisan starchmakers, for example, were soon lamenting that they were deprived of their livelihood " by the misgovernment and irregular proceedings of the new Company."[5] And that seems to have been the common experience of artisans who attempted to co-operate with outside investors.[6] Most of these associations were swept away, in actual fact, by the consumers' revolt which accompanied the Long Parliament, but all prospects of their permanent success had disappeared even earlier. Nor does it seem that this line of experiment was ever resumed. The post-Restoration capitalist preferred, not a regulated gild embracing new and old

[1] The best account is still that in Price, *English Patents of Monopoly.*
[2] S.P.D. Chas. I., vol. cccxli., no. 92.
[3] Privy Council Register, vol. li., p. 198.   [4] Unwin, *op. cit.*, chaps. v. and vi.
[5] S.P.D. Chas I., vol. cccciii., p. 114; Privy Council Register, vol. li., p. 87.
[6] Unwin, *op. cit.*, p. 171.

manufacturers, but a joint-stock company in a field where established producers were either negligible or non-existent.

Not merely did these companies break new ground by incorporating together speculative capitalists and skilled manufacturers; they also parted from strict orthodoxy in obtaining jurisdiction over areas wider than that of a single town. The authority of the soap and starch companies, for example, was national in its scope; the salt companies ruled that industry along the south and east coasts; and most of the combinations of London artisans and investors had powers extending at least into the home counties.   In this respect, however, they merely reflected the general contemporary tendency to draw within the gild system the hitherto unorganized rural worker. The coincidence of town and gild jurisdictions had arisen and had been natural in an age when nearly all industry was carried on within a town and for a narrow local market.   Once that situation had passed away, there were few reasons for keeping them closely wedded, and many for divorcing them and reorganizing the gild system upon a territorial basis more in accord with economic realities. A movement in that direction had already begun in the later Middle Ages, when the goldsmiths and pewterers of London,[1] for example, had obtained national rights of search, and had continued under the Tudors. It was not, however, until the seventeenth century that such a movement became general.

Except in a few unimportant cases,[2] the inspiration for all these expansions came from town industrialists, or at least from producers in an important industrial centre, who sought to bring under their control the whole area—suburbs, county or nation, as the case might be—from which serious competition was being felt.   Thus many London companies obtained, from either James or Charles, charters extending their authority for several miles beyond the city and its immediate suburbs.[3]   And the importance of London as a market and industrial centre led to a number of requests for an even wider jurisdiction, requests which were successful in the case of the shipwrights,[4] starch-

---

[1] Prideaux, *Memorials of the Goldsmiths' Company*, vol. i., p. xxii; Welch, *History of the Pewterers' Company*, vol. i., p. iii.

[2] The chief exceptions were the Hallamshire cutlers' company, which controlled the cutlers in and around Sheffield (Leader, *The Cutlers of Hallamshire*, vol. ii., p. 7); the Thames fishermen, who exercised authority west of Staines and between London Bridge and the Medway but not in the city itself (Patent Roll, 10 Chas. I., pt. 36, no. 39); and the corporations for brewers and maltsters proposed for every county as part of a scheme for licensing and taxing the drink trade (S.P.D. Chas. I., vol. ccccviii., nos. 18-20).

[3] Privy Seal Docquet Books, 1603-40, *passim*.

[4] Patent Rolls, 3 Jas. I., pt. 22, no. 15, and 10 Jas. I., pt. 9, no. 2.   The demands for these charters came, not from the small yards in the city, but from the suburban yards of Blackwall and Rotherhithe.

makers,[1] silkmen,[2] silkweavers,[3] vintners[4] and framework knitters,[5] all of whom obtained some measure of national authority, but unsuccessful in that of the cutlers,[6] plumbers[7] and haberdashers.[8]

In the provinces, however, this movement for extra-mural powers was confined almost entirely to the textile industry. The brewers of Lincoln[9] and Gloucester[10] and the tailors of Oxford,[11] it is true, obtained some measure of control over their immediate neighbours. But in most cases where the problem was only that of meeting the competition, within the local market, of those " whoe like drone bees to the hyve, paying nether scot nor lot, lye lurking in the suburbs, and other secret places in and aboute the towne,"[12] the provincial craftsman preferred other methods. For, on the one hand, extra-mural juris- diction could be obtained only by means of a royal charter. And a royal charter was often so fiercely attacked by the town magistrates, who resented the independence of their control which it conferred,[13] that it brought greater troubles than those it was designed to dispel. The officers of the Chester drapers, for example, were imprisoned when they spoke of obtaining such a grant,[14] and the charters of the Reading weavers,[15] Bristol bakers[16] and Ipswich clothworkers[17] were all cancelled or revised after a struggle before the Council and the courts. On the other hand, as long as the problem was simply one of suburban competition in a small local market, a number of other expedients promised as much, if not more, relief. Countrymen might be subjected to strict market regulations, or informed against for non-apprentice- ship; citizens might be punished for employing them; the town authori- ties themselves might seek to extend their own jurisdiction; and in cases of particular urgency direct appeal might be made to the Privy Council.

In the textile centres, however, conditions were different, and approximated more closely to those in London. The markets fought

[1] *Ibid.*, 5 Jas. I., pt. 20, no. 20; and 20 Jas. I., pt. 10, no. 13.

[2] *Ibid.*, 7 Chas. I., pt. 3, no. 1.   [3] *Ibid.*, 14 Chas. I., pt. 12, no. 1.

[4] Privy Council Register, vol. xlix., p. 402.

[5] Chambers, " The Worshipful Company of Framework Knitters," in *Econo- mica*, vol. viii., p. 303.

[6] Leader, *op. cit.*, vol. i., p. 20.   [7] S.P.D. Jas. I., vol. lxii., no. 56.

[8] *Acts of the Privy Council*, 1618-19, pp. 149-50.

[9] Sign Manual Warrants, vol. xvi., no. 62.

[10] Privy Seal Docquet, February, 1630-31.   [11] *Ibid.*, November, 1629.

[12] *Records of Leicester*, 1603-88 (ed. Stocks), p. 238.

[13] Cf. the report of Sir Thomas Edmunds and Sir Julius Cæsar that " we are of the opinion in the generall that theis under Corporacons in Townes and inferior Cities are seldom of goode use, but do rather disturbe the generall government of such places " (Lansd. MSS., vol. 165, f. 195).

[14] Harl. MSS., vol. 2,354, ff. 37-47.   [15] Guilding, *Records of Reading*, vol. ii., 9

[16] Latimer, *Annals of Bristol in the Seventeenth Century*, p. 58.

[17] Privy Council Register, vol. xxx., p. 510.

for were no longer local, and therefore were not subject to direct local regulation. The town authorities were more complacent. And demands for control over rural producers found disinterested support in the fashionable theory that the cloth industry could be saved only by an extension to the countryside of the regulations for searching and sealing which still obtained in Colchester, Canterbury and other towns.[1] As a consequence, a number of provincial clothing companies followed the example of the Londoners and extended their jurisdiction. Quite early in the century companies were set up in Bury[2] and Colchester[3] with control over the most important textile areas in Suffolk and Essex respectively. In 1631 the dornix weavers of Norwich had their authority extended over the whole of Norfolk and Suffolk.[4] Nineteen years later, after years of agitation, the worsted weavers of the same city had their county powers strengthened and confirmed.[5] And in 1662, as Professor Heaton has related, a corporation was set up in Yorkshire to control the clothing industry throughout the West Riding.[6] By the 'sixties, therefore, the bulk of the eastern textile industry, rural and urban alike, had been brought, at least in theory and for a time, under the regulation of one or other of five companies—the clothiers of Leeds, Bury and Colchester and the worsted and dornix weavers of Norwich. In the west of England, where the town clothier was a less important figure, the growth of extra-urban jurisdiction was far less marked. For a few years, until their charter was cancelled at the request of the local magistrates, the Reading weavers enjoyed a limited suburban authority.[7] And in 1603 the weavers' companies in the corporate towns of Wiltshire were given, by the county J.P.s in Quarter Sessions, a measure of control over all weavers within three miles of their respective towns.[8] But the only county organization was that set up in 1637, whereby the worsted combers of Exeter extended their sway over the whole of Devon.[9]

For success, these combinations of town and country, or of London and provincial, workers depended, as had those of capitalists and artisans, upon the effective reconciliation of the interests of the two parties concerned. The alternative, the drastic enforcement of the new privileges by the townsmen against the opposition of their rural

[1] See, for example, Misselden, *Free Trade*, p. 27 *et seq.*; *H.M.C., Portland MSS.*, vol. viii., pp. 2-3; S.P.D. Jas. I., vol. cxx., no. 75; vol. cxxi., no. 35; vol. cxxxiii., no. 35.   [2] *Vict. County Hist., Suffolk*, vol. ii. 263.

[3] Sign Manual Warrants, vol. ix., no. 11; Defoe, *Tour through England and Wales*, vol. i., p. 31 (Everyman Edition).   [4] Privy Council Register, vol. xli., p. 107.

[5] Scobell, *Acts and Ordinances*, 1640-56, p. 146.

[6] Heaton, *The Yorkshire Woollen and Worsted Industries*, chap. xi. Apparently, during the Long Parliament, a similar corporation was proposed for Kent (*Diary of Thos. Burton*, vol. i., p. 126).   [7] Patent Roll, 2 Jas. I., pt. 12, no. 26.

[8] *H.M.C., Var. Coll.*, vol. i., pp. 74-5.

[9] S.P.D. Chas. I., vol. cccxli., no. 114; vol. cccxlviii., no. 20.

competitors, was too expensive and unpopular to be of permanent value.[1] Yet it is difficult to see on what basis any effective reconciliation could be built. There was no question of a narrow monopoly. The only powers conferred by the new charters were those of searching and sealing and generally regulating the quality of work, and the desire to avoid such regulations had been an important factor in attracting industry from the towns to the countryside. The prospects of co-operation, moreover, were still further diminished by the manner in which the control of the new companies was often engrossed in the hands of the townsmen, and by the use to which that control was sometimes put.[2] " Wee were," later wrote the Canterbury weavers, " besett in the yeares 1638 and 1639 by the weavers hall of London, if in case it had not beene for the Magistrates of this Cittie we had become att that time their slaves,"[3] and the complaints of tyranny and extortion raised against the shipwrights,[4] the Norwich worsted weavers,[5] the Bury clothiers[6] and the Exeter worsted combers[7] were only a shade less bitter. Not all companies, it is true, gave rise to such protests; but the silence of the records makes it impossible to decide whether this is to be attributed to the attainment of some degree of harmony or to the non-enforcement of the new powers. Generally, the attempts to bring the rural manufacturers within the gild system failed less spectacularly than those to admit the passive investor; most of the companies mentioned above lasted at least until the later years of the century. But it is difficult to believe that their success was more than moderate and temporary; had these extraurban jurisdictions been exercised at all widely and regularly they must surely have left some mark on industrial history.

A second group of experiments were aimed at changing, not merely the company's financial and social structure, but its very purpose·

[1] The London pewterers, for example, appear to have abandoned their provincial rights of search after the middle of the century owing to the charges and lawsuits to which they gave rise (Welch, *History of the Pewterers' Company*, vol. ii., p. 103). The shipwrights are said to have spent £750 in a vain attempt to enforce their jurisdiction in the outports (Chanc. Procs., Series III., 373/45).

[2] The constitutions of the companies varied. In most cases the governing power was definitely placed in the hands of the townsmen or Londoners, and the provincials had nothing to do but to obey. In a few both parties were equally represented on the central court, but even in those cases the townsmen could dominate, since it was highly inconvenient for the country representatives to make repeated journeys to be present at meetings.

[3] Cross, *History of the Walloon and Huguenot Churches at Canterbury*, p. 241.

[4] *Commons Journals*, vol. i., p. 563; *H.M.C., Cowper MSS.*, vol. i., p. 111.

[5] *The Humble Petition of the Worsted Weavers in Norfolk and in the City of Norwich. The Arguments against the Bill for Regulating the Stuffs in Norfolk and Norwich.*   [6] *Vict. County Hist., Suffolk*, vol. ii., 264.

[7] Hamilton, *Quarter Sessions from Queen Elizabeth to Queen Anne*, pp. 116-17.

The gild had evolved in an age when industry was conceived as something static; its purpose was merely to regulate what already existed. But by the seventeenth century, thanks to the lessons of experience and the growth of mercantilist thought, industry was seen to be dynamic, something demanding not merely regulation, but encouragement, development, creation. To set the poor on work, to foster manufactures, was a major commandment of the economic gospel of the time. And the teachings of the theorists were driven home by that fear of an unemployment problem which haunted every seventeenth-century administrator, and to which the exhortations, the reprimands and the orders of the Privy Council, the reports of the J.P.s, the strict anti-settlement laws of the towns, and the petitions of the distressed themselves all bear eloquent testimony. In striving for that end it was only natural that attempts should be made to use the traditional instrument of industrial policy, the chartered gild or company. For the key problem in any attempt to promote industry was, quite clearly, that of directing the stream of capital investment into the desired channels. That such a stream existed was obvious from the contemporary activities in trade, money-lending, Government finance and land speculation. That on occasion it could be turned into industry was proved by the monopolies and the developments in mining. The difficulty was to persuade the investor to widen his interests, and to enter fields which offered neither the relative security of a patent nor the possibilities of immense wealth which imagination associated with coal. In particular it was necessary to persuade him to finance those great givers of employment, those twin foundations of English trade—the textile manufactures, already well capitalized, and the herring fishery, a hazardous trade in which the Dutch were already strongly entrenched and which, whatever pamphleteers might say, had few attractions for shrewd men of business. For this purpose, the traditional methods of Government interference were of little value. Financial reasons made any generous system of bounties impracticable. The time-honoured searching and sealing for the maintenance of quality were more likely to repel than to attract capital. And, in so far as both fish and cloth would have to be marketed, for the most part, abroad, tariffs, sumptuary legislation and political lents were largely irrelevant; while arbitrary regulations, such as those associated with Cockayne's scheme, were positively harmful. The industrial company, however, held a promise of better things. On the one hand, it might conceivably be endowed with privileges or powers sufficient to obtain the necessary capital. On the other, its very structure made it a suitable channel through which the funds of the passive investor could be applied to productive purposes.

Apart from the New River and Bedford Level Corporations, public utility undertakings formed respectively to supply London with water and to drain the Lincolnshire fens, the ostensibly creative companies of the early Stuarts fall quite clearly into two groups. First, there were the monopolistic corporations, such as those in the soap and salt industries, all of which were established at the request of the investors themselves, and all of which, at least according to their professed intentions, were designed to promote " the benefit of the King, the good of the Commonwealth, and the employment of 1,000 poor people."[1] But as they have already been discussed from the point of view of their significance in bringing together the investor and the skilled producer within the gild system, and as the taxes and abuses which accompanied them give rise to a legitimate doubt as to the honesty of their professions, they need no further consideration here. Secondly, there were certain schemes for developing industry by means of a network of regional joint-stock associations which, under some form of public control, should mobilize for industrial purposes part of the surplus funds of the gentry and merchants of their respective localities. In the phraseology and provisions of their charters these companies followed the orthodox gild pattern, but in other respects they represent a violent breach with tradition. Like the corporations already discussed in this article, they were designed to admit the capital of the passive investor and to be organized on a basis wider than that of a single town. Unlike most of them, their declared purpose was not merely to regulate, but to establish, industries; and a complete absence of graft leaves no room for suspecting their honesty. Other companies were formed at the request of producers, or would-be producers, who were prepared to join and operate them; these were initiated by the Government and had to seek for members. Whereas the old system had been built up piecemeal, corporations being chartered when and where the demand arose, these were part of a co-ordinated national plan. Most of these schemes, moreover, embodied a high degree of public control, amounting in some cases to direct public trading. And, quite apart from their significance in gild history, these projects are interesting as revealing Stuart mercantilism in its most ambitious form, anticipating some of the most grandiose ideas of Colbert, and representing the nearest approach to national planning and state capitalism ever made in England.

Company systems along these lines were proposed for several industries,[2] but were seriously considered only for two, herring fishing and

---

[1] *The Hog's Character of a Projector*, p. 2.

[2] In 1660, for example, they were suggested for developing England's mines of " Sea Coales, Tinn, Lead, Brasse, Iron, Allum and the like " (S.P.D. Chas. II., vol. xxii., no. 73 [i.]).

clothmaking. In these, the schemes seem to have been worked out quite independently of each other, but their basic principles and their fortunes showed a fundamental similarity. They both began in a projector's brain; they both became significant when they were taken up by the Privy Council and sealed as representative of the considered political thought of the time; they both failed because they provided no motive power to set their machinery in action. In the case of the fishing, the pioneer of these ideas was possibly Robert Hitchcock, who, in 1581, advocated in his famous " Politique Platt "[1] the establishment of eight fishing associations centred respectively in London, Yarmouth, Hull, Newcastle, Chester, Bristol, Exeter and Southampton, controlled by the chief officers of those ports, and financed, to the extent of £10,000 each, by loans from " the Lords, Bishops, Knights, Gentlemen, Merchants and other rich men spiritual and temporal " of the neighbouring counties. Under the Stuarts many variations upon that theme appeared,[2] and it formed the basis of the Fishery Society actually set up in 1632.

In its original form, embodying as it did ideas drawn from both at home and abroad,[3] this undertaking was far more ambitious than the emasculated version actually set up would suggest. As in some of the earlier proposals, " it was not held fesible or convenient to mesnage this commoun business and joynt stocke bot rather in severall

---

[1] The idea of a chain of fishing companies, but with their members trading as individuals and not in a joint stock, was certainly older than this. In 1549 an anonymous pamphleteer had suggested that the expansion of the fishing industry might " be right well brought to passe, if in evry shire adioininge upon the See and in every other shire adioininge uppon eney greate water, ther were a brotherhede made and a fraternite of fishermen havinge souche lyke copporation as the fraternite of occupacons have in London, and that all other shires which adioine not uppon the See nor uppon eney other greate water were so equallie allotede unto the foresaid fraternites that the circute belonginge unto evry fraternite myght be mouche of lyke quantitie." These companies were to sell licences for men to eat flesh on the official fish days within their areas, the money going half to the local poor and half to the *bona fide* fishermen of the company. It was argued that if men bought these licences, recruits would pour into the fishing industry in order to share the purchase money, and the poor would consequently be supplied with plenty of cheap fish (Goldsmiths' Library, MS. no. 10, pp. 37-8).

[2] See, for example, Misselden, *The Circle of Commerce*, p. 140; Malynes, *The Maintenance of Free Trade*, p. 101; S.P.D. Jas. I., vol. xlviii., no. 95; vol. lxxi., no. 89; vol. cxxxix., no. 66; vol. clvii., no. 46.

[3] There were " lait erected formes both in Spaine, France and the Low Countries which show the necessitie of settling a common counsell . . . to make and execute ordinances . . . for the ordering, taking and vending of the fish and . . . Lykwayes in everie province in that citie or burrow where a companie sall be sattled there must be a court of assistants to correspond with the common counsell " (*Acts of the Parliament of Scotland*, v., 222-3).

companies or members which not withstanding may have relatioun to one bodie or corporatioun "; and the scheme sent north to enlist the co-operation of the Scots proposed " in everie province to sattle a severall companie in the cheefe citie, town or burrow and to take order that all adventurers of that province may joyne with that companie both in the charge and contribution for setting forth the shippes and in sharing the benefite qlk sall be raised by the fishing."[1] In other words, the original ideal of the Government was to girdle England and Scotland with a belt of joint-stock fishing companies, financed by the local magnates, and co-ordinated by a common subjection to a central board of Privy Councillors. There was to be a gild of gilds, a national company composed of local companies, with each local company mobilizing the capital of its neighbourhood and directing it into the fishing industry, while the central council co-ordinated all these local efforts into a coherent national policy.

The scheme was magnificent in conception, but its weaknesses were both obvious and fundamental. It provided the machinery of investment; but it did nothing to attract the capital for which that machinery was created. The capitalist asked how the English were to reduce their costs to the extraordinarily low level of the Dutch. For this the scheme made no provision, and its supporters had to fall back on a variety of arguments ranging from an exposition of England's superior geographical position and cheaper supplies of raw materials to the more dubious claim that " noe man but knows . . . that one Hollander eats more then one and a halfe of our Englishmen at sea." The capitalist asked where markets were to be found. For this also the scheme made no provision, and the answers had to be found outside of it, ranging from a pious hope of racing the Dutch to the European buyers to the development of regional marketing schemes for increasing and satisfying the home demand. The capitalist asked for guarantees that he would not be defrauded, as the investors in the Virginia, East India and other companies had been defrauded. And such guarantees could be given only by making membership of the joint-stock companies voluntary and allowing adventurers, if they wished, to fish on their own.[2]

In face of these objections, and of the determined efforts of the Scots to sabotage the whole project,[3] the Council's ambitious schemes collapsed miserably. In actual fact, only three small companies were

---

[1] *Ibid.*

[2] Monson, *A Discovery of the Hollanders Trade of Fishing and the Circumventing us therein.* (Printed in *Monson's Tracts*, vol. v., by the Navy Records Society.)

[3] For an account of Anglo-Scottish disputes and negotiations over this business, see Elder, *The Royal Fishery Companies of the Seventeenth Century.*

set up,[1] and they were not organized on any local basis. The methods used for obtaining subscriptions have been described by the Earl of Pembroke. " I undertooke," he wrote, " to draw in as many Adventurers as possible I might to subscribe to a Booke framed to contayne the names and Adventures of such Noble personages and others as would be under my subordinacon . . . but at lengthe fyndeing the summe of Adventures so subscribed to be lower then it might effect anything considerable . . . we fell upon a second expedient of sendeing severall Bookes to the number of 30 and to perswade as many Gent. (wherein we made Choyse of the best in quallity and affection) to bring as many into theire severall bookes as they could." Apparently the canvassers thus selected carried on their missionary labours at the Assizes.[2] The spirit in which subscriptions were made can be gathered from the records of the Levant Company and Trinity House. The former made a corporate investment of £600 because no member would subscribe as an individual.[3] The latter promised £50 " in regard of his Mats. Zeale in furtherance of the worke; our respect and honor to yourselfe, and lastly the nature of the business."[4] And it is not unreasonable to suppose that most of the individuals who subscribed did so more through a desire to stand well at court than through any conviction of the economic soundness of the business. Companies thus recruited naturally took on a definite social tone. Of the 45 known members of the Earl of Pembroke's association, 4 were peers or peeresses, 16 knights or baronets, and the rest mostly country gentry;[5] of the 80 partners of the Earl of Portland, 15 were peers or peeresses, 23 knights or baronets, and the rest mostly country gentry.[6] For the rest, the story of their miserable fortunes during the few years in which they functioned has already been told and does not need repetition here.[7] Their experience testified to the wisdom of those who had criticized the Government's proposals.

The plan to develop the textile industries by a similar network of public joint-stock companies was in some ways more interesting, but even less successful. Its fullest expression is to be found in the draft of a Bill, drawn up early in the reign of James I., which is worth dis-

---

[1] Scott, *English Joint Stock Companies*, vol. ii., p. 369.

[2] S.P.D. Chas. I., vol. ccxliv., no. 49.   [3] MS. Court Book, 1631-40, p. 76.

[4] Transactions, 1625-35; Letter of February 23, 1632-33.

[5] S.P.D. Chas. I., vol. ccxci., no. 25; vol. cccxvii., no. 42; Privy Council Register, vol. xlvii., p. 229.

[6] S.P.D. Chas. I., vol. ccxxxi., no. 15 (i.).

[7] Scott, *op. cit.*, vol. ii., pp. 365-71. Professor Scott seems to have misinterpreted the constitution. The central board was not an active trading body, and the figures and fortunes which he ascribes to it actually relate to the Lord Treasurer's association.

interring if only for its opening passage, where, with a refinement of logic to which its advocates have seldom risen, the theory of the balance of trade is applied, not merely to the country as a whole, but to each separate county and important town. For, after lamenting that

" the general conceaved oppynion of the vulger sorte hath ben and still is stronge that wee stand no need of any manner of foraigne commodetyes, That havinge bredd a greaté discouragement of all industry especially to rayse Commodetyes for Transportation and thereby abandoninge all Commerce and Traffique as alsoe use of shippinge and soe consequently soe farre as in them lyeth debarre their sovereign and themselves of all hope of earthly safety,"

it proposes that commissioners be appointed

" to enquyre, heare, examyne and informe themselves by all fitte wayes and meanes whether each proper County, City or towne Corporate doth yearely affoord soe much manufacture and Commodety raysed by the industry, laboure and invention of that particular people by their ymployment vendible and vented by being Transported to foraigne nations as doth any way equalize and balance the foraign Commodetyes dispended in such County, City or Town Corporate, yea or no, if yea to certefy in and by what Commodetyes, if not, then to certefy upon mature Consideration firste had what materiales every such County doth or may affoord and what manufacture and what manner of proffitable and usefull ymployment may moste aptly and fittly in such Commissioners opinion be established and used for settinge on woork the poore men, weomen and Children."

Throughout their enquiries the commissioners were to keep before their eyes the glorious example of the county and people of Devon, " whose soyle is generally Baren, yett it with their good husbandry, industry, ymprovement of their owne materials by manufacture, doth returne yearely more quoyne and Commodetyes then some other forty Countyes putt togeather." Then, wherever an unfavourable trade balance was discovered, the commissioners were to

" selecte, nominate and appointe in every such County, Citty, and Towne Corporate such person and persons as are of habillity inhabiting within the sayd County who shalbe injoyned by virtue of this Acte to be of the Company and Corporation of that County for such manufacture as is or shalbe so thoughte fitte to be establishte And to adventure and bringe into Banck or Stocke, within the compasse of 4 yeares, that is every yeare one equall fourth parte, soe much money as the said Commissioners shall thinke fitte . . ., the same to be rated and taxed uppon them that shalbe of the sayd Corporation by such portions . . . as the Commissioners . . . shall sett downe and appoynte which sums or Banck of money shalbe wholly and only employed in taking of the said Commodetyes from off the hands of such as doe worke them within the county as alsoe for the venting of them into foraigne Countries or to such persons as will undertake to vent and transport or otherwise dispose the same."

Whatever other industries it might possess, every county was to establish, upon the basis of the existing Poor Law machinery, some branch of the textiles. All the necessary spinning was to be provided for by the churchwardens, who in each parish were to set on work a certain quota of women and children, supplying them with raw material and paying them a fixed rate of wages. The yarn was then to be sold to the new corporation, whose business it was to settle a sufficient number of skilled artisans within the county, to supply them with yarn, and to take off all their finished wares at reasonable prices. Any corporation finding it difficult to obtain sufficient skilled craftsmen were to apply to the commissioners, who were to provide them from elsewhere, if necessary by means of the press-gang. And, apart from these purely economic functions, every corporation was given powers to draw up all necessary regulations, to search and seal all textiles made within its area of jurisdiction, and to punish any artisan, churchwarden or other officer guilty of negligence or misdemeanour.[1] The Bill apparently never came before Parliament, but twice during the second and third decades of the century the Council attempted to set up a modified form of the system which it advocated.

The origin of the whole scheme seems to have been a public-spirited investment of the Earl of Salisbury, who, in 1608, engaged a certain Walter Morrell to establish " the art of clothing, weaving, spinning, carding or any such like commendable trade which the said Walter shall think good " in the parish of Hatfield.[2] In itself, that undertaking was not particularly important; except that it was financed privately by Salisbury instead of by a public rate, it did not differ greatly from other attempts elsewhere. But it at once became significant when Morrell tried to expand it to embrace all Hertfordshire and then to repeat it in every county, casting a corporation of local gentry for the rôle which Salisbury played alone on the smaller stage of Hatfield. In 1615 Morrell, who probably had at least some voice in drawing up the Bill already mentioned, petitioned the King with a proposal for incorporating the chief men of Hertfordshire with the power and duty of establishing and regulating the manufacture of the new draperies throughout that area. Certificates from the county magistrates and the farmers of the customs were produced in its favour, and after long consideration the Privy Council sanctioned it in principle.[3] On March 27, 1616, Bacon was ordered to work out the details of a charter, and later in the same year he, Salisbury and twenty-seven of the leading county gentry were incorporated as the " Master, Wardens, Assistants and Comminaltie of the Company of Drapers of the ars trade and

---

[1] S.P.D. Jas. I., vol. xx., no. 32.   [2] *Vict. County Hist. Herts*, iv., 250.
[3] *Acts of the Privy Council*, 1615-16, p. 464.

misterie of the new Draperie of Hatfield in the Countie of Hertford."
The government was vested in a master, four wardens and twenty-four
assistants. All the officers were nominated in the charter, Salisbury
being first master, Bacon a warden and Morrell the clerk. The assistants were to hold office for life, and each year were to elect four wardens
from among themselves and a master from among the ex-wardens.
Any officer, however, was to be removable by the majority of the
J.P.s at any Quarter Sessions. Quoting the testimony of the J.P.s
to the success of the Hatfield experiment, and that of the London
merchants to the necessity of ensuring the high quality of manufactures,
the charter gave the new company the twin duties of setting the poor
on work and of preventing deceits in drapery. The officers were to
admit any English-born subjects whom they might think desirable,
to appoint deputies to search and seal all draperies made in the county,
to draw up regulations and a schedule of fines for their non-observance,
and to collect the amercements by distraint, if necessary. The company might make any fabrics not made elsewhere in the kingdom,
might ship them wherever existing charters did not forbid, and might
prosecute any who counterfeited their seals or used their chosen trade-
marks for cloths made outside the shire.[1]

But establishment by administrative action necessitated one
vital change in the original scheme; it meant that capital would have
to be obtained by voluntary subscriptions instead of by a compulsory
levy, which only Parliament could grant. And that alteration spelled
failure. For, as in the case of the fishery project, the new company
provided only the bare machinery of investment. The incentive
necessary to set it in motion was lacking, and everywhere the appeals
for capital met with great " coldness and neglect." The Deputy
Lieutenants summoned the wealthier gentry and yeomen in their
divisions, but they refused to subscribe " unless they might be secured
of their principall to be repaid them howsoever the projecte should
succeede."[2] Their objections were very similar to those raised against
the fishing companies. It was argued that, far from the undertaking
yielding profits, the difficulty of finding markets, the losses while the
poor were being taught, and the probable dishonesty of the officers,
would steadily deplete the capital invested and soon lead to demands
for further subscriptions.[3] In the face of such opposition, all the
exhortations of the Council were in vain. A temporary compromise
was arranged, by which eight of the chief towns in the county were
ordered to furnish stocks, as by law they ought, for the employment
of their poor in the new draperies, Morrell being given the contract

1 Patent Roll, 14 Jas. I., pt. 23, no. 6.
2 S.P.D. Jas. I., vol. cxv., no. 13.   3 *Ibid.*, vol. xcvi., no. 39.

for the supply of raw materials. But when that failed, the whole project had to be abandoned for the time being.[1]

The second attempt to establish a system of joint-stock companies in the textile industry came shortly afterwards, when the trade depression of the early 'twenties provided a favourable atmosphere for schemes of national development. In 1622 a committee investigating the decay of the cloth trade advised " that a Corporacon in every County be made of the most able and sufficient men of the same whereby they may be authorized to look fullie to the true making, dyeing and dressing of cloth and stuffe in every shire,"[2] and commissioners of trade were appointed to carry out their recommendations.[3] That was Morrell's opportunity. He spent the next three years advocating his ideas at Whitehall,[4] and the fruits of his advocacy are obvious. The companies suggested by the committee had been merely to regulate the existing industry; the plans laid by the commissioners before the Council were for corporations, of which all county inhabitants were to be members and all J.P.s governors, and which were to establish and expand various branches of the textile manufactures by means of a joint stock.[5] Drafts for companies in Hertfordshire, Essex, Middlesex, Berkshire, Devon, Dorset and Shropshire were approved by both King and Council early in 1625, only to be held up by the former's death two days before they were to have passed the Great Seal.[6] Under Charles the project was soon resumed and expanded, and on April 15, 1625, charters were ordered to be prepared for thirty-two counties.[7] But the fates were unkind, for this time the scheme was pigeon-holed by the pressure of foreign affairs.[8] And this check was final. Walter, and his relative Hugh, Morrell raised the matter several times during the following years, and in 1638 it was recommended to Parliament by a committee of merchants,[9] but never again was it considered seriously by the Government.

Despite their almost uniform lack of success, these experiments make the early seventeenth century a significant period in company history. It is easy to see that, had they succeeded, had they been able to bring within the gild system the passive investor and the rural

[1] *Ibid.*, vol. cxv., no. 13.   [2] Stowe MSS., vol. 554, ff. 45-9.
[3] Rymer, *Foedera*, xvii., 410-15.   [4] S.P.D. Chas. I., vol. dxxxiii., no. 86.
[5] *Ibid.*, vol. i., no. 24; vol. dxxxiii., no. 86 (iii.).   [6] *Ibid.*, vol. x., no. 66.
[7] *Ibid.*, vol i., no. 62. The counties were Herts, Essex, Suffolk, Norfolk, Devon, Somerset, Dorset, Wilts, Hants, Berks, Surrey, Notts, Leicester, Durham, Sussex, Kent, Lincoln, Salop, Yorkshire, Lancashire, Cheshire, Worcester, Gloucester, Bucks, Northants, Bedford, Huntingdonshire, Cambridgeshire, Warwick, Cumberland, Northumberland, and Middlesex.
[8] *Ibid.*, vol. x., no. 66.
[9] *Ibid.*, vol. dxxxiii., no. 86; vol. dxxxvii., no. 60; S.P.D. Chas II., vol. xxii., no. 73.

manufacturer, had they been able to serve the creative purposes of Stuart mercantilism, they might well have opened a new and not unimportant chapter in gild history, and have exercised a not inconsiderable influence on industrial development. In actual fact, it is true, these experiments were confined to a comparatively few industries; but had they succeeded they would almost certainly have been imitated. For under the early Stuarts nearly everything was in their favour. The desirability of public interference in economic life was still accepted almost as an axiom. The desirability of the chartered company as the instrument of that interference was almost as great a commonplace, partly by virtue of tradition, partly because of the absence of any alternative machinery. Under such conditions failure was in itself significant. It could be attributed only in part to the abuses and taxes which accompanied some of these experiments. Fundamentally it was due to a fatal rigidity within the gild system itself; that system simply was not flexible enough to adapt itself to the new conditions and the new needs. Self-governing corporations could not function in fields where competition and the clash of conflicting interests were sweeping away the foundations upon which self-government had to be built. No matter that the soap and salt companies experimented with the quota systems, the central selling boards, and the price-fixing agreements upon which the trusts and cartels of the nineteenth and twentieth centuries were to be based; however successful those methods were to be two and a half centuries later, they were ineffective under the early Stuarts, when competition was in its infancy rather than its dotage. And for the promotion of industry, the chartered company, by itself and without a monopoly of its market or its equivalent privileges, was simply irrelevant; its powers bore no relation to the problems which had to be met. Seen from the vantage point of today, these lessons seem obvious truths. But like all lessons they had to be learned, and it was primarily the experiences of the early seventeenth century that taught them. After the Restoration the regulated company was to be far less popular as an instrument of industrial policy than before, and was to play a far smaller rôle in national industry than in national trade. It is not, surely, unreasonable to attribute that situation, at least in part, to the lessons learned from the experiments of the early Stuarts.

4

The Development of the London Food Market, 1540-1640

O F the factors that mark the transition from the medieval to the modern economic system, three are, by general consent, outstanding—the aggregation of capital, the improvement of technique, and the increase in the size of the market. The last number of *The Economic History Review* contained an illuminating article by Dr. Nef on the operation of the first and second in English industry during the century preceding the Civil War.[1] The purpose of this more modest essay is to consider the development of one particular market—the London food market—in the same period. By the seventeenth century, and even earlier, there were in England a number of commercial and industrial centres of sufficient size and concentration to have a considerable influence, as markets, upon both agriculture and the trade in agricultural produce. London and the larger provincial towns, the embryonic Black Country, the Tyneside mining area, the textile districts of York-shire, East Anglia, and the west must all have been important in this respect. Each meant a considerable body of consumers relying upon purchases for the majority of their victuals. Yet the study of their influence has been curiously uneven. On the one hand, the repercussions of their demand for wool have been the subject of lengthy, if somewhat barren, discussions. On the other, the repercussions of their demand for food have been almost entirely neglected. The course of history, nevertheless, has not been entirely unaffected by the fact that men, as well as looms, need food ; agrarian history is rapidly approaching the point where further advance must wait upon the study of the reactions to these growing markets.

Essentially, of course, this must be a problem for the agrarian specialist, when he can free himself from his peculiar obsession with the more recondite niceties of land tenure. But in the case of London—the most populous, the most rapidly growing, the wealthiest, and the most compact of all these centres of consumption—the reactions were so clearly marked that their trend is apparent even to the more general historian. A mass of evidence, not specifically agrarian in character, shows the direction in which things were moving. Complete statistics of food imported

[1] J. U. Nef, " The Progress of Technology and the Growth of Large Scale Industry in Great Britain, 1540-1640," *The Economic History Review*, 1934, vol. v, pp. 3-24.

coastwise into London exist for only six of the hundred years in question and are therefore too few to be in themselves conclusive. Yet their story is sufficiently corroborated by the customs records of the outports and by other more miscellaneous material to be substantially beyond question. The perpetual concern of the authorities for the city's food supplies casts, by inference, considerable light upon the agricultural system whence those supplies were drawn. And, under the early Stuarts, comments on the problem began to creep into contemporary agricultural literature. Consequently, a student of London history may perhaps be excused of presumption in writing of a subject of admittedly more than municipal significance.

In the first place, it is quite clear from Tables I and II that the

TABLE I

COASTWISE CEREAL IMPORTS INTO LONDON (QUARTERS)

From	1579-80[1]	1585-6[2]	1587-8[3]	1615[4]	1624[5]	1638[6]
N.E. Coast	345	914	25	33	672	4,840
Lincolnshire	293	1,238			757	
Norfolk	550	12,439	390	7,670	10,873	19,550
Suffolk	807	2,696	458	258	2,127	1,843
Essex	1,797	2,732	4,463	10,368	12,765	5,532
Kent	13,546	28,004	12,080	41,823	27,957	57,187
Sussex	2	258	100	7,604	5,722	3,807
Hants	40		250	670	464	208
S.W. Coast		120	10	170	312	2,747
Totals	17,380	48,401	17,776	68,596	61,649	95,714

NOTES TO TABLES

[1] Exch. K.R., Port Books, bdle. 6, no. 8.
[2] *Ibid.*, bdle. 7, no. 6.
[3] Exch. K.R., Miscellanea, bdle. 15, no. 5.
[4] Exch. K.R., Port Books, bdle. 18, no. 1.
[5] *Ibid.*, bdle. 28, no. 5. The returns for July and August are missing from this volume. The totals for the remaining ten months have therefore been increased by 20 per cent. to provide an estimate of the trade of the whole year.
[6] *Ibid.*, bdle. 41, no. 6.

TABLE II

COASTWISE DAIRY IMPORTS INTO LONDON (Unit for butter: barrel. Unit for Cheese: wey.)

From	1579-80[1] Butter	1579-80[1] Cheese	1585-6[2] Butter	1585-6[2] Cheese	1587-8[3] Butter	1587-8[3] Cheese	1615[4] Butter	1615[4] Cheese	1624[5] Butter	1624[5] Cheese	1638[6] Butter	1638[6] Cheese
N.E. Coast	6		11		2		102		1,394	26 tons	4,132	20 tons
Lincolnshire	16	83	11		29		65				500	
Norfolk	68	30	218	2	235	1	152	4	547		459	
Suffolk	1,457	2,317 (21 loads)	4,179	3,768 (10 loads)	2,984	2,629 (12 loads)	1,563	1,545 (7 loads)	1,739	1,580 (38 loads)	1,656	2,303 (128 loads)
Essex	6	352 (756 wey)	41	188 (925 wey)		663 wey	1	70 (438 loads)		76 (352 loads)	6	92 (580 loads)
		742 wey		2,194 wey		2,190 wey		460 wey		188 wey		498 wey

TABLE III

CEREAL IMPORTS INTO LONDON (Unit : 100 quarters)

From	1579-80[1]			1585-6[2]			1587-8[3]			1615[4]			1624[5]			1638[6]		
	Wheat	Malt	Oats	Wheat	Malt	Oats	Wheat	Malt	Oats	Wheat	Malt	Oats	Wheat	Malt	Oats	Wheat	Malt	Oats
N.E. Coast	3·5	2·8		2·8	6·1		·3			·3			·2		4·8	11·3	5·3	31·2
Lincolnshire		1·4	3·5	·4	5·8	·3							1	·7	5·9	13·1	172·1	9·8
Norfolk	·3	7·4	·6	9·7	46·4		1·5	1·4	1	·5	71·2	3·9	31·6	50	23·6	2·7	6	4·6
Suffolk		1	7·6	3·5	22·8	·6	·8	3·5		·3	·7	1·6	11·5	3·3	6·3	18·1	4·8	32·2
Essex	1·5	12	4·8	4·8	·3		5	2·9	34·5	21·6		79·9	26·2	·4	96·6	331·7	190·9	48·5
Kent	129·4			240·6	38·4	22·1	99·5	16·5	39·2	105·6	279·4	32·4	46·5	151	80·7	32	4·6	1·6
Sussex		·4		2·6			·5	·5		44·7	16·4	4·8	41·3	6·3	5·2	·4		1·7
Hants					1·2		1·7	·8		4·5	2·2		2·4	1·6	·4			
S.W. Coast							·1					1·7	2·9				7·6	19·8
Total	134·7	25	16·5	264·4	121	23	109·4	25·6	74·7	177·5	369·9	124·3	163·6	213·3	223·5	409·3	391·3	149·4

area from which the city obtained its food was growing, and that by 1640 it was large. For obvious geographical reasons, the home counties were, no doubt, always the chief source of supplies. At the very end of the sixteenth century, London was said still to be fed " principallie . . . from some fewe shires neare adioyninge,"[1] and as late as 1632 it was argued that the assize of bread should be regulated by the price of wheat in the neighbouring markets of Uxbridge, Brentford, Kingston, Hampstead, Watford, St. Albans, Hertford, Croydon, and Dartford.[2] But as the years pass it is possible to watch the city's tentacles spreading over the provinces until by the middle of the seventeenth century they reached to Berwick, Cornwall, and Wales.

As one would expect, the evidence is most abundant, and the process of expansion most easily traced, in the corn trade. By the middle of Elizabeth's reign, the city was already drawing to a considerable degree upon the south midlands.[3] The growth of the down-river trade from Berkshire and Oxfordshire was reflected in the increasing importance of Queenhithe as a meal and grain market.[4] But, save in years of scarcity, both coastwise and foreign imports were comparatively slight.[5] In 1573, the Lord Mayor and aldermen could speak of foreign imports as negligible save in times of dearth, and of heavy demands upon the maritime counties as something exceptional, due to the fact that " the contrey about them doth not bringe corne to the markett there in such plentie as they were wonte and as will suffice the Citie."[6] Of the three years 1580, 1586, and 1588, it was only the scarcity year of 1586 that shewed considerable coastwise supplies. In the more normal years, the total was well below 20,000 quarters, of which Kent alone supplied nearly 75 per cent. The next half-century saw a striking change. Imports continued to fluctuate with prices. Foreign, and the more distant provincial, sources were still drawn upon more heavily when harvests were bad. But by now the mean around which the coast trade fluctuated was much higher. Neither 1615, nor 1624, nor 1658 was a year of scarcity ; yet each saw coastwise imports around 60,000 quarters, well above the famine level of 1586.[7] Under the early Stuarts, north-east Kent was a vast granary for the city's service. Both Norfolk and Essex were sources of regular, as well as of exceptional, supplies. The Sussex grain

[1] S. P. D., Eliz., vol. ccliv, no. 10.   [2] *Ibid.*, Chas. I, vol. ccxxiv, no. 64.
[3] N. S. B. Gras, *The Evolution of the English Corn Market*, 1915, p. 109, and see below, p. 60.
[4] City Repertories, vol. xvi, *ff.* 10, 133, 147.
[5] Table I ; Gras, *op. cit.*, p. 275.   [6] Gras, *op. cit.*, p. 105.
[7] For statistics of foreign imports see Gras, *op. cit.* p. 275 ; for those of coastwise imports see *ibid.*, p. 319, and Table I above.

trade rose from insignificance into some prominence. In times of dearth, both the north-east and the south-west coasts made substantial contributions.

Except that foreign imports were always slight, the story of the dairy trade is very similar. Milk and fresh butter, no doubt, always came from the neighbouring countryside ;[1] yet already by the sixteenth century there was a well-developed trade in cheese and salt butter from Essex and Suffolk. In the seventeenth, the city's feeders crept steadily northwards up the coast to Norfolk, Lincolnshire, Yorkshire, Durham, and Northumberland.[2] Some of the city's eggs and poultry came from Bedfordshire and Northamptonshire.[3] Above all, the city's meat trade was organised upon a national basis. Sheep were brought in from as far away as Gloucestershire and Northampton.[4] Many of its cattle were bred in Wales, or the north or west of England, and fattened in the midlands, East Anglia or the home counties before being sold to the city butchers.[5] In 1724, Defoe was to write of the " general dependence of the whole country upon the city of London—for the consumption of its produce."[6] The situation which obtained a century earlier differed from that described by him in degree rather than in kind.

In the second place, it seems highly probable that the growth of the London market gave a definite stimulus to English agriculture. Its increased demands for food were, quite clearly, not met to any noteworthy degree by larger supplies from abroad. Small quantities of foreign cheese trickled in,[7] but otherwise imports of meat, poultry, and dairy produce were negligible. The trade in foreign fruit and vegetables, which had shewn signs of decay even under Elizabeth,[8] rapidly dwindled under the early Stuarts.[9] Save in years of scarcity, the consumption of foreign corn was not heavy

---

[1] See below, p. |70.   [2] See Table II.

[3] Lansdowne MSS., vol. xlvi, *f.* 207 ; *His. MSS. Comm., Var. Coll.*, vol. iii, p. 93.

[4] A. J. and R. H. Tawney, " An Occupational Census of the Seventeenth Century," *Economic History Review*, 1934, vol. v, p. 27, note 2 ; J. Gutch, *Collectanea Curiosa*, 1781, vol. i, p. 222.

[5] See C. J. Skeel, " The Cattle Trade between Wales and England from the Fifteenth to the Nineteenth Century," *Trans. R. His. Soc.*, 1926, series iv, vol. ix, pp. 135-58 ; Cotton MSS., Faustus, C. ii, *f.* 164.

[6] *A Tour through England and Wales* (Everyman ed.), 1928, vol. i, p. 3.

[7] Ct. of Request, Proceedings, bdle. 64, no. 80 ; Exch. K.R., Port Books, bdle. 40, no. 2 ; Letter Books, vol. FF, *f.* 81 b.

[8] In 1582 the fruitmeters complained that " nowe there cometh verie small stoare of fruite from beionde the seas," Letter Books, vol. Etc., *f.* 106.

[9] *Samuel Hartlib, His Legacy*, 1652, p. 9 ; Hops and onions, however, continued to come in (Exch. K.R. Port Books, bdle. 40, no. 2).

and showed no tendency to grow.[1] Merchants in the Netherlands, Germany, and the Baltic, carefully watched the London grain market,[2] and their shipments helped to steady prices.[3] But under anything approaching normal conditions, foreign grain went in serious danger of finding no purchaser. Freights were high, the risk of deterioration was great, and even in years of dearth promises of free re-export were sometimes necessary to attract substantial imports.[4] Nor is there any evidence that the city's demands were met to any considerable extent by the diversion of supplies previously exported. It is possible that there was some slight falling off in the exports of English corn during this period. But the evidence is doubtful, and, even on the most liberal interpretation, suggests no decline comparable to the city's increased consumption.[5] The conclusion, therefore, seems inevitable that there was an important net increase in the output of English agriculture.

In certain commodities this increase is beyond all doubt. In many places within easy reach of the city, the production of fruit, hops, and vegetables, rose from the position of insignificant and neglected branches of general farming almost to the status of independent industries. " Gardening," wrote Fuller in 1660, " was first brought into England for profit about seventy years ago ; before which we fetched most of our cherries from Holland, apples from France, and had hardly a mass of rath ripe peas but from Holland which were dainties for ladies, they came so far and cost so dear. Since gardening hath crept out of Holland to Sandwich, Kent, and thence to Surrey where, though they have given 6*l*. an acre and upwards they have made their rent, lived comfortably, and set many people on work. . . . 'Tis incredible how many poor people in London live thereon, so that in some seasons the gardens feed more people than the field."[6] The testimony of Hartlib was the same : " Market-gardening," he wrote in 1652, " is but of few years standing in England, and therefore not deeply rooted. About 50 years ago, about which time Ingenuities first began to flourish in England, This Art of Gardening began to creep into England, into Sandwich and Surrey, Fulham and other places. Some old men in Surrey, where it flourisheth very much at present, report that they knew the first Gardiners that came into those parts to plant Cabages, Colleflowers, and to sowe Turneps,

[1] Gras, *op. cit.*, p. 275 ; *Calendar of S.P., Venetian, 1607-10*, p. 146.

[2] Cranfield MSS., no. 2020 ; I am indebted to Professor R. H. Tawney for this reference.

[3] S.P.D., Chas. I, vol. ccccl, no. 14.

[4] S. P. Docquet, 25 March, 1608 ; *Cal. S.P.D., 1611-18*, p. 261.

[5] Gras, *op. cit.*, Appendix C.

[6] Quoted by D. Lysons, *The Environs of London*, 1792, vol. i, p. 28.

Carrets and Parsnips, to sowe Raithe (or early ripe) Rape, Pease, all which at that time were great rarities, we having few, or none, in England, but what came from Holland and Flaunders. These Gardiners with much ado procured a plot of good ground, and gave no lesse than 8 pound per acre ; yet the Gentleman was not content, fearing they would spoil his ground, because they did use to dig it. So ignorant were we of Gardening in those dayes. . . . In Queen Elizabeth's time we had not onely our Gardiners ware from Holland, but also Cherries from Flaunders ; Apples from France ; Saffron, Licorish from Spain ; Hopps from the Low-Countreys : . . . whereas now . . . the Licorish, Saffron, Cherries, Apples, Peares, Hopps, Cabages of England are the best in the world."[1]

Probably both, as historians are wont, exaggerated the novelty of what they described. Small quantities of English fruit and vege-tables had for many years been trickling into the city from the orchards and gardens of the neighbouring gentry ;[2] quite early in Elizabeth's reign that trickle became a stream of some proportions.[3] The fruit and hop industries of Essex and Kent seem to have begun earlier and to have developed more slowly than either Fuller or Hartlib suggests. Essex hops were commented upon by Harrison in 1587 and were being grown around Colchester at least sixteen years earlier. Kentish fruit was praised by Lambarde in 1576, and some orchards dated back to the times of Henry VIII.[4] But their main argument stands. It was in the early seventeenth century that the orchards of Kent and the hop-grounds of Kent, Essex, Suffolk, Sussex, and Surrey, became really prosperous. And that they were called into being primarily to serve the London market is scarcely open to doubt. To all of them, a temporary closing of that market meant " such a dampe in the trade as will be in short tyme the undoing of many Farmers and other labouring men . . . and a greate losse to the lords and owners of the lands in their rents and revenues."[5]   Equally, it was in the early seventeenth century

---

[1] *Op. cit.*, pp. 8-9.

[2] H. T. Riley, *Memorials of London and London Life*, 1868, p. 228.

[3] Letter Books, vol. Y, *f.* 251.

[4] *V.C.H., Essex*, vol. ii, pp. 366-7 ;   *Kent*, vol. iii, pp. 420-1 ; J. F. Bense, *Anglo-Dutch Relations*, 1925, p. 114.

[5] S.P.D., Addend., vol. xlii, no. 63.   *Cf. ibid.*, nos. 64-5 ;   and *The Essex Review*, 1908, pp. 173-4. Since most of these commodities came into the city by land, adequate statistics are unobtainable. But the coast trade figures at least shew the direction in which things were moving. In the 1580's London imports of English fruit and hops were negligible; by 1638 the former amounted to 621 baskets and the latter to 1,594 bags. (Exch. K.R. Port Books, bdle. 41, no. 6).

that the suburban market-gardeners first rose to prominence. In 1605 they obtained a royal charter of incorporation with jurisdiction over all gardening within six miles of London, a charter of which the city disapproved and which was to be questioned as a grievance in Parliament.[1] Already by 1617 they claimed to be employing " thowsandes of poore people, ould menn, women and children in sellinge of their Commodities, in weedinge, in gatheringe of stone, etc." ; in the middle of the century they estimated their labour force more specifically at 1,500 men, women, and children, and 400 apprentices. By that time they had contrived a minor revolution in the ordinary citizen's diet and their gardens clustered thickly in the suburbs.[2]

To a degree that makes some criticisms of open-field farming read strangely, this increased production of fruit and vegetables was fitted into the common-field routine of the neighbouring villages. An aldermanic report of 1635, on the agriculture of Chelsea, Fulham, and Kensington, relates of the husbandmen there that

" they sowe seedes for parsnipps, turnopps, carriotts and the like in their Comon feildes whereof most of them they plough upp and others they digge upp with the spade according to the nature and ritchness of their grounds. And ye same feilds sometymes sowe with corne whereby the grounds are the more fruitfull And ... by this manner of Husbandry and ymployment of their groundes the Cittys of London and Westminster and places adiacent are furnished with above fower and twenty Thousand loades yearely of Rootes as is credibly affirmed. . . . whereby as well the poore as the ritch have plenty of that victuall at reasonable prices and ... some of them have belonging to their houses one two or three acres of ground in orchards and gardens which they ymploy and husband in setting forth and planting of Roses, Raspesses, strawberries, gooseberries, herbes for foode and Phisick which besides their owne necessary use they bring to the Marketts both of this Citty, the Citty of Westminster and other places adiacent."[3]

But the significant developments which struck the imagination of contemporaries were the work, not so much of open-field farmers, as of specialists working enclosed holdings by intensive methods, often borrowed from abroad, and by the heavy expenditure of both capital and labour.

[1] *Proceedings and Debates of the House of Commons in 1620 and 1621*, 1766, edited by T. Tyrwhitt, vol. i, pp. 132-3.
[2] C. Welch, *History of the Gardeners Co.*, 1900, p. 28 ; W. T. Crosweller, *The Gardeners Co.*, 1908, p. 15.
[3] Repertories, vol. xlix, *f.* 262.

Individual market-gardens in Bermondsey, Battersea, Stepney, Lambeth, and the other suburbs, do not seem to have been large ; the Gardeners Co. established a maximum of ten acres.[1] Some members, however, held other gardens elsewhere in the home counties ; one, with a plot in St. Martins-in-the-Fields, had others as far apart as Wandsworth, Woking, and Dunmow (Essex).[2] And the suburban gardens were obviously highly cultivated. Two hundred pounds, for example, were estimated to have been sunk in improving a four-acre holding in Stepney.[3] The labour employed upon them was great.[4] Dressings of the city's street soil were regularly applied.[5] Despite high rents, it was estimated that an able man could keep a family and even employ outside labour on a holding of three acres or even less.[6] And save that their holdings were probably larger, the hop-masters and fruit-growers were working along the same lines. Their grounds were enclosed. They depended on wage labour. They paid rents that only intensive farming could make possible.[7]

The benefits of the London market, moreover, were not confined to the growers of fruit and vegetables. The city diffused throughout Middlesex a prosperity that could be shared by all willing and able to provide the " small acchates " that it needed. " Such as live . . . in body or hart of the Shire, as also in the borders of the same," wrote Norden, " for the most part are men of husbandrye, and they wholy dedicate themselves to the manuringe of their lande. And theis comonlye are so furnished with kyne that the wife or twice or thrice a weeke conveyeth to London mylke, butter, cheese, apples, peares, frumentye, hens, chyckens, egges, baken, and a thousand other country drugges, which good huswifes can frame and find to gett a pennye. And this yeldeth them a lardge comfort and releefe. Besyds the husbande castinge the quantetie of his corne, and proporcioninge the same with the expens of his howse, of the overplus he maketh monie to mayntayn his family and to paye his rent.

" Another sort of husbandmen or yeomen rather ther are, and that not a few in this Shire, who wade in the weedes of gentlemen ; theis only oversee their husbandrye, and give direction unto their servauntes, seldome or not at all settinge their hand unto the

---

[1] Crosweller, *op. cit.*, p. 16.   [2] *Ibid.*, p. 13.

[3] Chancery Proceedings, Series i, Chas. I., bdle. B. 14, no. 6. This prosperity was naturally reflected in the rents paid, and in 1621 the copyholders of Stepney and Hackney took a private bill to Parliament to confirm their customary rights of sub-letting (House of Lords MSS.).

[4] See above, p. 69.

[5] Welch, *op. cit.*, p. 28 ; Norden, *Surveyors Dialogue*, 1618 ed., p. 226.

[6] Hartlib, *op. cit.*, p. 8.   [7] *Ibid.*, p. 15.

plowgh, who havinge great feedinges for cattle and goode breede for younge, often use Smythfelde and other lyke places with fatt cattle, wher also they store themselves with leane. And thus they often exchaunge, not without great gayne, wherby and by their daylye increase at home they comonly become very riche."[1]

The glimpses that we catch of their economy suggest that the same description would fit quite well the nearer parts of Hertfordshire, Essex, Kent, and Surrey.[2]

Outside of this area concentrating on the production of butter, milk, poultry, eggs, fruit, vegetables, pork, bacon, and other " country drugges," for the London market, the influence of the capital can only be suggested with diffidence. Diffused over too large an area to be spectacular, it was too entangled with other factors to be easily discernible. One conclusion, however, seems justified. London's demands on the more distant sources of supply were selective rather than indiscriminate. It drew on each district, not so much for food in general, as for those victuals in particular which the district was best fitted to produce. Its stimulus, that is to say, was not merely in the direction of increased production but also in that of specialisation ; and in that direction lay agricultural progress.

The coast books show that the corn and dairy regions were distinct. Suffolk, the chief source of cheese and butter, was negligible as a supplier of grain. Sussex and the great granary of Kent sent almost no dairy produce at all. Norfolk and the north-east coast sent both, but from different parts. Corn came chiefly from Berwick, Hull, Wells, and Yarmouth ; butter from Stockton, Whitby, Boston, and Lynn. Within the cereal areas themselves further specialisation tended to appear. Sussex was primarily a source of wheat, Essex of oats, Norfolk of malt. Kent supplied all three, but shipped most of its malt through Sandwich, most of its wheat and oats through Faversham and Milton. Under the prevailing system of farming the raising of cattle was widespread, but its relative importance varied from place to place. Fattening was a major industry in the south midlands,[3] parts of East Anglia[4] and on the marshes which fringed the coast from Romsey to Lincoln and where it was the annual practice for men to lay out money

[1] *Description of Essex*, ed. Ellis, Camden Society, 1840, p. xii. In his introduction Ellis prints a description by Norden of " The meanes most usuall how the people of Myddlesex doe live " to be found in manuscript in Harl. MSS. 570 but not included in the printed description of Middlesex.

[2] Norden, *Surveyors Dialogue*, 1618 ed., p. 215 ; Lansdowne MSS., vol. xlvi, *f.* 193 ; vol. lxxx, *f.* 91 ; vol. lxxxi, *f.* 145.

[3] Privy Council Register, vol. xl, p. 356.

[4] S.P.D., Chas. I, vol. cclvii, no. 121 (i).

"uppon Heiffors and such other young ware, emptying their purses of Crownes to cram the Fens with Cattell."[1] Breeding was more practised in Wales, the north and the west.[2]

Specialisation along such lines was, of course, inherent in local soil conditions ; its explanation must be framed primarily in terms of economic geography. But inherent specialisation becomes actual only when there is at hand some market to act, in the words of Burleigh, as " an encouragement to the husbandmen to apply and follow their tillage with confort of gayn."[3] And it was becoming more and more the lot of the capital to supply that encouragement and thereby to promote, in some degree, agricultural specialisation and the most profitable use of the soil. It would, of course, be absurd to exaggerate the importance of London in this respect. In some districts, such as Norfolk, it was only one among several alternative markets ; in others, its influence was too slight to be of much effect. Nevertheless, in some regions, and those not the least highly specialised, its influence was paramount. The corn-growers of Cambridgeshire,[4] south-east Essex,[5] and north-east Kent,[6] the dairy farmers of Suffolk,[7] the graziers of the south midlands,[8] all looked to the London market as the hub of their economic universe.

With these developments in agriculture there went, of necessity, others in the organisation of the trade in foodstuffs. Like all townsmen, the Londoner purchased many of his victuals in the common market places in the city ; and as the population grew, so there was an increase in the volume of this market trade. The growth of river and coastal traffic necessitated the development of Queenhithe to handle the overflow from Billingsgate.[9] The growth of the meal trade led to the extension of the markets at Newgate and Leadenhall, and the opening of new ones at Bishopsgate and Queenhithe.[10] In 1615, the creation of a common market place in

---

[1] *A True Report of certain wonderful Overflowings of Waters in Somerset, Norfolk and other parts of England*, reprinted 1884, p. 26.

[2] G. Markham, *Cheap and Good Husbandry*, 1631, p. 88; *Hist. MSS. Comm., Rep. iii*, p. 6; *Calendar of Wynn Papers*, nos. 627, 1228, 1406.

[3] S.P.D., Eliz., vol. xxxvi, no. 69.   [4] *Ibid.*

[5] *Ibid.*, Chas. I, vol. clxxxii, no. 67.

[6] *Ibid.*, Jas. I, vol. cxii, no. xii (i) ; In the reign of Charles I London was taking two-thirds of the cereal exports from Sandwich (Gras, *op. cit.*, p. 311), and over 90 per cent. of those from Milton and Faversham (Exch. K.R., Port Books, bdle. 659, nos. 2 and 4).

[7] *Ibid.*, bdle. 474, nos. 10 and 20 ; bdle. 604, no. 15.

[8] Privy Council Register, vol. xl, p. 356.

[9] Letter Books, vol. V, *f*. 57 ; vol. CC, *ff*. 161-2.

[10] Repertories, vol. xvi, *ff*. 10, 133, 147; vol. xxii, *ff*. 315b, 364b ; vol. xxxi, *ff*. 175, 178 ; vol. xxxviii, *f*. 188.

Smithfield was almost agreed upon " by reason that Newgate Market, Cheapside, Leadenhall, and Gracechurch Street were unmeasurably pestred with the unimaginable increase and multiplicity of market-folkes."[1] Yet all this evidence of growth is, in a sense, misleading. It suggests that the city was fed by a simple expansion of the orthodox medieval marketing system ; in actual fact, London had long passed and was rapidly leaving behind the stage when its needs could be even approximately satisfied in any such way.

A comparison between the city's food trade and that of the ordinary provincial town, in which the medieval system continued almost unchanged, reveals two important differences. In the first place, the London markets relied to a far greater degree upon middlemen for their supplies. Their corn was handled almost entirely by country mealmen.[2] Much of their meat was brought in by suburban butchers who competed with the free butchers in the purchase of cattle and probably sold indifferently in Leadenhall or the suburban shambles.[3] Even the trade in poultry, eggs, and dairy products, the traditional sphere of the country wives, was shared by a swarm of petty higglers. In the second place, a large and increasing proportion of the capital's food passed, not through the common market places, but through the hands of the free retailers. Every town, of course, had its bakers, brewers, and butchers ; craftsmen processing the wares which they sold rather than simply dealers. But no other town could show a body of retailers comparable to the fishmongers, fruiterers, poulterers, chandlers, and cheesemongers of London. The common market places formed a bottle-neck through which the trade from the provinces and abroad, as distinct from that of the nearer parts of the home counties, could not easily be squeezed ; as more distant sources were drawn upon for food, so the influence of the city retailers grew. And this growth, reacting as it did on the organisation of the food trade, was during this period the most important feature of London's alimentary system.

Most significant was their development of channels of supply other than those which fed the common market places. The often lamented forestalling in city inns and suburban lanes seems, for the most part, to have been the work of hucksters and other small fry. More substantial men were primarily concerned with supplies of more distant origin, which they normally obtained by one or other of two methods. Much was simply purchased in the city from producers and middlemen, who, for various reasons, were tacitly,

---

[1] Stowe, *Survey of London*, ed. Howes, 1631, p. 1023.   [2] See below, p. 75.
[3] Letter Book, vol. EE, *ff.* 88, 179. There were shambles at Temple Bar, Holborn Bars, Smithfield Bars, Whitecross Street, Bishopsgate Bars, Aldgate Bars, East Smithfield, and St. Katheⅰines (Harl. MSS., vol. 6363, *f.* 22).

and sometimes explicitly, excused from selling by retail. Butchers bought heavily in Smithfield, and as late as 1612 it was thought that an additional market day there would enable them to obtain all the cattle they needed " without further travell or expence."[1] The growth of waterborne traffic was reflected in the development along the riverside of a flourishing wholesale trade in fish, fruit, and grain. The brewers obtained nearly all, and the bakers a large part, of their corn from provincial dealers.

These purchases were made from a variety of sellers. Imports from abroad were brought in by alien merchants ; save in years of scarcity English merchants do not seem to have taken any considerable interest in the provision trade.[2] Cattle were sold either by graziers or by drovers who " leavinge their accustomed order to buy leane ware in the remote partes where Cattell are better cheape and to bringe the same to places nearer to serve the grasiers and feaders of Cattell...do now bothe buy of the grasiers in places and marketts neare the Cittie and also do buy fatt cattell to sell the same againe."[3] As Professor Gras discovered, the coastal corn trade was for the most part in the hands of men who confined their interests to occasional and rather speculative shipments. In 1638, prices were high and therefore favourable to regular trading. Yet of the 481 men who brought corn from the coast into London, only 80 brought more than two, only 25 brought more than five, and only ten brought more than eight consignments. Prior to the Civil War, the growth of the coastwise trade in corn was not accompanied by the rise of a class of grain merchants.[4]

[1] Letter Books, vol. EE, *f.* 179b.
[2] Exch. K.R., Port Books, bdle. 15, no. 5 ; bdle. 18, nos. 3 and 6 ; bdle. 40, nos. 2 and 6 ; Lansdowne MSS., vol. lxxxi, *ff.* 88, 119b.
[3] Cotton MSS., Faustus, C ii, *f.* 164 ; Letter Books, vol. EE, *f.* 179b.
[4] Some idea of the relative importance of large and small traders can be obtained from the following analysis of coastwise imports for the years 1580, 1586, 1615, and 1638.

Quarters imported per merchant	1580		1586		1615		1638	
	No. of mch'ts	*Imports*	*No. of mch'ts*	*Imports*	*No. of mch'ts*	*Imports*	*No. of mch'ts*	*Imports*
1–100	72	3,473	145	6,701	228	10,137	212	11,840
101–200	14	1,942	64	9,330	91	13,476	136	20,328
201–300	4	920	21	5,282	56	13,857	52	12,884
301–400	1	340	6	2,199	13	4,419	32	11,299
401–500	1	500	11	5,003	9	3,971	16	7,116
501–1,000	2	1,380	11	8,029	18	11,962	27	17,342
Over 1,000	5	8,654	5	11,694	5	7,540	6	12,538

The overland trade in corn, however, was organised on rather different lines, dictated, to a considerable degree, by the fact that it was more convenient to process grain before, rather than after, it came to the city. Not merely were transport costs thereby reduced ; London had no facilities for malting, and, in the absence of adequate running water, few for milling. Consequently, a number of country towns found their major employment in the processing of the city's corn, and their inhabitants a regular occupation as middlemen. To the north, Enfield was famous for its mealmen and maltmen.[1] Hertford was a flourishing milling centre.[2] Hatfield, Hitchin, St. Albans, Hexton, Cheshunt, Aldenham, Elstree, Luton, Shefford, and Dunstable collected the surplus grain of Bedfordshire, Buckinghamshire, and Northamptonshire and " were onely upholden and maynteyned by the trade of making of Maults and of the cariage therof up to London by horse and carts."[3] By the time of Charles I, the more distant Royston was buying " a very great parte of the Corne in Cambridgeshire " and sending 180 great malt waggons to the city every week.[4] To the west, Henley,[5] High Wycombe,[6] and Brentford seem to have been important entrepôts. Kingston, Croydon, and Reigate, played the same role in Surrey. And the river Wandle supplied the power for a highly prosperous milling industry. Its 24 mills returned gross annual earnings of £5,252 and ground, not only for the Surrey mealmen, but also for those of Brentford and for many city bakers.[7] The mere carriage of cereals enabled many inhabitants of Middlesex " to live verye gaynfully."[8]

It will be noticed that the group of big men bringing in over 1,000 quarters each a year showed no marked tendency to grow. Those handling between 500 and 1,000 quarters increased considerably ; but the proportion of total imports handled by these two upper groups declined. It was 58 per cent. in 1580, 41 per cent. in 1586, only about 30 per cent. in the early seventeenth century. The expansion of the corn trade was primarily the work of smaller men. (These figures are taken from the same port books as those in Table I. The slight discrepancies between the totals for the various years arise from imperfections in the manuscripts, whereby some consignments can be ascribed to a shipper but not to a port, others to a port but not to a shipper).

[1] Norden, *Description of Essex*, p. xii.

[2] *Cal. S.P.D., 1595-7*, pp. 126, 336.

[3] S.P.D., Eliz., vol. clxxvii, no. 8.

[4] *Ibid.*, Chas. I, vol. i, no. 70 ; vol. cxciii, no. 3.

[5] Gras, *op. cit.*, pp. 105-6.

[6] S.P.D., Chas. I, vol. clxxvii, no. 50. In 1699 the trade of Wycombe was said to consist chiefly in buying of corn and sending the same to London. (*Commons Journals*, vol. xii, p. 615.)

[7] M. Giuseppi, " The River Wandle in 1610," *Surrey Archaeolog. Collections*, 1908, vol. xxi, pp. 170-91.

[8] Norden, *Description of Essex*, p. xii.

There seems to have been considerable variation in both the status and methods of these town middlemen. Some maltmen were obviously wealthy, engrossing " into their handes out of manye of the best maultinge townes verie greate quantities of Malte— wch they sent to London daylie, eyther out of their howses or els from their private shopps in market townes,"[1] and giving credit to brewers up to as much as £1,500.[2] At the other extreme were the petty and would-be independent carriers who " used to take up money and graine of maltsters and other corne men upon trust."[3] Most seem to have sold to brewers under a contract for weekly deliveries over a period of months, or even years.[4] Mealmen purchased not meal but grain, which they either milled themselves or had milled for them, and sold not only to bakers but also directly to consumers in the open city markets.[5]

Wholesale purchases within the city, however, did not solve all the problems of the retailers. Allowed by the authorities to the butchers, brewers, and bakers, they were less acceptable when made by the non-craftsmen victuallers, who on occasion had to submit to arbitrary interference in the interests of the consumers. And whether craftsman or not, the man who waited to buy in the city must face the risk of being disappointed. Consequently there was a steady permeation of the countryside by London retailers purchasing for resale in their shops. The poulterers' ordinances forbade them to buy rabbits except from breeders under annual contracts ; their other poultry had to be obtained from chapmen who were little more than their servants.[6] Fish was obtained directly both on the coast and from the ponds of country gentlemen.[7] Fruit, hops, butter and cheese, were all bought up in the

[1] Lansdowne MSS., vol. 48, *f.* 116.   [2] *Ibid.*, vol. 32, *f.* 104.

[3] *Ibid.*, vol. 38, *f.* 84.

[4] In 1574, nearly all the alebrewers of London were obtaining malt in this manner from Cambridgeshire, Hertfordshire, and Bedfordshire (Cotton MSS., Faustus, C ii, *ff.* 162-3). For specimen contracts see Court of Requests, Proceedings, bdle. 60, no. 88 ; bdle. 63, no. 99 ; bdle. 65, no. 62 ; bdle. 116, no. 31 ; bdle. 119, no. 25 ; bdle. 168, no. 61 ; bdle. 488, Jellyman *v.* Hamond ; Chancery Procs., Ser. i, Chas. I, bdle. C. 13, no. 35.

[5] Lansdowne MSS., vol. 48, *f.* 139 ; *Cal. S.P.D.*, 1595-7, p. 126 ; S.P.D., Chas. I, vol. ccxxiv, no. 64 ; Giuseppi, *loc. cit.*

[6] Letter Books, vol. Z, *f.* 207 ; vol. AB, *f.* 300 ; Repertories, vol. x, *f.* 331 ; For specimen contracts see Court of Requests, Proceedings, bdle. 38, no. 3 ; bdle 181, no. 61.

[7] *Losely MSS.*, pp. 276-7 ; Norden, *Surveyors Dialogue*, 1618 ed., p. 226 ; Lansdowne MSS., vol. xxxiv, *f.* 58. For a description of a London fishmonger going to Yarmouth " to buy fish uppon the coast to make his provisions for the whole yeare," see Court of Requests, Proceedings, bdle. 487, Gense *v.* Heron ; and *cf.* bdle. 192, no. 19 ; Chancery Proceedings, Early, bdle. 1008, no. 13.

country ;[1] the coast trade in dairy produce, in striking contrast to that in corn, was dominated by a handful of London dealers.[2] In their anxiety to obtain supplies, the butchers not only established direct contact with the graziers on their farms[3] but, in the early seventeenth century, transferred an increasing portion of their market trade from Smithfield to Barnet.[4] Bakers, chandlers, and brewers, all bought in the provinces.[5] And except in the case of grain and cattle, few of these purchases seem to have been made in the open markets.

The process of permeation, moreover, did not stop with direct buying on the part of retailers. There grew up a body of London wholesalers who resold at least part of their country purchases to the smaller city shopkeepers. They were not welcomed by the authorities, but glimpses of them can be caught in the meat, fish, fruit, dairy, poultry, and hop trades.[6] Another aspect of the matter is disclosed by the complaint of the Hertfordshire magistrates that " wheras diverse of our Countrye Inhabitants (being by trade Badgers and Loaders) dyd usuallye goe from markett to markett and ther dydd buye Corne and grayne, wch they weekly carryed to the Citye of London for the provision thereof : whereby many of them grewe to be men of good wealthe and abilitye, and dyd set verye many poore men a worke—Now thos Bakers and Brewers of London, not content to receive thos comodities from thes Loaders as heretofore they have donne, doe dailye come downe into the countrye and verye greadely doe buye great quantities of corne and grayne and doe offerr such deare and high prices for the same . . . that . . . they have utterly overthrowne the former trade of the Loaders and getting the gayne from them doe make the loaders their servauntes and carriers."[7]

---

[1] Court of Requests, Proceedings, bdle. 58, no. 22 ; bdle. 61, no. 39 ; S.P.D., Addend., vol. xlii, nos. 63-5 ; Repertories, vol. x, *f.* 319b ; Letter Books, vol. Q, *f.* 86b ; vol. X, *f.* 48.

[2] Exch. K.R., Port Books, bdle. 18, no. 1 ; bdle. 41, no. 6.

[3] Court of Requests, Proceedings, bdle. 12, no. 56 ; bdle. 27, no. 156 ; bdle. 61, no. 55 ; bdle. 127, no. 53 ; Chancery Proceedings, Early, bdle. 940, no. 17 ; bdle. 986, no. 32.

[4] Letter Books, vol. EE, *f.* 88.

[5] S.P.D., Chas. I, vol. clxxxii, nos. 7 and 81 ; vol. clxxxiii, no. 37 ; vol. clxxxix, no. 79 ; vol. cxc, nos. 44 (v) and 66. For sample transactions see Court of Requests, Proceedings, bdle. 29, no. 42 ; bdle. 491, Beasley *v.* Harding.

[6] Repertories, vol. xv, *ff.* 289, 293 ; Chancery Proceedings, Early, bdle. 1004, no. 64 ; Letter Books, vol. AB, *f.* 301 ; *Acts of the Privy Council, 1615-16,* p. 524 ; S.P.D., Addend., vol. xlii, nos. 63-5.

[7] S.P.D., Eliz., vol. ccliv, no. 10. *Cf.* the complaints from Kent (Lansdowne MSS., vol. lxxviii, *f.* 153), High Wycombe (S.P.D., Chas. I, vol. clxxvii, no. 50) and Kingston (*Ibid.,* vol. clxxxii, no. 7.)

Direct buying meant, in fact, a tendency to depress formerly independent rural middlemen into the employees of London dealers.[1] And in some cases the process of penetration culminated in the Londoners obtaining an interest in the actual production of food. Poulterers made loans to warreners and themselves bred poultry.[2] Fruiterers helped to establish orchards and leased them when established.[3] Butchers themselves became graziers.[4]

Naturally, there were obstacles. Particularly in the sixteenth century, the city authorities objected both to the rise of the city wholesalers and to direct purchase of certain victuals in the country.[5] They found it difficult to distinguish between harmless direct buying and forestalling. County justices occasionally made themselves a nuisance by their efforts to protect rural consumers.[6] At different times the trade in grain, hops, and dairy produce was seriously embarrassed by the statutes against middlemen.[7] The growing coast trade was vulnerable to both the weather and to foreign enemies.[8] And the rural vested interests disturbed by the changes periodically caused trouble. The rise of the Barnet cattle market brought loud protests from Leighton Buzzard and Smithfield; its desertion meant complaints from the Barnet men themselves.[9] The butchers' experiments in fattening their own cattle brought them, at the suit of the outraged graziers of the south midlands, before Parliament, Council, and the Star Chamber.[10]

[1] Every London poulterer, for example, had to undertake not to buy from another's chapman; the chapmen were allowed to change their customers only once a year (Letter Books, vol. AB, *f.* 300).

[2] Repertories, vol. xv, *f.* 223; vol. xxiii, *f.* 512; Letter Books, vol. Z, *f.* 207.

[3] Add. MSS., vol. 33,924, *f.* 32; Court of Requests, Proceedings, bdle. 34, no. 38.

[4] *Ibid.*, bdle. 12, no. 56; Privy Council Register, vol. xl, p. 356.

[5] Repertories, vol. xiii, *f.* 341; Letter Books, vol. Q, *f.* 86b; vol. X, *f.* 48; vol. AB, *f.* 301; S.P.D., Chas. I, vol. ccxxiv, no. 64.

[6] Lansdowne MSS., vol. xlix, no. 5; vol. li, *f.* 97; S.P.D.,C has. I, vol. v, no. 2; vol. lx, no. 49.

[7] *Ibid.*, Jas. I, vol. cxii, no. 12 (i); Addend., vol. xlii, nos. 63-5; Repertories, vol. xxxii, *f.* 271b; *Acts of the Privy Council, 1615-16*, p. 524.

[8] S.P.D., Chas. I, vol. clxii, no. 41. Curiously enough, the difficulties of land carriage do not seem to have impressed contemporaries. They were simply accepted to a degree which historians, debauched by the standards of a pampered age, are apt to forget. The normal way of bringing fish from the Cinque ports to London, for example, was not by river, but by packhorse. The road was divided into stages of fifteen miles, and one set of carriers worked from the coast to Chepstead, another set from Chepstead to the city. (Court of Requests, Proceedings, bdle. 74, no. 4.)

[9] *His. MSS. Comm., Rep. iii, Appendix*, p. 7; Letter Books, vol. EE, *f.* 88; Privy Council Register, vol. xl, p. 356.

[10] *His. MSS. Comm., Rep. iii, Appendix*, p. 31; Privy Council Register, vol. xl, p. 356, vol. xli, pp. 37-8; A. Pearce, *The History of the Butchers' Company*, p. 95.

When the bakers bought from mealmen they offended the suburban millers; when they bought in the country they aroused the opposition of the rural middlemen.[1] The famous struggle over the navigation of the river Lea was only in part a clash between rival transport interests; in part it was a struggle between a group of London brewers and the middlemen of Enfield for control of part of the trade in midland grain.[2] Yet none of these things could stop development along the lines sketched above. London had to be fed, and no practical alternatives were ever suggested. Vested interests could only delay what they could not prevent. City, county, and national authorities all learned in time to tolerate what they had previously damned.

It is, of course, impossible to measure and easy to exaggerate the novelty, rapidity, and efficacy of these various responses to the growing London market. Medieval research will, no doubt, reveal in embryo much of what has been described above. By the early seventeenth century, there was a general feeling that the city's appetite was developing more quickly than the country's ability to satisfy it. Imports from abroad, it is true, do not appear to have risen. But the complaints of the rural justices show that the trade to London was placing an increasing strain on local resources; the high profits of landlords and farmers were obtained in part by pinching the bellies of the local poor. Under the early Stuarts, the theory that the city was too large became generally accepted, partly because of this difficulty of obtaining food, and it became usual to fight unduly high prices by limiting the city population. But when all reservations have been made, the fact of these repercussions remains beyond dispute. The city retailers won a new importance and an increasing control over the trade in agricultural produce. Suburban farming was revolutionised. Prosperity was diffused through the nearer parts of the home counties and south midlands. And a powerful impetus was given to the forces that were working for the commercialisation of agriculture in England at large.

[1] Letter Books, vol. X, *f.* 378; and see p. 47 above.
[2] Lansdowne MSS., vol. xxxii, *ff.* 91-2, 104-10; vol. xxxviii, *ff.* 84, 88-90, vol. xli, *f.* 188. For a similar struggle between the bakers, brewers, and victuallers of Bristol and the merchants of Gloucester for the control of the corn trade to Bristol, see MSS. Records of the Corporation of Gloucester, vol. 1450, *f.* 93.

5

Commercial Trends and Policy in
Sixteenth-Century England

BY now it is almost an axiom of historiography that each generation must re-interpret the past in terms of its own experience, and in accordance with that principle much has recently been done to transform the accepted views of Tudor history. To men brought up in a world of liberalism and *laissez-faire* it was possible to endow sixteenth-century policy with an impressive consistency of both theory and practice ; to think of Tudor despotism and mercantilism as coherent entities ; and to imagine the pattern of English life as being slowly moulded from above in accordance with some preconceived plan. During the last fifty years, however, historians have been given abundant opportunities to learn at first hand of the piecemeal methods by which the mosaic of official ideas and actions is, in fact, built up, and in the light of that knowledge the earlier views of sixteenth-century statesmanship have undergone a gradual change. More than twenty years ago Unwin questioned the right of mercantilism to be considered a " system," and Marshall reduced it from " a body of definite doctrines which arose suddenly, quickly overcame all minds, and after a time was wholly discarded " to a " tendency of thought and sentiment which had its roots in the past ; which never, even at the height of its power, completely dominated all minds ; and which has not yet completely disappeared."[1] More recently, Professor Allen has shown that the sixteenth-century was characterised less by any positive theory of the state than by a naïve belief in " the ability of centralised government to realise its ends. . . . Emergence, or even partial emergence, from the anarchic conditions of the fifteenth century brought with it an accession of faith and hope in the shaping power of government. Whatever men in large numbers desired, whether mere peace and order, or wealth, or justice, or true religion or even happiness, they tended to look to the Prince to supply it. . . . Reformers tended to think that everything was possible to this strange thing, a government able to enforce obedience."[2] By now it is a commonplace of undergraduate essays that the Tudor state was more forced than forceful, and that the origins of its actions are to be found less in any theories held by its rulers than in the pressure to

[1] A. Marshall, *Industry and Trade*, pp. 719-20.
[2] J. W. Allen, *English Political Thought, 1603-60*, vol. i, pp. 59-60.

which it was subjected from vested interests and urgent social and financial problems. The twentieth century, in short, is busily recreating the sixteenth in its own image and the purpose of this article is to suggest that any such process should logically include some enquiry into the possible connection between state policy and the fluctuations in foreign trade. For no one who has studied the great depression of the eighteen-seventies and 'eighties and lived through that of the nineteen-thirties can doubt the influence of commercial crises to influence policy; in sixteenth-century England foreign trade was already important; and the correlation that can be established between trade fluctuations and the various phases of government policy is close enough at least to be suggestive.

Tudor trade statistics are notoriously imperfect and misleading; but a reasonable guide to the main commercial trends of the time is to be found in the figures of shortcloths exported from London, for throughout the sixteenth century cloth was by far the most important commodity exported and by far the greater proportion of English cloth went out through London.

TRIENNIAL AVERAGES OF SHORTCLOTHS EXPORTED FROM LONDON.[1]
(The figures in italics relate to single years.)

1500-2	49,214	1536-8	87,231	1568-70	93,681
1503-5	43,884	1539-41	102,660	1571-3	73,204
1506-8	50,373	1542-4	99,362	1574-6	100,024
1509-11	58,447	1545-7	118,642	1577-9	97,728
1512-14	60,644	*1550*	*132,767*	1580-2	98,002
1515-17	60,524	*1551*	*112,710*	1583-5	101,214
1518-20	66,159	*1552*	*84,968*	1586-8	95,087
1521-3	53,660			1589-91	98,806
1524-6	72,910	1559-61	93,812	1592-4	101,678
1527-9	75,431	1562-4	61,188		
1530-2	66,049	1565-7	95,128	1598-1600	103,032
1533-5	83,043				

And a glance at the cloth figures is sufficient to show that English overseas trade in the sixteenth century passed through three clearly defined phases. As can be seen from the above table, the first half of the century was marked by a meteoric rise in the number of shortcloths exported. That rise, it is true, was not unbroken. With an almost cyclical regularity war, or the danger of war, produced a depression at the beginning of every decade save

[1] The statistics for 1550-2 have been taken from the Exchequer Miscellaneous Customs Accounts, bundle 166, nos. 1 and 8, and bundle 167, no. 1. The remaining figures are from the enrolled accounts of which those for the reigns of Henry VII and Henry VIII have been printed in Schanz, *Englische Handelspolitik gegen Ende des Mittelalters*, vol. ii, pp. 86-7.

one. But as against the general trend these politically-induced set-backs were of no significance ; the vital fact was that in fifty years the cloth trade grew in volume by 150 per cent.[1] By contrast, the third quarter of the century saw not only a contraction of some 25 per cent. in exports, but also two catastrophic slumps in which those exports were halved. Finally, the Tudor age ended with three decades of comparative stability in which London cloth exports remained fairly steadily at a level some 20 per cent. below that reached at the peak of the boom. To analyse those changes and the reaction of the business and political worlds to them is to suggest a clue, albeit a minor one, to the development of Tudor economic policy.

Of the expansion which took place in the first half of the century by far the most significant feature was the change which gradually came over it after the middle of the 'twenties. Until then its story was simple enough and there is no difficulty in enumerating the more important factors of which it was the result. Something, no doubt, was due to the peace which the Henries were able to maintain. Something, also, must be attributed to that process whereby the lines of the international division of labour were being redrawn, and the manufacture of certain types of cloth was migrating from the Netherlands to this country.[2] But the major impetus came from another source. It was a commonplace of the age that English commerce was overwhelmingly dependent upon the Low Countries and that economically London was a satellite of Antwerp. It was upon the looms of Flanders that most of the exported wool was woven ; it was through Antwerp that English cloth reached its consumers not only in the Netherlands themselves, but also in Germany, eastern Europe, Italy and the Levant ; it was from Antwerp that nearly all imports came. " If English men's fathers were hanged at Andwarpes gates," ran a contemporary Flemish proverb, " their children to come into that towne would creepe betwixt their legges."[3] Therefore, it is hardly fanciful to see a connection between the growth of London trade and the fact that it was during these years that Antwerp was climbing to the zenith of its power as the commercial and financial centre of the western world. As the moon of Antwerp waxed the laws of nature dictated that the tide of London trade should rise, and as English

[1] Neither the figures of provincial exports nor those of goods other than cloth sent out from London rose at anything like that pace, so that the London cloth statistics rather exaggerate the general growth in trade.

[2] It would not, however, be strictly true to say that during these years England was abandoning the trade in wool for that in cloth for the wool figures remained fairly stable.

[3] S.P.D. Eliz., vol. xxxvi, no. 34.

cloths were among the major commodities handled in the Flemish city it is not surprising that the export of them increased as the business of that city grew.

Nor are the results of that expansion much more difficult to discover than its causes. On the one hand, there was a marked diversion of national resources into new channels. Arable land was converted to pasture; the textile industry spread over the countryside; the ranks of the merchants were swollen with new entrants. On the other, the growth of exports brought with it a corresponding growth of imports. For the latter no complete set of statistics appears to exist, but some light is thrown on their behaviour by at least three sets of figures. There are the official values of the goods paying subsidy; and although the Henrician accounts do not always distinguish between exports and imports, they are useful because the contribution of the former to their total was comparatively small. There are, in the second place, the official values of the goods brought in by Hanseatic and other foreign merchants; and although the aliens' share in London trade was by no means a constant proportion of the whole, the records of exports suggest that its variation was not great enough to rob these values of all significance for this purpose. Finally, there are the statistics of wine imports. No two of these groups, it is true, moved in exactly the same manner but, until the late 'twenties, all three rose at a pace in some degree comparable to that of the soaring exports.[1] And their story can be confirmed from other sources. Foreign imports were among the grievances of the rioting apprentices in 1517,[2] and one of Armstrong's bitterest complaints was that England " is in such maner alwey stuffid, storid and pesterid so full of straunge merchaundise. . . . It is over long to describe the myschief that merchaunts werkth thorowt the reame by bryngyng such quantite of straunge merchaundise and artificiall fantasies." If Armstrong is any criterion, contemporaries found little cause for rejoicing in the direction which the country's economic life was taking.[3] To a less righteous and possibly more enlightened age, however, it is clear that there was another aspect to the matter. In the same words in which they prophesied disaster contemporaries unconsciously bore witness to a rise in their standard of living, a rise that was emphasised by the sumptuary legislation designed to check its most obvious manifestations. And there seems little doubt that the first quarter

[1] Schanz, *op. cit.*, vol. ii, pp. 62, 63, 146-8.

[2] Tawney and Power, *Tudor Economic Documents*, vol. iii, p. 83.

[3] *Ibid.*, pp. 90-114. The whole of Armstrong's *Treatise Concerning the Staple* is the description of a commercial boom by one who disliked everything which that boom implied.

of the sixteenth century must be regarded as essentially a period of commercial prosperity.

The influence of Antwerp upon London trade continued to operate until the 'sixties, but in the 'twenties it was joined, and in the 'forties it was overshadowed, by a far less healthy stimulus— that of exchange depreciation. By now, the story of that depreciation is well known. The fall of sterling began with the French war of 1522, and its first stage was crystallised by the reduction of the weight of coins in 1526, by which time the value of the pound had dropped from 32s. Flemish to 26s. 8d. During the 'thirties the exchanges probably weakened still further, and with the successive debasements of the 'forties they finally collapsed until, in the early months of 1551, the pound was worth only 13s. 4d. Flemish.[1] Nor were the effects of that decline completely nullified by the accompanying rise in the internal price level. The fall in the external value of the pound began before inflation,[2] and always kept ahead of it.[3] The result was inevitable. During the second quarter of the sixteenth century, and particularly during the 'forties, silver prices slowly fell in England while they rose on the continent[4] and, as English goods thereby became relatively cheap, there was a natural increase in their sales abroad. The relevant statistics are too imperfect and the intrusion of other factors is too great for any exact correlation to be possible, but the connection between the fall of the exchanges and the rise of exports is reasonably obvious. The depreciation of the early 'twenties was followed by a distinct jump in the cloth figures ; that of the 'forties was accompanied not only by a boom in textiles, but also by a recovery in wool shipments ; and it is perhaps of some significance that when the revaluation of the currency restored its silver content to approximately that of the early 'forties the cloth figures gradually stabilised themselves at a level not far removed from that which obtained in those years.[5]

As the expansion of exports grew to depend more and more upon exchange depreciation, so its economic significance gradually changed. An immediate result of the new impetus to trade was to accelerate the diversion of national resources into the exporting industries. The conversion of arable land to pasture was already an established phenomenon, but in the 'thirties and 'forties it took

---

[1] Feavearyear, *The Pound Sterling*, p. 64.   [2] *Ibid.*, p. 47.

[3] Ricardo, *Principles of Political Economy* (Everyman Edition), p. 239. I am indebted to my colleague Mr. J. K. Horsefield for this reference.

[4] Wiebe, *Zur Geschichte der Preisrevolution des xvi und xvii Jahrhunderts*, Appendix A.   [5] *Vide* the statistical table on p. 82.

on a new magnitude, and the Tudor government was driven to vastly more energetic attempts to handle the problem.[1] The growth of the textile industry was not new, but it was the 'thirties and 'forties that produced an embryo factory system under men such as William Stumpe. And as the pace of economic change grew, so the strain which it put upon the comparatively rigid structure of Tudor England grew with it. In the earlier years of the century that strain had been tolerable, although the enclosure agitation and apprentice riots of 1517 must in part be laid to its charge. But as, under the stimulus of exchange depreciation, cloth exports reached new high levels and even the trade in wool revived, the pains of adaptation became increasingly acute. It would, of course, be foolish to attribute all or even most of the troubles of those times to the developments in foreign trade. Far more important, no doubt, was the rise in the internal price level. But the connection between exchange depreciation and the agrarian problem was obvious even to an age not unusually gifted with economic insight. As Lane once wrote to Cecil :

> " The fall of the exchange within thys iiii dayse hathe cawsyd
> and wyll cause to be boughte clothes at lvi *li*. the packe
> wyche before wold not have byn bowghte for lii *li*. the
> packe ; so that yow may perseve that the exchange doth
> ingender dere clothe, and dere clothe doth engendar dere
> wolle, and dere wolle doth ingendar many scheppe, and
> many scheppe doth ingendar myche pastor and dere, and
> myche pastor ys the dekaye of tyllage, and owte of the
> dekaye of tyllage spryngythe ii evylls, skarsyte of korne
> and the pepull unwroghte, and consequently the darthe of
> all thynges.[2]

And it was by no mere chance that Starkey, Latimer, Hales, Crowley and the " commonwealth party " were most vocal when overseas commerce was booming or that Norfolk rose in rebellion when London exports were greater in physical volume than they had ever been before or were to be again for more than half a century.

Moreover, as exports became more costly in terms of the social changes needed to produce them, so they tended to become less lucrative in terms of the foreign wares which they purchased. Contemporary complaints against the excessive volume of imports still continued, yet the customs figures already mentioned as

[1] Tawney, *The Agrarian Problem in the Sixteenth Century*, p. 358.
[2] Tawney and Power, *op. cit.*, vol. ii, p. 184.

throwing some light on the subject all suggest that, for most of the 'thirties and 'forties, that volume was either stable or declining. Certainly the volume of imports did not grow as rapidly as that of exports, and its failure to do so seems to admit of only three explanations, all of which were probably in some measure operative and none of which were conducive to general prosperity. That failure may have been due in part to a net increase in the inflow of bullion although, despite the raising of the Mint price, the tendency to smuggle abroad all the better coins must have prevented that ever becoming great and the writers of the time were not aware of any such increase. It was undoubtedly due in part to the growth of invisible imports such as the alien shipping services against which the navigation laws of 1532 and 1540 were directed, the interest on the royal debt abroad, and the expenses of the French wars in the early 'forties. Finally, the natural result of the depreciation of sterling was to alter the terms of trade in a direction unfavourable to this country. Contemporaries were aware of the extraordinary dearness of foreign goods even to the point of attributing to it the rise in the domestic price level; Wiebe has shown that there was in fact a marked divergence between silver prices here and abroad; and it is not difficult to believe that as the exchanges declined an ever larger volume of exports was needed to purchase a given quantity of foreign wares. Because of that change in the terms of trade, together with the increasing strain which the provision of exports placed upon the whole economic structure, it is not, perhaps, too fanciful to argue that by the 'forties commercial expansion had changed from a force making for general economic progress into one of the causes of that distress and discontent which were such outstanding features of those years.

Yet, although the first two quarters of the sixteenth century were rather less alike than the export figures at first sight suggest, they had one major characteristic in common. Together they formed, especially in contrast with the years which followed, one of the great free trade periods of modern English history. They were preceded by the famous statute of 1497 which temporarily curtailed the power of the Merchant Adventurers;[1] they were marked by the collapse of the usury laws,[2] the relaxation of the restrictions upon the export of unfinished cloth,[3] and by the virtual cessation of the attacks upon the Hanseatic merchants;[4] there was a period in the 'thirties and 'forties when the differential

---

[1] 12 Hen. VII, c. 6.   [2] 37 Hen. VIII, c. 9.   [3] 27 Hen. VIII, c. 13.

[4] J. A. Williamson, *Maritime Enterprise, 1485-1558*, ch. 7.

duties imposed on aliens were abolished ;[1] and none of the spas-
modic efforts of the government to interfere in commercial affairs
seems to have been more than half-hearted. For that comparative liberalism the reasons were doubtless several. Something
must be attributed to the worldly wisdom of the early Tudors.
Certainly Henry VIII, than whom no man was more adept in the
art of cloaking private ends in the decent robes of public sentiments, had no illusions about " the inordinate desire of gaynes . . .
naturally given to merchaunts." As he once explained to the
Emperor, he made it his policy " to give no further credit unto them
in their sutes, clamours and complaynts thenne is convenient." [2]
More important, no doubt, was the delicate international situation
which made it dangerous in any way to antagonise the Emperor
upon whose subjects the brunt of any trade restrictions must inevitably fall. Of still greater moment was the fact that England was in
no good position for economic warfare. The only foreign
merchants worth penalising were those of the Hanse towns and
Flanders. Mediæval experience suggested that to interfere with the
privileges of the former was to enter into a struggle which was sure
to be long and likely to be unsuccessful. To molest the latter was
to cross swords with the Emperor, whose economic armoury
included weapons deadlier than any that Henry could command.
He could close the Antwerp market to English goods and he could
extend the conflict by penalising English traders in Spain. Yet
later sovereigns as astute as the Henries and in no better position
to risk offending their neighbours were soon to reverse their policy
of free trade, and the ultimate explanation for that policy must be
sought elsewhere. It is to be found in the simple fact that at no
time during the first half of the century was strong and consistent
pressure brought to bear on the government drastically to interfere
in commercial affairs. On the one hand those, and they were many,
who thought it the duty of the State to promote English mercantile
interests had little cause for action when trade was so continuously
growing. In every minor slump they clamoured for and obtained
legislation but the enforcement of that legislation was probably as
transitory as the depressions which produced it. On the other hand
those, and they were also many, who thought it the duty of the
State to keep commercial expansion within reasonable bounds
found, as Americans were to rediscover in the nineteen-twenties,
that stables are seldom locked until their horses have been stolen
and that booms, like floods, can seldom be controlled until the
waters have begun to subside of their own accord. They obtained

[1] *L. and P. Henry VIII*, vol. xvi, no. 13.

[2] Add. MSS., 25,114, f. 122 b.

some largely ineffectual legislation against enclosures, but for more drastic measures they had to wait. They did not have to wait for ever.

In so far as the later stages of the export boom had been based upon currency devaluation they had been inherently unstable. As internal prices rose the advantages of exchange depreciation were bound to dwindle and already in 1550 there were complaints of overproduction.[1] Unless the process of debasement was continued indefinitely the physical volume of exports was in time certain to fall, and there was a point beyond which debasement could not be taken without endangering the whole economic and social system. But although some decline in exports was inevitable, its pace and severity depended largely upon whether internal and external prices were left to adjust themselves or whether that adjustment was hastened by a change in currency policy. The merchants, eager to reap the benefits of devaluation for as long as possible, were all for allowing matters to take their own course. To the government, however, the matter appeared differently. Faced with the necessity of checking the rise in domestic prices and of repaying its heavy debts abroad, it saw a bitter truth in the dictum that " the exchainge is the thing that eatts ought all princes to the wholl destruction of their commonweal." Therefore, despite mercantile opposition, the currency was called down in 1551, the exchanges shot up, and there was a drastic fall in the sterling equivalent of the prices reigning upon the Antwerp market. " The exchange in King Edward's time," wrote Gresham, " was but 16s. Dyd I not raise it to 23s. ? . . . Whereby wool fell in price from 26s. 8d. to 16s. and cloths from lx *li.* to xl *li.* and xxxvi *li.* a packe."[2] Unfortunately, as the merchants pointed out, English internal prices fell neither as rapidly nor as far, and there followed a painful and protracted struggle until a new equilibrium could be reached. At first the physical volume of exports shrank quickly ; the number of short-cloths sent out from London fell from 132,767 in 1550 to 112,710 in 1551, and to 84,969 in 1552. Then, as costs were slowly adjusted, as the international bickerings of the early 'fifties died down, and as the exchanges once more collapsed exports shot up once more to reach a new record in 1554.[3] But in the following year there was an epidemic of bankruptcies in the city;[4] in 1556 all shipments to the Netherlands had to be stayed for four months in order to ease

---

[1] *Acts of the Privy Council, 1550-2*, p. 20.

[2] J. W. Burgon, *Life of Sir Thomas Gresham*, vol. i, p. 261.

[3] See statistical table on p. 82, and Exchequer Miscellaneous Customs Accounts, bdle., 175, no. 4.

[4] *Hist. Mss. Comm. Report III*, p. 37.

the glut there ;[1] and the opening years of Elizabeth's reign found the cloth trade at a level some 30 per cent. below the peak of the boom, a level which was not to be substantially exceeded until the next century. The great expansion of trade was over.

To see in that change any great national catastrophe would, no doubt, be absurd. The appreciation of the exchanges meant a change in the terms of trade in favour of this country. The value of exports must have fallen less than their volume. It is conceivable that imports and the national income were scarcely diminished. But the mere falling-off in the physical volume of exports meant that in trade, in the textile industry, and in shipping there was left a body of unemployed resources that had in some way to be liquidated or relieved. And in attempting to solve the problems thus created men at first succeeded only in damaging commerce still further. In the early 'sixties and again in the early 'seventies, partly because of the measures taken in the 'fifties, Antwerp was closed to English goods, the major prop of London trade was knocked away, and exports fell to levels which they had not known for a generation.[2] Followed as they were by those even greater setbacks, the maladjustments of the 'fifties opened a new chapter in English economic history. It is a platitude that periods of intense or repeated depression are fertile in changes in both economic thought and economic practice, for it is when men's established expectations are not fulfilled that they become most critical of the system under which they live and are most readily led to experiment. The depressions of the early nineteenth century were a potent factor in the development of classical theory and *laissez-faire* practice; those of the 'seventies and 'eighties had their fruit in economic imperialism, tariff reform and the rise of collectivism; those of the nineteen-thirties have stimulated changes of which the effects are bound to be immense ; and those of the third quarter of the sixteenth century had repercussions which make that period comparable to any of the other three in its significance. On the one hand, it saw an outburst of economic discussion which, although it drew heavily on the past for its ideas, was carried on in a different language and with a different emphasis from those of the 'thirties and 'forties. Then the important thinkers had been preachers and social reformers but now they were merchants and statesmen ; then the characteristic vehicle of expression had been the sermon and the treatise but now it was the more technical memorandum ; then the criterion

[1] *Acts of the Privy Council, 1554-6*, p. 295.

[2] For a discussion of these later depressions see Unwin's lectures on the Merchant Adventurers in his *Studies in Economic History*.

by which contemporary life was tested had been that of social justice but now it was that of economic expediency; then the great topic of discussion had been agriculture but now it was trade and industry. Faced with the problem of recurrent depressions the men of the 'fifties, 'sixties and 'seventies fused the ideas and prejudices of the middle ages into a loosely co-ordinated body of doctrine, and in applying that doctrine they imposed upon the economic system a set of regulations that were substantially to affect its working for the next two generations.

Some measure of adjustment to the new circumstances took place without any major interference on the part of the government and without any radical departure from established habits. Land that had been converted from tillage to pasture could easily enough be reconverted to tillage.[1] It is possible that some mercantile funds went into the privateering which grew into such evil prominence under Mary. Certainly, to judge by the outcry against them, both merchants and clothiers transferred some of their capital to land and, willingly or otherwise, many of the former invested in government loans. More spectacular were the attempts of the government to bring under control the foreign exchanges which, in a sense, had been the original cause of all the difficulty. As Professor Tawney has shown, the third quarter of the sixteenth century was marked by almost ceaseless discussions about the international money market, and every falling-off in trade produced some scheme for reducing that market to order. However loudly Gresham might repeat his father's axiom that " merchants can no more be without exchanges and rechanges than ships at sea without water," the demand for exchange control appeared in every slump with the automatic regularity of a reflex action. It was part of the revaluation policy of the early 'fifties, when private exchange business was banned as from June 1551. It re-appeared in the commercial crisis at the end of the decade and in 1559 private exchange business was suspended once more. The depression of the early 'sixties led to the Royal Commission of 1564 ; that of the early 'seventies led to the ban of 1576.[2] Save as a nuisance, however, exchange control probably exercised little influence on trade and the more important results of the depression have to be sought elsewhere.

---

[1] Miss Bradley (*The Enclosures in England*) has suggested that the reconversions after 1550 were due to the recuperation of soil which had been put down to grass because of its exhaustion. They may equally well be attributed to the fall in the demand for wool.

[2] *Vide* R. H. Tawney's introduction to Thomas Wilson's *Discourse on Usury*, pp. 145-50. It is significant that usury was once more prohibited in 1552.

An obvious measure was to seek new markets for English cloth and in the 'fifties, when the problem was essentially one of a shrinkage in the effective European demand, those markets were of necessity sought further afield. The immediate result of the slump induced by the over-production of the 'forties and the revaluation of 1551 was, in fact, to launch England on the quest for Eastern and African trade. Previously, despite the country's favourable geographical position and the activity of a few enthusiasts, English interest in the search for and the exploitation of new lands had been of the slightest. On the one hand, the fear of Spanish hostility made the government cautious. On the other, the profits to be earned at Antwerp left merchants content to be tied to Europe and reluctant to face the retaliation that any infringement of the Spanish and Portuguese monopolies might bring. During the first half of the century it had been only in periods of slack trade that projects for more daring ventures could hope for the attention of business men, and with every check to commercial expansion such projects had appeared. In the early 'twenties Henry VIII had proposed to the Londoners that they should finance a company to trade to Newfoundland and beyond ;[1] in the early 'thirties Thorne and Barlow had joined forces to work out their scheme for a northwest passage ; in the early 'forties Barlow had revived that scheme and a pilot had actually been brought from Seville in the hope of discovering a way between Iceland and Greenland.[2] But all those depressions had been too brief for the merchants' interest to be seriously captured and it was not until the 'fifties, when men saw quite clearly that under the impetus of exchange depreciation the cloth trade had reached dimensions which could not be maintained upon the basis of purely European markets, that effective action was taken. Then, in 1551, a ship was sent to Morocco ; in 1553 others went to Guinea ; and in the latter year Chancellor and Willoughby sailed in search of a north-east passage and thereby opened up trade with Russia. The later depressions served only to intensify the movement. To see more than a coincidence in the fact that the traffic in slaves to the West Indies began when cloth exports were once more falling would, no doubt, be dangerous. But the overtrading of which men were complaining in Africa by 1567 may well have been due to the closing of Antwerp in 1562 and the following years ;[3] and the same crisis almost certainly encouraged the Russian merchants in their efforts to establish an

---

[1] Williamson, *Maritime Enterprise, 1485-1558*, pp. 245-6.

[2] *Ibid.*, p. 265. For a full account of the Thorne-Barlow project see Professor Taylor's introduction to Barlow's *Brief Summe of Geographie*.

[3] S.P.D. Eliz., vol. xlii, no. 49.

overland trade with Persia, for those efforts were more and more directed to obtaining the spices which previously Antwerp had supplied. Finally, the slump of the 'seventies had the most important result of all for it led to the reopening of direct trade with the Levant.[1] England was at last launched upon the pursuit of world commerce. Nor was such enterprise peculiar to trade. The textile industry, unable for technological reasons to meet depression by drastically reducing its costs, met it in some measure by diversifying its products. For it was these years that saw the beginning of the " new draperies " in England ; and although those draperies owed much to Protestant refugees from abroad there is no reason either to believe that all the new cloths were introduced by foreigners or to doubt that the welcome which those foreigners were given was in some part due to the employment which they could create. The depressions of the third quarter of the sixteenth century, in short, resembled those of the last quarter of the nineteenth in turning the eyes of English merchants to more distant markets and the hands of English manufacturers to new commodities.

The immediate relief to be expected from such developments was, however, but slight and for the most part men pinned their faith on other and more dubious remedies. The most obvious characteristics of the 'fifties were an outburst of economic nationalism aimed at maximising the Englishmen's share of such trade as there was and a crop of restrictions designed to protect certain vested interests from the necessity of contraction, to bolster up prices, and to make impossible any repetition of the feverish expansion of the preceding decades. Neither of those phenomena was, of course, by any means new. But during the first half of the century, although they had not lacked occasional expression in either words or action, they had been generally held in check by the prevailing prosperity. When trade is booming the sting of economic inequality is magically softened and the interests threatened by restrictions and xenophobia are too powerful to be lightly ignored ; the danger comes with depression. When, for other reasons, markets are shrinking, the fear that they will be closed in retaliation for nationalistic measures obviously loses some of its potency ; when sales and prices are falling the compulsory restriction of output and the bridling of competition acquire a specious rationality which it is difficult to resist ; and as profits dwindle the former champions of liberty lose both their convictions and their influence. Therefore it is not surprising that the

[1] Cotton Mss., Nero B. xi, f. 292.

'fifties opened a period which saw, if not a complete reversal, at least a drastic refashioning of economic policy.

The revival of economic nationalism was, of course, by no means confined to merchants and in 1563 a general prohibition was placed upon all that foreign haberdashery against which pamphleteers had been railing for a generation.[1] But the great protagonist of economic nationalism was still the merchant rather than the manufacturer. Imports were still complementary to rather than competitive with the products of England, and the really urgent problem was not whether they should be admitted but who should bring them in and carry out exports in exchange. Whereas in the twentieth century the aim of economic nationalism has been to limit international co-operation, in the sixteenth it was rather to decide upon the agents by whom that co-operation should be carried on. And inevitably the major enemy in that struggle were the Hanseatic merchants, for by virtue of their tariff privileges those merchants were more important than all the other foreigners engaged in English trade and by virtue of their opposition to the growing English penetration of the Baltic it was against them that most bitterness was felt. One of the first results, therefore, of the depression of the early 'fifties was a recrudescence of that anti-Hanseatic feeling which had been smouldering ever since the great eruptions of the fifteenth century but which the early Tudors had never permitted to come to a head. As in the fifteenth century, the opposition to the Hanse turned partly on the question of parity of treatment for English merchants in the Baltic; but now there was added a new element. For the centripetal tendency which had drawn the Londoners towards Antwerp had also been felt by the Hanse merchants, so that the Low Countries which had earlier been a refuge from their competition now became its very centre.[2] Armstrong had drawn a sharp distinction between the Prussian merchants trading " owt of the cold contreys in the este parties " and those of western Germany who carried on their trade through Flanders,[3] and when the storm broke in the 'fifties it was upon the latter that its greatest violence fell. That development, which contemporaries dated from the 'twenties, was important because it ranged against them not only the Baltic traders but also the much more powerful Merchant Adventurers just at the time when the Adventurers were rendering important financial services to the

[1] 5 Eliz., c. 7.

[2] For the tendency of Hanseatic exclusiveness to divert English trade to the Netherlands see Power and Postan, *English Trade in the Fifteenth Century*, pp. 150-3.

[3] Tawney and Power, *op. cit.*, vol. iii, pp. 108-9.

government and were therefore in a position to press for favours. To that situation there could be but one outcome ; the special privileges of the Hansards were at last curtailed. In 1552 they were abolished entirely ; but that was no more than the opening to a wearisome series of negotiations during which those privileges were restored, modified and again cancelled before, in 1560, a settlement was reached on the basis of a new tariff that left the Hansards more favourably placed than other aliens but with no advantages over native merchants. In their business with their own towns they were to pay as Englishmen, but in that with Antwerp they were to be taxed at a rate only slightly below that for other foreigners.[1] Those other foreigners had fewer privileges to lose but, even so, their position was steadily undermined. The early 'fifties were full of complaints from Low Country merchants about their ill-treatment in England ;[2] Italian, Ragusan and French merchants were forced to enter bond not to sell English cloth in Antwerp or elsewhere save in their own countries and beyond ;[3] the petty obstacles in the way of aliens were multiplied ; and the policy reached its climax in the new tariff and the navigation act of 1558. " The natives here," reported the Venetian ambassador, " have laid a plot to ruin the trade of all foreign merchants,"[4] and in the next twenty years there were repeated attempts to hamper those merchants by enforcing the statutes of employment, by making them host with Englishmen and employ English brokers, by excluding them from retail trade and by limiting the types of goods which they might export.[5]

Even more spectacular than this outburst of economic nationalism was the wave of restrictionism which accompanied it. In great crises the cost of industrial and commercial expansion seems disproportionately large and, in the spirit of caution which those crises bring with them, it seems the epitome of wisdom to control production and to avoid the curse of plenty. Thus the great depression of the twentieth century has produced its restrictive planning to act as a brake upon progress ; that of the late nineteenth

---

[1] Williamson, *op. cit.*, ch. 7.

[2] *Cal. S.P. Spanish, 1550-2, passim.* For the general wave of anti-foreign feeling which, based on hatred of the Spaniards, swept over the country, see *Cal. S.P. Venice, 1555-6,* pp. 1056 and 1066 ; *1557-8,* p. 1544.

[3] *Cal. S.P. Domestic, 1547-65,* p. 518 ; Baschet Transcripts, bundle 23, letter of January 8, 1557.

[4] *Cal. S.P. Venice, 1556-7,* p. 1011.

[5] *Cal. S.P. Foreign, 1560-1,* pp. 91-2 ; *Cal. S.P. Domestic, 1547-65,* pp. 531-2 ; *Acts of the Privy Council, 1577-8,* pp. 281, 379, 401 ; S.P.D. Eliz., vol. lxxx, no. 61 ; vol. lxxxiii, nos. 35-6 ; vol. cvi, nos. 27-8 ; vol. cxxx, no. 25 ; Harl. Mss., vol. xxxvi, ff. 81 *et. seq.*

produced its cartels and its trusts ; and that of the sixteenth proved a worthy forerunner of them both by inspiring a similar flight from competition towards organisation. As the boom of the first half of the century had been largely confined to the textiles, it is not surprising that the policy of restraint was first elaborated in the cloth industry. Attacks upon the rapid expansion of that industry were not new. It had created, and threatened to create in the future, problems to which men could not remain blind, and all the arguments now used in favour of restriction had, in fact, been heard in the days of prosperity. But although they had been heard they had not been seriously heeded, for Tudor governments seldom met their difficulties before they became acute. While the industry was flourishing and profits were easy the diversion of resources into it imposed a serious strain only upon agriculture and the government contented itself with trying to check the conversion of arable land to pasture. It was only in the depression, when those resources had to be rediverted, that attention was seriously turned to industry itself. That " experience hath taught that overmuche draperie, besydes divers other inconveniences, hath destroyed more necessarie Artificers than it hath bred " became a bitter platitude of which the truth became ever more obvious with each successive collapse in trade. And as the long term costs of rapid industrialisation became more apparent men began to devise means for making such industrialisation impossible.

The arguments for restriction came mainly from three sources. There were, in the first place, those conservatives to whom all change was necessarily suspect and to whom the rise of a new class of industrialists implied a threat to the whole well-ordering of society. Complaints about the contemporary confusion of social classes were many, and to some the greatest of all offenders was the clothier " whoe doth most harme of all other degres in this land by purchasing lande or leses, or by maynteyning in his sonne in the Ynes of Cort like a gentleman or by byeng offices for him."[1] To the progressive landlord deriving much of his income from the sale of wool those views may have seemed extreme ; but there were plenty of men in the Commons to whom they appealed and the restrictions on the cloth trade were voted partly in the spirit in which the Tory squires of the nineteenth century were to fasten the Factory Acts upon the cotton lords.

There was, in the second place, the approach of the statesman concerned for the preservation of law and order and for the maintenance of those conditions which made law and order possible.

[1] Rawlinson Mss., D., vol. 133, f. 13.

Their views were expressed by Cecil:

> " It is to be thought that the diminution of clothyng in this
> realme were proffitable to the same for manny causes : first,
> for that therby the tilladg of the realm is notoriously decayed,
> which is yerly manifest in that, contrary to former tymes, the
> realme is dryven to be furnished with forrayn corne, and
> specially the Citee of London. Secondly, for that the people
> depend uppon makyng of cloth ar worss condition to be
> quyetly governed than the husband men. Thyrdly by con-
> vertyng of so manny people to clothyng the realme lacketh
> not only artificers, which were wont to inhabitt all corporat
> townes, but also labours for all comon workes."[1]

Experience showed that such fears were by no means imaginary.
The dependence of London upon French corn was an important
factor in Anglo-French relations during the 'fifties ;[2] the repeated
danger that Philip might bring England to heel by the use of
economic sanctions illustrated the political inexpediency of industrialisation ;[3] and the results of unemployment in the textile
industry were, to say the least, disconcerting. It was found
that whenever trade fell off :

> " infinite nombers of Spynners, Carders, Pickers of woll are
> turned to begging with no smale store of pore children, who
> driven with necessitie (that hath no lawe) both come idelie
> abowt to begg to the oppression of the poore husbandmen,
> And robbe their hedges of Lynnen, stele pig, gose, and capon,
> and leave not a drie hedg within dyvers myles compas of the
> townes wher they dwell to the great destruction of all mannor
> of grayen sowen and to the spoile of mens meadowes and
> pastures, And spoile all springes, steale fruit and corne in the
> harvest tyme, and robb barnes in the winter tyme, and cawse
> pore maydes and servantes to purloyne and robbe their masters,
> which the foresayd spynners etc. receve Besides many other
> myscheifes falling owt the Weavers, Walkers, Tukkers,
> Shermen, Dyers and suche being tall lusty men and extreame

---

[1] Tawney and Power, *op. cit.*, vol. ii, p. 45.

[2] Baschet Transcripts, bundle 23, ff. 279, 281, 290.

[3] In the early 'sixties the policy of sanctions found a powerful advocate in
Cardinal Granvelle, the virtual ruler of the Netherlands and the man most
responsible for the embargoes placed upon English cloth in 1562 and 1563
(Rich, *The Ordinance Book of the Merchants of the Staple*, pp. 45-51). In the later
'sixties and early 'seventies Norfolk, Arundel and Ridoli all wanted a similar
ban in support of their conspiracies (*Cal. S.P. Spanish, 1568-79*, p. 136 ;
Cal. S.P. Rome, 1558-71, p. 338). For the influence of trade depression on the
rising of 1569 see *Cal. S.P. Venice, 1558-80*, p. 437.

pore streyght being forced by povertie stele fish, conies, dere, and such like, and their streight murmur and rayse comocions as late experience in Suffolke shewed."[1]

On occasion, as in 1563, the government might meet such a position by purchasing cloth with public funds ;[2] but the temptation to avoid the problem by checking the growth of the industry was irresistible.

Finally, there was the pressure of those vested interests who could make restriction serve their purpose and increase their profits. The established manufacturers had never looked kindly upon newcomers and, when contraction became inevitable, they immediately demanded that it should be so regulated as to fall entirely upon those whom the boom had drawn into production. When examined by the Privy Council in 1550 they immediately explained the glutting of the Antwerp market and consequent collapse in prices by " finding great fault with the moltitude of clothiers lately encreased in the realme."[3] And the Staplers could be relied upon to welcome any scheme that, by diminishing the home consumption of wool, would leave more for export.

When Parliament met in 1551 the depression was already upon the country and during the next twelve years the policy of restriction was slowly given legislative form. On the one hand, the pressure upon landlords to reconvert their pasture land to tillage became stronger.[4] On the other, the textile industry itself was subjected to stricter control. The first suggestion was to limit the industry by confining it to towns.[5] For some reason, however, that device was abandoned. Instead, after consultation with clothiers, merchant tailors and representatives of the finishing trades, two other bills were preferred and passed. The first established a detailed code of regulations for the maintenance of the quality of English woollens, for as prices fell manufacturers had as usual resorted to the debasement of their workmanship in an effort to reduce their costs.[6] The second allowed broadcloths to be woven only by such persons as had either served an apprenticeship or followed the trade for seven years, for in that way the most recent recruits to the industry could be weeded out.[7] Unfortunately, however, the problem of enforcing that contraction was complicated by the desire of the government to preserve urban interests from loss and to make the burden fall entirely upon their rural

---

[1] Rawlinson Mss., D., 133, f. 4b.   [2] *Cal. S.P. Spanish, 1568-79*, p. 113.
[3] Tawney and Power, *op. cit.*, vol. i, p. 184.   [4] Tawney, *op. cit.*, p. 354.
[5] *Commons Journals*, vol. i, p. 16.   [6] 5 and 6 Ed. VI, c. 6.
[7] 5 and 6 Ed. VI, c. 8.

competitors. For that purpose the statute of 1552 was too general for it created unemployment in town as well as country and within three years it had to be twice modified. In 1553 towns and cities were exempted from its operation.[1] And in 1555, when the Antwerp market was again glutted, the policy of discrimination and restraint was carried a stage further by limiting the number of apprentices and looms that even a qualified rural manufacturer might employ.[2] Finally, when the slump of the early 'sixties made all existing restrictions seem inadequate and all arguments against industrialisation appear unanswerable, the sphere of State action was widened and, in place of the further regulation of textiles as such, there appeared the famous Statute of Apprentices applying to trade, industry and agriculture alike.[3] Like all great measures of social reconstruction that statute had many roots and, in the absence of the debates upon it, it is impossible to trace all the causes to which it was due. But among its results was one so obvious that it could not have been unpremeditated. By insisting upon apprenticeship in trade and industry, by defining the classes from which apprentices might be taken, by fixing wages, and by prohibiting the sudden termination of contracts between employer and employed, it made illegal that mobility of labour without which rapid industrialisation and spectacular commercial expansion are impossible. Had the Statute of Apprentices been in effective operation in the 'thirties and 'forties the boom of those years could not have taken place ; in view of the economic opinions which prevailed in the 'fifties and 'sixties it is, perhaps, not unreasonable to see in that fact one of the motives which inspired it ; and to that extent it stands as a classic example of the restrictive legislation which great depressions tend to produce.

But although the policy of restriction found its most obvious manifestations in industry it by no means left commerce free. An immediate result of the crisis had been to strengthen among merchants not only their hostility to foreigners but also their insistence that the quintessence of economic wisdom lay in raising prices by controlling sales. The attraction of that device has always varied inversely with the prosperity of trade. While the boom kept prices buoyant and profits high it had languished. Now, as those conditions passed, that idea became the basis of commercial policy and its acceptance as such, although owing much to the financial services which its champions were at this time affording to the government, was made infinitely easier by the attempts to deflate

---

[1] 1 Mary, sessio tertia, c. 7.   [2] 2 and 3 Ph. and Mary, c. 11.
[3] 5 Eliz., c. 4.

the cloth industry itself. In the first place, the textile legislation provided an obvious instrument whereby the volume of cloth coming on to the market could be controlled at its source.[1] What was even more important, that legislation answered the most obvious objection to the merchants' programme. To allow them to control sales meant, as contemporary critics did not fail to point out, the sacrifice of the manufacturers to them. It was, therefore, highly convenient for them that the revival of their policy of restriction coincided with a public opinion temporarily biassed against the manufacturer and inclined to see the limitation of production rather as a blessing than otherwise. Finally, the same school of thought that advocated a reduction in the number of textile workers welcomed the attempts of the merchants to reduce their own.

During the boom years new capital and labour had flowed into commerce as into industry, and the increase in merchants had been as conspicuous and as unpopular as the multiplication of clothiers. It presented a similar challenge to the established order of society ; it aroused a similar opposition among both the established traders and the gentry ; and with the advent of the depression that opposition flared up into a general attack upon the newcomers. Upon their misdemeanours there was no disagreement. By their competition they raised the prices of imports and lowered those of exports ; by their purchases of land they undermined the social hierarchy of the countryside ; in so far as they were young men without capital they were forced to trade with borrowed money and thereby weakened the exchanges ; coming as many of them did from the ranks of the artisans and retailers they complicated the problems of those among the gentry who looked to commerce for the employment of their younger sons. Nor was there much doubt about the remedies. Trade should be restricted to those who had served an apprenticeship ; apprenticeship should be restricted to the sons of the well-to-do ; and for each branch of trade there should be established a company to enforce those restrictions and to regulate the conduct of such merchants as were admitted to it. One of the major results, therefore, of the depressions in the third quarter of the sixteenth century was to fasten upon English commerce a framework of companies which were to dominate its history for the next half-century.

Of the growth of those companies the story is too well known to need repeating in any detail.[2] For the most part it marched in

---

[1] For a discussion of the attitude of London merchants to this textile legislation see Miss Gay's article on " Aspects of Elizabethan Apprenticeship " in *Facts and Factors in Economic History*, pp. 134-163.

[2] Most of the facts mentioned here have been taken from Unwin's lecture, already referred to, on the Merchant Adventurers.

step with the fluctuations in trade and each successive slump added
its quota of restrictions. Ever since 1497 the Merchant Adventurers had been divided into the " Old Hanse " of old-established
firms and the " New Hanse " of those admitted under the statute
of that year. Theoretically, the status of the two groups was the
same. But the former had always contrived to determine the
company's byelaws and to dominate its court of assistants, and with
the depressions of the 'fifties they used their power to cramp the
activities of the others, to multiply the obstacles to the admission
of new members, and to punish any who should appeal to the royal
courts against their policy of discrimination and restraint. The
particulars of the resulting struggle are confused, but from the
recrimination to which it gave rise it is clear the restrictions were
aimed primarily at those whom the boom had drawn into trade.
To the objections of the New Hanse it was replied, no doubt with
some truth, that

> " some of the parties that do complayne have not bene in the
> said company passing iiii or v yeares, and many of them not
> passing thre or two yeares, and some of them not passing one
> yere. . . . The chief of the same complaynants were clothe-
> workers and of other handy crafts and so brought up."

And it was taken as an axiom that old-established ought of right
to be protected from the competition of newcomers who combined
retail with overseas trade and, in their thirst for business, sank to
bartering their wares and paying illegal taxes. It was a contest in
which the Old Hanse held all the winning cards. There was growing a general sentiment in favour of restriction ; the financial
services which they were rendering the government assured them
of official support against the English as well as their foreign
competitors ; and the elimination of the new traders formed an
integral part of Gresham's policy for raising the exchanges. Against
such an array of forces the opposition could do nothing ; its
leaders were either imprisoned or expelled from the company ;
and with each succeeding depression the system of control
was carried a step further.[1] During that of the early 'sixties the
Russia Company was able to obtain a ban on the trade of non-
members to Narva ; the shifting of the cloth staple from Antwerp
to Emden was favoured partly because it would eliminate the
weaker merchants whose existence depended upon the quick
returns which could be had from the Netherlands ;[2] both the

[1] Rawlinson Mss., c. 394, pp. 121 *et seq.*, Burgon, *Life of Gresham*, vol. i,
p. 463.
[2] S.P.D. Eliz., vol. xxxv, no. 33.

Adventurers and the Staplers obtained new charters ; the latter, if not the former, immediately used their new powers to tighten their control over trade ;[1] and an unsuccessful attempt was made to incorporate the merchants trading to Barbary.[2] The slump of the 'seventies in turn produced a Spanish and an Eastland Company ; for although the former was not set up until 1577 it was suggested as early as 1574 to check the influx of new merchants when Philip removed his embargo and that trade was reopened ;[3] and although the latter was not created until 1579 it had as one of its objects the exclusion from the Baltic of those who had begun trading there after the closing of the Spanish market after 1568.[4] Nor were these developments confined to London, for many of the companies also covered the outports and during these years the merchants of Chester, Exeter, Bristol and York all acquired chartered corporations of their own.

To complete that story one thing more was necessary. As entry to trade and industry was made progressively more difficult there disappeared the hope that unemployment would speedily be cured, and it is no mere coincidence that it was during these years that the system of poor relief was revolutionised by the introduction of a compulsory poor rate and a system of public relief works. Thus the depressions of the third quarter of the sixteenth century were a not unimportant episode in English economic history for they saw an erratic attempt to mould the economic system according to something like a pattern. And the details of that pattern . . . economic nationalism, the opening of distant markets and the organisation of those already in existence, the encouragement of new industries and the control of production in the old, the regulation of the whole pace of economic change and the public provision for the unemployed . . . give it familiar appearance. It is, in many respects, the pattern of the mercantilism of the textbooks and of the economic policy of more than one country since 1929. What, finally, was the result of it all ? To answer that question would require an article in itself but perhaps three broad generalisations might be hazarded. In the seventeenth century, although not before, the new extra-European markets and the new draperies were to be of great importance to this country, and in that way the depressions may be said to have given a stimulus to economic progress. By the end of the sixteenth century the London export trade was almost entirely in the hands of English merchants and in

---

[1] Rich, *op. cit.*, pp. 30-1, 87 *et seq.*   [2] S.P.D. Eliz., vol. xlii, no. 49.

[3] *Ibid.*, vol. xcix, nos. 8 and 9.

[4] Deardorff, *English Trade to the Baltic during the Reign of Elizabeth*, p. 258.

that fact may perhaps be seen one of the fruits of economic national-ism. During the last quarter of the century the general trend of the cloth trade showed a remarkable stability.[1] Partly, no doubt, that was due to the war with Spain. But it may also be attributed in part to the regulations which had been expressly designed to preserve stability and to prevent rapid growth. Certainly that was the ex-planation favoured by contemporaries, for as the years passed and commerce failed to expand there arose a free trade agitation which reached its climax in the May of 1604 when the Commons passed two bills for greater freedom of trade.[2] That vote did not mean that men had changed their views on economic causation, for the relation between freedom and commercial expansion was a truism to the Tudors. What had changed had been men's scale of values. By the end of the sixteenth century the stability that had seemed so desirable a generation earlier had been found irksome ; as condi-tions for trade expansion once more came into being the feeling against such expansion declined ; and the uprooting of those vested interests that had grown behind the restrictions of the great depression became one of the major tasks of the seventeenth century.

[1] Scott (*English Joint Stock Companies to 1720*, vol. i, ch. v) argues that the period 1587-1603 was one of depression. In the export trade, however, that depression showed itself in the form not of a downward trend but of wider fluctuations around a fairly stable average.

[2] *Commons Journals*, vol. i, p. 218.

6

The Development of London as a Centre of Conspicuous Consumption in the Sixteenth and Seventeenth Centuries

OF all forms of historical writing, that which deals with particular places is perhaps the most pregnant with the possibilities of boredom, for the general reader can seldom hope to share the parochial enthusiasms by which the study of local history is so often inspired. But local history, and particularly urban history, can be approached from two different points of view. It can seek to portray the changing pattern of life within the few square miles which it takes for its field of study. Or it can endeavour to interpret that changing pattern as a symptom of greater changes in the nation as a whole. For, as the sociologists are never weary of reminding us, a town is essentially a social product. It is brought into being by forces external to it. It continues to exist because, and only so long as, it serves a social purpose. During the sixteenth and early seventeenth centuries the population of London and its immediate suburbs grew much more rapidly than the population of the country as a whole. Confronted by that fact, one of the obvious tasks of the historian is to make clear the purposes which that metropolitan expansion served ; to indicate the wider developments of which it was a symptom ; and to explain why, to contemporaries, it appeared as a symptom of disease rather than of health in the body politic. For that the growth of London was widely considered to be a morbid growth is incontestable. Topographers and chroniclers might write with admiration and affection of the city whose contours they described and whose history they told. But the pride of the city fathers was tinged with dismay at the problems of housing, public health and poor relief which they saw mounting before them. And outsiders were openly abusive. ' Soon,' wrote King James, whose dislike of the city was notorious, ' London will be all England ', and for once he echoed the sentiments of a large proportion of his subjects.

The major reason for the growth of the metropolis is obvious enough, and needs to be mentioned merely in order to give the rest of the story some degree of perspective. Giovanni

Botero, the translation of whose work on the magnificence and greatness of cities is itself indicative of the rising interest in urban problems, confidently laid it down that the largest towns were always based on trade and usually built on the banks of navigable rivers.[1] To that generalization, London was clearly no exception. All contemporary descriptions emphasized its commercial importance. Most of them pointed out the degree to which that importance was due to the river on which the city stood. In that respect, the growth of London was a symptom both of the expansion of English trade as a whole and of the concentration of that trade upon the Thames. It was widely held to be a morbid symptom, for many contended that London waxed fat at the expense of the outports, and grew rich only by sucking the wealth of the country to itself. To explain that expansion and concentration and to examine that contention would, no doubt, be fruitful tasks, but would lead into more purely economic fields than that with which this paper is concerned.

For the city and its suburbs had a second function. Not only did they constitute a centre of production where substantial incomes were earned from industry and trade ; they were also a centre of consumption where men expended the revenues which they had acquired elsewhere. During the sixteenth and early seventeenth centuries a number of factors combined to swell the volume of that expenditure. Irrigated by the fertilizing tide of provincial money, the metropolitan economy not only expanded but began to bear new fruit. And to that extent the development of the capital became a symptom of something more than the nation's commercial progress. The factors which combined to produce that result are not far to seek. Botero postulated three conditions under which cities tend to develop as centres of consumption. Each of those conditions can be shown, not only to have existed in Tudor and Stuart London, but to have considerably increased in influence. In the first place,

> It doth infinitely availe to the magnifyinge and making Cities greate and populous [to have] the Residency of the Prince therein, . . . for wheare the Prince is resident there also the Parliaments are held and the supreame place of justice is kept. All matters of importance have recourse to that place, all Princes and all persons of account, Embassadores of Princes and of Common weales . . . make theire repaire thither . . . All such as aspire and thirst after offices and honors run thither

[1] G. Botero, *A Treatise Concerning the Causes of the Magnificencie and Greatness of Cities* (trans. R. Pearson, 1606), ch. x.

overcome with emulation and disdaine at others. Thither are the revenues brought that appertain unto the state, and there are they disbursed out againe.[1]

Many years ago Professor Tout pointed out the importance in London history of the fact that the seat of government was established at Westminster.[2] As the policy of centralization increased the work of that government, and as the mounting extravagance of court life increased its social expenditure, so the significance of that fact grew.

In the second place, Botero insisted upon the economic implications of the law courts.

> Cities, that have Courts of Justice must needs be much frequented as well for concourse of people that have cause of Suite unto it as also for the execution of Justice. For it cannot be ministered without the help of . . . advocates, proctors, sollicitors, notaries and such like. Nay more than that (which it greeves me to think on) Expedition of justice cannot be made these our daies without ready money.[3]

Judicial history is a field in which a mere economic historian must obviously hesitate to tread, but at least there seems to be a prima-facie case for arguing that the sixteenth and early seventeenth centuries saw a significant increase in the amount of judicial business conducted in the capital. Looking back from the later seventeenth century, Hales noted a long-term tendency for common law cases to be heard at Westminster rather than in the provinces. If the volume of extant records is any criterion, there was a substantial growth in the work of Chancery. Clearly, the age of the Tudors and early Stuarts was the heyday of the prerogative courts. And on two points, at least, contemporary comment leaves no room for doubt. The first was the growth in the number and wealth of London lawyers—a growth which it is difficult to explain except as the result of a similar growth in the volume of the business which they handled. The second was the vital importance to the economy of Westminster of the tide of men and money that flowed in with every term.

But it is Botero's third postulate that throws most light upon the factors which were operating to mould the pattern of London life.

> Experience teacheth that the residence of noblemen in cities makes them to be more glorious and more populous, not onely

---

[1] Botero, *op. cit.*, p. 65.
[2] T. F. Tout, *The Beginnings of a Modern Capital ; London and Westminster in the Fourteenth Century* (British Academy, Raleigh Lecture, 1923).
[3] Botero, *op. cit.*, p. 45.

by cause they bring their people and their families unto it, but also more by cause a nobleman dispendeth much more largely through the accesse of friends unto him and through the emulation of others in a Citie where he is abiding and visited continually by honourable personages then he spendeth in the country where he liveth amongst the brute beasts of the field and converseth with plaine country people and goes apparelled among them in plain and simple garments.[1]

A significant feature of the sixteenth and early seventeenth centuries was the increasing extent to which the revenues spent in London were the revenues of that junior branch of the nobility, the country gentry. If the rise of the squirearchy to social and political pre-eminence was a major theme of the history of those times, their growing urbanization was a minor theme upon which contemporary comment was abundant and which the historian cannot afford to ignore.

It was a curious development, for it sprang from two immediate causes that were contradictory, although in a sense they shared a common origin. By the early seventeenth century two streams of gentry can be seen converging upon the capital, the one carried along by its growing wealth, the other driven by its growing poverty. It was, no doubt, the former who inspired Hume's comment that ' could humanity ever attain happiness, the condition of the English gentry at this period might merit that appellation '. And Professor Tawney has recently shown how, faced by a secular rise in prices, a substantial section of that class not only held their own but raised themselves to new levels of affluence, partly at the expense of the Crown, the Church and the peerage whose estates they acquired, partly at the expense of the tenants whose rents they raised and whose faces they ground.[2] But as they acquired the estates of their betters, so they took on some of their social habits. As their revenues rose, so their eyes turned citywards and they established ever closer social contacts with the capital.

In many cases, those contacts began early in life for, by the early seventeenth century, London had become an important educational centre and more than one country squire obtained his first taste of London life as a schoolboy. Some may have gone to St. Paul's ; some certainly went to the Merchant Taylors' School ; more probably went to Westminster, although the imperfections of the records make

---

[1] Botero, *op. cit.*, p. 63.
[2] R. H. Tawney, ' The Rise of the Gentry, 1558-1640 ', *Economic History Review*, xi (1941), pp. 1-38.

generalization dangerous. But, in addition to those foundations, there were private schools which catered for the sons of the nobility and gentry. Of these by far the best known is that of Thomas Farnaby, who, after an adventurous youth spent voyaging with Drake and Hawkins and soldiering in the Low Countries, became a leading classical scholar of his day and established a school in Goldsmith's Alley where he is said to have had upwards of three hundred noblemen and others under his care.[1] Farnaby was no doubt exceptional both in the reputation which he acquired and in the colourful life which he led, but he was not unique in his occupation. Nor was a London education a masculine monopoly. For Sir Simon D'Ewes tells us that his sisters were sent to school in Walbrook,[2] and the niece of Andrew Overton, among others, was sent to London to learn ' her needle, dauncing, and such qualities becoming a gentlewoman '.[3]

For most of the gentry, however, the significant introduction to the capital must have come when they enrolled at one of the Inns of Court, partly to obtain that minimum knowledge of the law essential to a landowner and justice of the peace, but principally to acquire that modicum of the social graces without which no gentleman's education could be considered complete. The role of the Inns of Court as schools of law and manners was not, of course, new. But in the sixteenth and early seventeenth centuries the number of their students rose. Admissions to Gray's Inn, for example, which had amounted to only two hundred in the third decade of the sixteenth century, had risen to seven hundred and ninety-nine in the last and to twelve hundred and sixty-five in the ten years between 1611 and 1620.[4] Already by the middle of Elizabeth's reign three of the four great Inns were faced by that too familiar symptom of educational expansion, an accommodation problem that could not be solved by the obvious device of doubling up in chambers.[5] By the reign of Charles, that champion of right thinking, Archbishop Laud, was insisting upon the necessity of appointing proper officials in the Inns because ' almost all young gentlemen spend part of their time in one or other of the Inns of Court and afterwards, when they return to live in their several counties, steer

[1] See the article on ' Farnaby ' in the *Dictionary of National Biography*.
[2] *The Autobiography and Correspondence of Sir Simonds D'Ewes* (ed. J. O. Halliwell), i. 157.
[3] Chancery Proceedings, Chas. I, bdle. 6, no. 3. Cf. Star Chamber Proceedings, Jas. I, bdle. 116, no. 1, and *Cal. S.P.D., 1637*, p. 422.
[4] J. Foster, *Register of Admission to Gray's Inn, 1521-1889* (1889).
[5] S.P.D. Eliz., xcv. no. 91.

themselves according to such principles as in those places are preached to them '.[1]   Under Elizabeth, Sir Humphrey Gilbert had complained that ' the estate of gentlemen cannot well traine upp their children within this Realme but eyther in Oxford or Cambridge ', where ' they utterly lose their tymes if they doe not follow learning merely, for there is no other gentlemanlike qualitie to be attained '.[2]   In 1615 Sir George Buck could write with some justification of a third University, the University of London, which offered a range of studies as extensive as it was peculiar.[3]   Although they might still waste part of their youth on the banks of the Isis and the Cam, by the reign of Charles I the majority of the country gentry were spending the most impressionable years of their lives on the banks of the Fleet and the Thames, in an area admirably situated for tasting the pleasures of both the City and the Court, and in institutions which, far from following learning only, were sufficiently of the polite world to cultivate a taste for music and the drama and sufficiently broad-minded to finance that taste by turning their libraries into gambling saloons.[4]

Once settled on his family estate, there was a multitude of reasons why the thoughts of the country squire should constantly return to the capital.   In one of the greatest ages of land speculation in English history, London was the very centre of the land market ; for the estates that were being sold were above all those of the Crown, and the normal method of sale was through the agency of London financiers.   In an age of universal borrowing, London was the great money market and London merchants the great lenders.   In an age when a judicious marriage was often the easiest way to fortune, London was not unimportant as a marriage market, and the widows and daughters of citizens were not the least attractive stepping-stones to affluence.   In an age of furious litigation, a substantial number of the gentry sooner or later found themselves involved before one or other of the courts at Westminster.   Above all, in an age which was characterized by the successful assertion of the claims of the gentry to a share in political power, Westminster was the very centre of the political map.   To say that the thoughts of the gentry constantly turned to the metropolis is not, of course, to argue that their bodies always followed.   Lands could be bought, money could be borrowed, marriages could be arranged and

---

[1] *Cal. S.P.D. 1633–4*, p. 340.   [2] Lansdowne MSS., xcviii, no. 1.
[3] J. Stow, *Annales* (ed. E. Howes, 1631), pp. 1063–87.
[4] *Cal. S.P.D. 1631–3*, p. 215 ; *1639–40*, pp. 304–5.

lawsuits could be fought without the physical presence of the landowner concerned. But three generalizations may be made with confidence. The squire who stayed in the country when such questions were at issue had of necessity to be represented by an agent in town ; an agent who was likely to be a member of his own family. Whoever the agent might be, his employment entailed the expenditure of money which helped to develop the capital as a centre of consumption. Above all, far from being reluctant to visit London on business, a substantial number of the gentry were anxious to do so even when business offered no pretext. ' I am resolved to spend the greatest part of the rest of my lyf for the wynter and springe quarter abowt london,' wrote John Wynn of Gwydir in 1605, and in so resolving he was no more than conforming to a fashion already well established.[1] Whatever else they may have learned from their sojourn at the Inns of Court, it had revealed to the landowners of England that rural delights did not span the whole gamut of human pleasures. By the early seventeenth century, in fact, there had developed a clearly defined London season which began in the autumn, reached its climax at Christmas, and was over by June. The Duchess of Newcastle, for example, has left it on record that her sisters spent nearly every winter in London.[2] Two sisters, no doubt, do not make a season. But from her account of their normal activities when in town it is clear that, in paying their annual visit, they were following less some personal idiosyncrasy of their own than the social habits of their class. Not every squire went to London every winter, or necessarily stayed for the whole season when he did go. But, by the early seventeenth century, from October to June London always contained a substantial population of rural landowners. And the more regular that system became the more it grew, for the more men could rely upon finding company to their taste.

The townward migration of the gentry, however, was not a purely seasonal phenomenon, and by the reign of Charles I a significant number had become permanent residents of the city and its immediate neighbourhood. And it is at this stage that the story becomes more complicated, for it is here that the second stream of the gentry begins to appear—the stream of those who were driven citywards by their poverty.

---

[1] Wynn MSS., no. 348. The Wynn MSS., in the National Library of Wales, are an invaluable source for illustrating the relations of a county family with the capital.
[2] H. B. Wheatley and P. Cunningham, *London Past and Present*, iii. 295.

It is reasonable to suppose that the bulk of the seasonal visitors were comparatively affluent and came because their revenues provided a surplus which could be spent on the pleasures of the town. Some, no doubt, who came to take up permanent residence did so from deliberate and unfettered choice. But many were driven by compulsion. For though the gentry as a class emerged victorious from the difficulties into which they had been plunged by the rise in prices, the struggle had not been bloodless and the victims had not been confined to the ranks of the peasantry and the peerage. More than one county family found its expenses rising above its income, and the author of *The Commonweal of this Realm of England* explains how many of them sought a way out of their dilemma. ' Seeinge,' he says, ' the charges of howshold so much as by no provision they can make can be holpen, they give over their howsholds and get them chambers in London or abowte the courte, and there spend there time, some with a servaunte or 2, wheare he was wounte to kepe 30 or 40 persons daily in his house.' [1] By the early seventeenth century it had become a commonplace that landowners were moving to London in order to save the charges of housekeeping in the country, although not all who did so were reduced to living in a single room, Moreover, even those families that successfully weathered the storm often did so only by means of a rigorous system of primogeniture. It was a system which often bore heavily on widows, and more than one moved Londonwards to ease the strain upon her scanty means. In particular, it was a system which bore heavily upon the younger sons who, to use Thomas Wilson's inelegant but expressive phrase, had only ' thatt which the catt left on the malt heape, perhaps some smale annuytie during his life or what please an elder brother's worship to bestowe upon us if wee please him and my mistress his wife '.[2] To such, London had obvious attractions. Thus the permanent residents which London recruited from the landowning classes were by no means a homogeneous group. Some were wealthy and able to support themselves with style if not with ostentation. Others were merely concerned to eke out a modest income. Others sought to supplement an income that was woefully inadequate to their needs. The efforts of this last group constitute a not unimportant factor in English history. On the one hand, they fertilized both commerce and the professions. On the other, they were largely responsible for the rash of patents

---

[1] *A Discourse of the Commonweal of this Realm of England* (ed. E. Lamond), p. 81.   [2] *Camden Miscellany*, xvi (1936), p. 24.

and monopolies which from time to time disfigured the political and economic complexion of England. Those who succeeded in making or mending their fortunes must, by that very fact, pass largely beyond the scope of this paper. For to them London became the milieu in which they earned an income rather than spent revenues acquired elsewhere. But to ignore them completely would be an error. For many continued to draw some income from the provinces and, in so far as they retained the tastes and habits of the class from which they came, they served to reinforce the influence which their more fortunate kinsmen had upon the pattern of London life.

Neither the chronology nor the volume of that townward drift is easy to determine. It had existed in some measure during the Middle Ages. A few attempts were made to check it in the first three-quarters of the sixteenth century. But if the volume of contemporary comment may be taken as a criterion, it reached significant proportions in the last two decades of that century, two generations after the rise in prices had burst upon the landowning classes and at a period when the processes of eviction, enclosure and rack-renting and the sale of royal and monastic lands had all progressed suffi-ciently for the factors outlined above to have had some effect. By the early seventeenth century it had become great enough to inspire James to an ungallant outburst against ' those swarms of gentry who, through the instigation of their wives and to new-model and fashion their daughters (who, if they were unmarried, marred their reputations, and if married, lost them) did neglect their country hospitality, and cumber the city, a general nuisance to the kingdom.' [1] More important, it led to a series of prohibitory proclamations which not only stirred to fury the gentry with whose social activities they interfered, but also stirred to remonstrance the city in whose economic life that influx had come to play a part of some moment. According to Salvetti it had become, by the early years of Charles's reign, the custom for the greater part of the gentry to winter in town. [2] Since both Wilson at the beginning of the century and King at the end estimated the total number of gentle families at between sixteen and seven-teen thousand, that statement, if true, would imply a seasonal influx of thousands of individuals. To take it literally would, no doubt, be naïve ; diplomatists are notoriously bad statis-ticians, and the Italians were worse than most. But at least it suggests that the numbers concerned were of some magnitude,

[1] I. Disraeli, *The Curiosities of Literature* (1849 ed.), iii. 402.
[2] *Cal. S. P. Venetian 1632–6*, p. 38, note.

and the same conclusion is borne out by the fact that, in 1632, some two hundred and fifty peers, baronets, knights and gentlemen were prosecuted in the Star Chamber for having been found in London after a proclamation had ordered them home.[1] For it would surely be to underestimate both the law-abidingness and the ingenuity of their class to suppose that a much larger number had not either obeyed that proclamation or else escaped detection when it became clear that the government intended to act.

By the early seventeenth century, therefore, the economy of London and its suburbs was called upon to adapt itself to a substantial seasonal immigration of rural landowners, many of them accompanied by their families. It had to accommodate itself to an ever-changing and steadily growing student body which had already, under Elizabeth, exceeded a thousand. It had to absorb an uncertain but not inconsiderable number who, from either poverty or choice, from either boredom or ambition, had abandoned their country seats for permanent residence in the town. The incomes of those immigrants no doubt varied, but their total revenues must have been substantial. The result of their expenditure was to create a series of demands which it became an important function of the metropolis to fulfil and which significantly increased the influence that the Court had for long exerted on the pattern of London life. As Botero had pointed out, an invariable characteristic of the gentleman come to town was his ostentatious display. Or, in the more homely words of Ben Jonson, ' First, to be an accomplished gentleman—that is, a gentleman of the time—you must give over housekeeping in the country and live together in the city amongst gallants where, at your first appearance, 'twere good you turned four or five acres of your best land into two or three trunks of apparell '.[2] From that tendency towards conspicuous consumption the luxury trades of the city inevitably waxed fat. As in all ages, the gentleman come to town required transport, and it was during the early seventeenth century that the coach became a familiar part of the London scene. By the reign of Charles I, not only were hackney coaches to be found in their hundreds, but the cab rank had become an institution and the sedan chair was ceasing to be a curiosity.

What was of greater moment than either luxuries or transport, the gentleman come to town needed entertainment. Some, no doubt, he found at Court. But the facilities of the

[1] Rushworth, *Historical Collections*, ii. 288–92.
[2] C. Knight, *London*, i (1841), p. 378.

Court were limited, and by the Civil War the visiting and resident gentry had begun to build, or to help build, the leisure institutions that were to be characteristic of polite society in London at least until the end of the eighteenth century.   The origin of English club life, it has been argued, is to be found in the associations of gentlemen, usually organized upon a county basis, who regularly met in their favourite taverns to drink, talk and criticize the government in the manner common to all club men at all times.   By the reign of James, the gentry were already manifesting that taste for parks and pleasure gardens that one normally associates with a later age.   By the reign of Charles, Hyde Park, which had still been used for hunting under James, had become a parade ground for the coaches of the fashionable, and, although Ranelagh and Vauxhall still lay in the future, the Spring and Mulberry Gardens were indicating the form which they were to take.   That the Spring and Mulberry Gardens were both, strictly speaking, part and parcel of the royal parks is no doubt true.   But that they were becoming commercialized is obvious from the contemporary descriptions which survive.   As Garrard wrote to Wentworth in 1634 :

> The Bowling in the Spring Garden was by the King's Command put down for one day . . . there was kept in it an ordinary of six shillings a meal (when the King's proclamation allows but two elsewhere) continual bibbing and drinking of wine all day long under the trees, two or three quarrels every week.   It was grown scandalous and insufferable ; besides, my Lord Digby being reprehended for striking in the King's Garden, he answered that he took it for a common bowling place where all paid money for their coming in.

When, in the next year, the Spring Garden was closed to the public, the immediate result was the opening of a new one as a private business venture.[1]   Above all, there was the theatre. Lord Keynes is reported once to have said that England obtained Shakespeare when she could afford him.   Presumably his meaning was that Shakespeare could flourish only in a commercial theatre, and that a commercial theatre could flourish only when there was sufficient surplus wealth to pay for it.   If that argument is valid, then perhaps the urbanized and semi-urbanized gentry of Elizabeth and the early Stuarts may claim at least some share of reflected glory, for it was their demand for entertainment that helped to bring the commercial theatre into being.   Describing how, in the days of

---

[1] Wheatley and Cunningham, *op. cit.*, iii. 294-5.

Charles I, her sisters spent their London seasons the Duchess of Newcastle wrote : ' Their customs were in the winter time to go sometimes to plays or to ride in their coaches about the streets to see the concourse and recourse of people, and in the springtime to visit the Spring Garden, Hyde Park and the like places, and sometimes they would have music and cup in barges upon the water.' [1] It was a routine which would have seemed familiar to the eighteenth century. It would have been incomprehensible to the fifteenth.

Moreover, not only did the demands of the newly urbanized country gentry for entertainment lead to a pattern of leisure activities that was to persist for generations, but their demand for accommodation eventually opened a new chapter in the history of architecture. To a large extent, of course, that demand was for purely temporary accommodation and was met by the expansion of what would now be called the hotel and catering trades, and references abound to the great inns that were going up in and around Holborn and to the taverns and cookshops to which the gentry proved such good customers. But of more interest to the historian was their demand for permanent accommodation, for by the time of Charles I that demand was being met in ways which were to leave a lasting imprint upon London topography. On the one hand, those who were content to live near rather than in the metropolis began to build up the old villages of Clerkenwell and Islington, Hampstead and Chelsea as residential suburbs. On the other, those who wished to be in the centre of things settled in the area which was being developed in the parish of St. Giles-in-the-Fields. As Mr. Summerson has recently pointed out, in developing that area Inigo Jones, the Earl of Bedford and William Newton laid the foundation-stones of two centuries of London taste. Lincoln's Inn Fields, Covent Garden and Great Queen Street inspired the work of the great builders of the eighteenth century. The character of the Georgian town house was fixed under Charles I, and it was fixed to meet the needs of the country gentry who were becoming townsmen.[2]

To discuss at length the process by which the spending of these rural revenues gradually modified the pattern of London life in one detail after another would, however, be to lapse into that parochial enthusiasm which the local historian should never parade in public. But two general remarks may perhaps be permitted. The new urban society that was growing up in the city and its suburbs, a society that still had its financial

---

[1] Wheatley and Cunningham, *op. cit.*, iii. 294-5.
[2] J. Summerson, *Georgian London*, ch. ii.

roots and many of its interests in the countryside, created an environment which helped to foster two of the most interesting phenomena of Tudor and Stuart England. The first was the development of the lay professions. Of all the unexplored fields of English economic history, none is less known than the story of the English professional classes, and where the historian knows little it behoves him to say less. But clearly, when that story comes to be written, an important chapter in it will of necessity be devoted to the sixteenth and early seventeenth centuries, for those years saw, not only the spectacular rise of the lawyers, but also a significant development of the doctors and architects, the scriveners and journalists. Nearly the whole of that development took place in London and Westminster, for it was only in the capital that the demand for professional services was sufficiently great to make their provision on any scale a source of profit. And a not unsubstantial part of that demand came from the gentry. In the second place, it was this period that saw firmly established the connection between the capital and scholarship, both professional and amateur ; the Academy which met weekly from 1572 to 1604 stands on record as the first of the learned societies of London.

By comparison with the rural tide which flowed towards the capital after the Restoration, this earlier movement may seem modest. To an age which takes urban life for granted, it may reasonably appear as a sign of economic progress. But to contemporaries it was a phenomenon of ill-omen. Some of the opposition which it encountered was, no doubt, inspired by motives which do not appear on the surface. For, as the Venetian ambassadors pointed out, an order that the gentry should disperse to their country homes could on occasion serve as a means for breaking up a Parliamentary opposition or as an instrument of taxation. But the major roots of official disapproval lay deeper, for the migration of the gentry towards London offended against some of the major social principles of the time. In an age when both economic and religious theory demanded a régime of some austerity, the gentleman come to town indulged in luxuries which not only threatened him with personal ruin but which endangered that favourable balance of trade to which so great importance was attached. In an age when the problems of city government were becoming ever more acute, the responsibility for those problems was in large measure laid at his door. For, it was argued, where the gentry went there the idle and dissolute among the lower orders were bound to follow. And in following the gentry to the capital they created problems of housing and poor relief, disease and high prices, which were intolerable in a well-ordered commonwealth. Above all, in an age when every social class was deemed to have its obligations as well as its rights, the gentry threatened to become parasites upon the body politic. As the Attorney-General argued in the Star Chamber :

> For where by their residency and abiding in several Counties where their Means ariseth, they served Your Majesty in several places according to their Degrees and Ranks in aid of Government, whereby, and by their Housekeeping in those Parts, the Realm was defended and the meaner sort of Your People were guided, directed and relieved ; but by their residency in the said cities, and parts adjoining, they have no employment, but live without doing any service to Your Majesty or Your People.[1]

By so neglecting their traditional functions, the gentry threatened to undermine the whole structure of local government. Consequently it is not surprising that sporadic efforts were made to discourage the new fashion, efforts that became more vigorous and more frequent as the fashion grew. Sometimes, those efforts were indirect. ' We have very plausible Things done of late,' wrote Gerrard to Wentworth in 1634. ' To encourage Gentlemen to live more willingly in the Country, all Game Fowl, as Pheasant, Partridges, Ducks, as also Hares are by Proclamation forbidden to be dressed or eaten in any Inns, and Butchers are forbidden to be Graziers.'[2]   More often, however, the method used was that of ordering the gentry back to their country residences. That in the long run those methods failed is obvious. But the efforts of the Crown were not entirely devoid of results. For the resentment which those orders aroused must be counted among the minor causes of the growing rift between the landowning classes and the monarchy.

[1] Rushworth, *op. cit.*, ii. 289.
[2] W. Knowler, *The Earl of Strafforde's Letters and Dispatches*, i (1739), p. 176.

7

London's Export Trade in the Early Seventeenth Century

To the student of English commercial development the seventeenth century must always present peculiar difficulties. Few aspects of commercial organization or policy can be fully understood unless seen against the background of the general commercial trends of their time. Long- and medium-term trends can seldom, if ever, be satisfactorily established without the aid of statistics. And the seventeenth century is the one period in modern English history for which no continuous series of customs or commercial statistics appears to have survived or, indeed, ever to have been made. The annual customs accounts ceased to be enrolled in the Office of the King's Remembrancer at the accession of James I. The Inspectors-General of Imports and Exports did not begin to compile their ledgers until 1696. For the intervening years, the historian is driven back to sources that are both discontinuous and difficult to correlate. There is a wealth of statistical memoranda prepared by contemporaries for specific and immediate purposes; but the methods by which those memoranda were prepared are so obscure, and the purposes for which they were prepared so diverse, that their comparison is more dangerous than profitable. There still remain a few of the original Port Books in which all imports and exports were required to be entered; but years of neglect have reduced a once complete series to a sample which, if sufficiently random to refute all charges of bias, is too small to permit the accurate measurement of general trends. From such materials no definitive table of trade figures can possibly be constructed. But it is the purpose of this paper to suggest that, at least as far as the first four decades of the century are concerned, the fragmentary statistics that have by chance survived can be combined in such a manner as to indicate certain trends for which there is considerable supporting evidence in literary sources; for which a plausible explanation can be offered; and which, therefore, may merit some considera-

---

[1] This article is based on a paper read on 15 April 1950 before the annual conference of the Economic History Society.

tion by those working in this particular field. The investigation has been confined to the export trade of London but, since throughout this period the capital handled some two-thirds or three-quarters of the nation's foreign trade, any conclusions that can be drawn from the London figures must obviously provide a major theme in the story of that trade as a whole.

By the beginning of the seventeenth century, shipments of wool, woolfells and leather were sufficiently small for them to be safely ignored in any calculation of broad general trends. For the purposes of taxation, all other exports were divided into two categories. The older forms of woollen textiles were measured in terms of a notional shortcloth and paid custom at the rate of 6s. 8d. per shortcloth; all other commodities paid subsidy at the rate of 5% *ad valorem* calculated on the basis of their official value as set out in the Book of Rates. Thus the records yield two sets of figures each; as is convenient for an age of rising prices, showing changes in the volume rather than in the value of the exports to which they relate. Neither set, it is true, would satisfy any rigid tests of statistical orthodoxy. The notional shortcloth was a clumsy unit for the measurement of fabrics which differed, not only in their weight and dimensions, but also in their fineness and their degree of finish. The figures for subsidy-paying exports would obviously be affected by any changes in the official values assigned to those exports in the Book of Rates and, although there was no general or substantial revision of export valuations during this period, it is impossible to be certain that none were altered. Yet, unsatisfactory though they may be, such are the figures which the historian must use. And although their division into two series makes the calculation of overall totals extremely difficult, as contemporaries found when they tried to assess the balance of trade,[1] it is convenient in so far as it is from the differences in behaviour between the two series that some of the more interesting aspects of London's commercial history in the early seventeenth century may be deduced.

As will be seen from Table 1, both branches of London's export trade shared in the expansion that reached its peak in the middle of the second decade of the century. But from then on they moved in different directions. Exports of shortcloths sank back to a level below that from which the expansion had started and for a generation showed a sluggishness comparable to that which had characterized them during the latter half of the sixteenth century.[2] Other exports continued to expand—whether steadily or erratically we do not know—until in 1640 they were some five times as great in volume as they had been during the closing years of Elizabeth's reign.

As can be seen from Tables 2 and 3,[3] the two branches of London's export trade differed in their geographical direction as well as in their

---

[1] For the calculations made by Cranfield and Wolstenholme, and the different conclusions to which they came, vide Lansdowne MSS., vol. CLII, f. 175.

[2] For the commercial trends of the later sixteenth century, see L. Stone, 'Elizabethan Overseas Trade', *Econ. Hist. Rev.* (1949) 2nd ser. II, p. 30; and F. J. Fisher, 'Commercial Trends and Policy in Sixteenth-Century England', ibid. x, p. 95 (1940); reprinted above, pp. 81-103.

[3] Both tables have been compiled from the Port Books.

Table 1. *Statistics of London Exports, 1598–1640**

(excluding wool, woolfells and leather)

Year	No. of 'Shortcloths' exported		Official value of other goods exported (£)	
	By natives	By aliens	By natives	By aliens
1598–1600 (av.)	97,737	5,295	119,415	
1601	100,380	3,643	120,860	
1602	113,512	5,072	133,688	
1603	89,619	2,366	136,695	
1604	112,785	5	—	
1606	126,022	—	—	—
1609	—	—	198,266	—
1612	—	5,199	275,140	81,072
1614	127,215	—	—	—
1616	88,172	—	—	—
1617	—	—	338,598	—
1618	102,332	—	—	—
1619	—	—	371,572	—
1620	85,517	—	—	—
1622	75,631	—	—	—
1626	c. 91,000	—	—	—
1627	c. 88,000	—	—	—
1628	c. 108,000	—	—	—
1631	84,334	—	—	—
1632	99,020	—	—	—
1633	80,844	—	—	—
1634	—	—	594,849	—
1636	—	1,256	—	65,745
1640	86,924	503	609,722	85,136

* The figures for the years 1598–1604 are taken from the Enrolled Customs Accounts. Those for 1626–8 are estimates based on the Abstract of the Accounts of the General Farm of the Customs to be found in the Shaftesbury Papers, bundle ii, no. 17; they are more likely to be too high than too low. The rest have been calculated from the Port Books. The figures for shortcloths are exclusive of duty-free wrappers. According to a memorandum among the papers of Lionel Cranfield, the total number of shortcloths exported from London was 142, 466 in 1614 and 126, 134 in 1615.

Table 2. *Distribution of Shortcloths exported by English Merchants from London*

Percentage shipped to	1614	1616	1620	1622	1632	1640
Russian, Baltic and N. Sea ports	76	76	78	80	77	73
Spanish, African and Mediterranean ports	16	18	17	16	18	25

long-term trends. The major markets for shortcloths were in northern, central and eastern Europe. Of the years examined for this purpose only 1640, when, under the pressure of the Thirty Years War, the trans-alpine route into central and eastern Europe was being used, shows the Spanish, African and other Mediterranean ports taking as many as a quarter of the total shortcloths exported. By contrast, it was to those southern ports that

Table 3. *Distribution of Goods Other than Shortcloths exported by*
English Merchants from London

Percentage shipped to	1609	1612	1619	1634	1640
Russian, Baltic and N. Sea ports	29	23	25	24	22
Spanish, African and Mediterranean ports	46	55	59	65	65

the bulk of the other exports went. The expansion of those other exports meant, above all else, the growth of trade with Spain and the Mediterranean.

Finally, from Table 4 it will be seen that most of the goods which paid subsidy were themselves woollen textiles. The differences between them

Table 4. *Official Values of Commodities, other than Shortcloths, Exported*
from London by English Merchants in 1640

	£
Woollen fabrics and hosiery	454,914
Other goods of English manufacture	26,973
Minerals	34,555
Agricultural produce	16,878
Re-exports	76,402
Total	609,722

and those goods classified as shortcloths and therefore paying custom was one of degree rather than of kind. The first half of the sixteenth century had seen a great expansion in the export of shortcloths; the first half of the nineteenth was to see an even greater expansion in the export of cotton goods; the most prominent feature of London's trade in the first half of the seventeenth century was the expansion in the export of what were known to contemporaries as 'the new draperies'—fabrics made of combed, long-staple wool and characterized by their light weight and their wide range of patterns.

Thus the figures to be obtained from the Port Books and other sources suggest certain obvious and elementary conclusions as to the development of London's exports during the early seventeenth century. Those exports consisted almost entirely of woollen textiles of one kind or another. During the first fifteen years of the century they prospered greatly. Then, for the next twenty-five years, the trade in shortcloths—a trade carried on mainly with northern, central and eastern Europe—languished at a level, not merely below that which they had attained at the peak of the Jacobean boom, but even below that which had obtained when the century opened. Meanwhile the export of the new draperies—mainly to southern Europe—continued to expand until, by the eve of the Civil War, the pattern of London's commerce had been significantly altered. By that time, the trade in the newer fabrics almost equalled in value the trade in the old, and the ports of Spain and the Mediterranean were taking as a large share of

London's exports as were those of Germany and the Low Countries. The Provost of Oriel has no doubt done well to warn us against excessive reliance upon the accuracy of the Port Book entries.[1] It is obvious, from internal evidence, that the London volumes were sometimes carelessly compiled. But it would be carrying scepticism to the point of credulity to suppose that the conclusions to which the London figures point were nothing but statistical illusions; the other evidence pointing in the same direction is too abundant. The preponderance of textiles among English exports was a commonplace of contemporary economic discussion. The opening years of the century have long been recognized as a period of commercial prosperity.[2] The depression in the cloth trade that followed Cockayne's disastrous scheme has been described in detail by Miss Friis;[3] that of the early 'twenties has left a wealth of evidence in the proceedings of Parliament and of the Privy Council, in the State Papers, and in the economic literature of the time; under Charles the complaints of distress in the cloth industry were sufficiently frequent to make it clear that his reign saw nothing comparable to the expansion with which that of his father opened. The history of the new draperies has still to be written; but there can be little doubt that their growth constituted the most important chapter in the story of English industrial development under the early Stuarts and little surprise that much of their output was sold abroad. The new significance of the Spanish market—a market made especially attractive by internal inflation and colonial purchases—was one cause of the revolution in Anglo-Spanish political relations. The economic penetration of the central and eastern Mediterranean by London merchants provides the major theme of the Venetian State Papers. The change in the pattern of London's overseas trade was reflected in the decline in the relative prestige and importance of the Merchant Adventurers and the rise in those of the Levant Company. By 1638 Lewis Roberts could declare that the latter organization had 'growne to that height that without comparison it is the most flourishing and beneficiall Company to the commonwealth of any in England of all other whatsoever'.[4] It is doubtful whether, even in 1638, that statement was strictly true; at the beginning of the century it would have been ridiculous.

The real task of the historian is less that of defending than that of explaining the conclusions to which the Port Books point. In some measure, no doubt, their explanation is to be found in the political history of the time. The expansion of trade with Spain and the Mediterranean was made possible by the peace of 1604; the sluggishness of the trade in shortcloths during the third and fourth decades of the century was partly the result of the Thirty Years War which impoverished some of its markets and broke the communications with others. In some measure, however, the explana-

---

[1] G. N. Clark, *Guide to English Commercial Statistics, 1696–1782* (1938), pp. 52–6.
[2] W. R. Scott, *The Constitution and Finance of English Joint Stock Companies* (1912) vol. I, ch. vii.
[3] A. Friis, *Alderman Cockayne's Project and the Cloth Trade* (Copenhagen, 1917).
[4] Quoted by A. C. Wood, *A History of the Levant Company* (1935) p. 43.

tion is to be found in more purely economic factors; one reason for accepting the evidence of the Port Books is that it coincides so closely with what might be theoretically deduced from the nature of English trade and industry in the early seventeenth century.

The outstanding feature of England's trade was that her exports consisted almost entirely of woollen textiles. The outstanding feature of her textile industry was that it operated under conditions of virtually fixed real costs. To say that is not, of course, to argue that seventeenth-century producers were not cost-conscious. 'The Cheapness of English cloth', declared the House of Commons in 1624, 'Together with the goodnes therof hath been in all tymes the true cawse that it hath bene so vendible.' In their efforts to keep money costs down clothiers and merchants protested vigorously against taxation, demanded that restrictions be placed upon the trade in raw materials, and cut wages until the sweating of labour in the textile industry became a major social problem. But, in the absence of real-cost-reducing inventions, reductions in money costs were necessarily limited and could not be continuous. Stuart finances were in no state to permit of considerable tax reliefs; interference with the trade in raw materials could have untoward results; wages could not be cut indefinitely. Moreover, pressure on money costs inevitably intensified the problem of adulteration; and in the debasement of materials and workmanship, to which both clothiers and their employees resorted in their struggle to keep costs low, lay one of the most vexatious problems of the time. The outcry against it filled a host of pamphlets and memoranda; the efforts to suppress it produced a not inconsiderable body of statutes, proclamations and council orders; the complications to which it gave rise were a constant source of embarrassment to the business world. In a theological age, it is true, men often ascribed that debasement to the peculiar wickedness that flourished in the hearts and minds of the manufacturing classes. But there were not wanting some shrewd enough to see that low prices and low wages were more to blame than any natural sinfulness of spinners and weavers.[1]

Thus the position of the seventeenth-century merchant was profoundly different from that of his nineteenth-century successor in so far as the expansion of his sales was not being constantly facilitated by cost reductions in the industry from which he drew his supplies. Even under such conditions, it is true, sales might on occasion be substantially increased even in well-established markets. Exchange depreciation, the difficulties of foreign competitors, unwonted interludes of peace in a world normally wracked by war, could all increase the demand for English cloth. But such conditions were of their nature temporary. Under normal conditions, the demand for English cloth in any area where the trade in it was well-established tended to grow but slowly. Under such conditions, the expansion of trade tended to be an extensive rather than an intensive process; a process of finding new markets rather than one of increasing sales in the old. The substitution of the export of cloth for that of wool had of itself introduced such a

[1] A. E. Bland, P. A. Brown and R. H. Tawney, *English Economic History; Documents*, (1920) p. 337.

tendency in London trade, for it is an obvious truism that the demand for consumers' goods is geographically wider than that for raw materials. The former exists, at least potentially, wherever men of prosperity are to be found. The latter is of necessity confined to a comparatively few industrial areas. So long as wool had been the staple export, trade had perforce been directed to the few great manufacturing centres on the continent; above all to Flanders and northern Italy. When cloth took the place of wool there arose the possibility of finding new markets to be served directly from London, and much of the history of the later middle ages and of the sixteenth century was concerned with their exploitation. By the end of the sixteenth century the cost-structure of the cloth industry had made the finding of even newer markets essential to commercial progress. Few things stand out more clearly from the economic discussions under Elizabeth and the early Stuarts than the twin ideas that the old outlets for cloth were glutted and that new ones must be found; to impute those ideas entirely to theoretical naivety would be to overlook the technological conditions of which a realistic age was only too keenly aware.

Not unnaturally, in their search for new markets men's thoughts turned first to the regions made accessible by the great geographical discoveries, where English textiles were as yet unknown and where the possibility of new sales seemed therefore to be greatest. The hope of tapping a new demand for English cloth was a motive appealed to both by those who would found colonies on the American continent and by those who sought to open direct trade with the Far East. Yet, apart from purchases made in Spain for re-shipment to the Spanish colonies, neither the New World nor the Far East contributed any immediate solution to the problems of English exporters. The nations of the latter were highly commercialized; but for them English broadcloth was too heavy. 'The English', wrote Sandys in 1610, 'have so ill-utterance for their warm cloths in these hot countries that I believe they will suffer their ships to rot in the river than continue that trade any longer.'[1] Sandys was writing of Egypt and the countries to the south rather than of the Far East itself; but the same cry came from India. 'English cloth', wrote Thomas Aldworth from Surat in 1614, 'will not sell; it was only bought at first by great men to cover their elephants and make saddles for their horses. But for garments they use none in these parts.'[2] The early history of the East India Company was to furnish repeated proof of those assertions. By contrast, although North America provided ideal climatic conditions for the wearing of heavy woollens, it as yet contained few communities sufficiently commercialized to purchase them. Until the middle of the seventeenth century, the new markets for English textiles were found in the Old World rather than in the New, in southern Europe and Asia Minor rather than in the Far East.

Spain and the Mediterranean countries also, as the quotation from Sandys shows, presented a climatic problem. Although they had long provided an outlet for a limited number of shortcloths, those fabrics were too warm and

[1] Quoted Wood, op cit. p. 33.
[2] *Cal. S. P. Colonial, East Indies, 1513–1616*, p. 317.

heavy for general wear. But it was a problem to which the English textile industry itself could offer a solution. For to think of that industry as technologically stagnant would be highly erroneous. The absence of labour-saving inventions meant, not that ingenuity was dead, but that it operated through other channels. Like the commercial expansion of the time, as also like the agricultural expansion of the time, it was extensive rather than intensive. Just as merchants sought to open new markets rather than more fully to exploit the old, just as agriculturists sought to bring more land under cultivation rather than to increase the yield of that which they already farmed, so clothiers sought to devise new types of cloth rather than to cheapen those which they were already making; a situation that is hardly surprising at a time when labour was cheap and capital scarce. Admittedly, with wool as their material and with no assistance from power-driven machinery in their major processes, they were unable to produce anything fitted for the Indian market. But in the new draperies they provided a range of fabrics admirably suited for the warm, but non-tropical, Mediterranean. Tradition has it that the new draperies were introduced by Protestant weavers from the Netherlands. But although they undoubtedly owed much to alien immigrants, by no means all came from abroad; and whatever their origin it is not unreasonable to see in their development an obvious and appropriate response on the part of the textile industry to the opportunities opened by the re-establishment of direct trade with the Mediterranean in the later sixteenth century and by the Anglo-Spanish peace of 1604.

The striking difference between the trade in the old draperies and that in the new suggests a relationship, not only with the conditions which obtained in the textile industry from which they both sprung, but also with the prevailing forms of commercial organization. Northern and central Europe, the area in which the sales of the old draperies were languishing, was the sphere of influence of the great regulated companies—the Russia, the Eastland and the Merchant Adventurers. By contrast southern Europe, where the sales of the new draperies were flourishing, was an area of relative freedom. For none of the seventeenth-century attempts to establish a Spanish Company seems to have been really effective, and the monopoly of the Levant Company never extended to the west coast of Italy. Moreover, even in Germany and the Netherlands, the trade in new draperies was for a considerable period left open to merchants not free of the Merchant Adventurers. The correlation between regulation and stagnation, between freedom and expansion, is too clear to be dismissed as pure coincidence. Yet the exact nature of the relationship between those phenomena is far from obvious. It is tempting to argue that it was one of simple causation; that the trade in shortcloths was sluggish because it was regulated and that the trade in the new draperies expanded because it was comparatively free. Yet it is doubtful whether the facts will support so simple an interpretation. The business correspondence of Lionel Cranfield does not suggest that the Merchant Adventurers had any policy of controlling prices or sales; the experience of the opening years of the century shows that regulation and expansion were not necessarily incompatible; it has been the purpose of this article to suggest that other reasons can be adduced to explain the different behaviour of the two branches of London's trade. In fact, it might be argued with some plausibility that the process of causation worked to some extent in the opposite direction; that regulated companies flourished in the northern European trade because there the problem was one of selling a well-established commodity in an area where the equilibrium point between supply and demand had been established by long experience and was unlikely to change with any rapidity; that the arguments for regulation were rejected in the case of Spain and much of the Mediterranean since there it was clearly possible to expand the sales of the new fabrics at current prices. Certain it is that men thought in different terms about the old and the new draperies. Throughout the later sixteenth century men looked upon the old cloth industry with suspicion as a breeding-ground of unemployment and distress; by the early seventeenth century some were pinning their hopes of solving the problem of destitution on the development of the new draperies.

To think of the new draperies purely in terms of the trade to Spain and the Mediterranean would obviously be contrary to the evidence of the Port Books. A minor, but not unimportant, proportion of them were sold in northern Europe and may have contributed something to the falling off in the demand for shortcloths. To think of the expansion of London trade purely in terms of the new draperies would also be to ignore one of the most significant pieces of evidence that the Port Books yield. The problem of increasing sales under conditions of comparatively rigid industrial costs invited not one solution, but two. Men could find new markets in which to sell their accustomed commodities; or they could find new commodities to sell in their accustomed markets. With respect to the latter solution the Port Books are suggestive rather than conclusive; but what they suggest is of some interest. In 1640, remarkably few English commodities other than textiles were exported by London merchants from their own port. England was still primarily an agricultural country; yet the agricultural produce shipped out by the city merchants was officially valued at less than £20,000. Professor Nef has shown that the late sixteenth and early seventeenth centuries saw a considerable expansion of English manufacturing industry; yet in 1640 Londoners exported less than £30,000 worth of manufactured goods other than textiles. Professor Nef and others have also shown that the same period saw a boom in mining; yet in 1640 the minerals exported from London were valued at less than £40,000. To some extent Londoners may have shipped their more bulky commodities from provincial ports—they certainly seem to have shipped fish from Yarmouth—yet the impression left by the Port Books is that the city merchants supplemented their trade in textiles, less by dealing in other forms of native produce, than by trading in foreign commodities. Of all forms of England's produce her wool, whether raw or manufactured, was the only one in great demand overseas. Outside of the trade in textiles, it was re-exports rather than exports that opened a road to fortune.

By 1640 Londoners were re-shipping East Indian wares to Russia, Germany, the Netherlands and even to Italy and the Levant; Virginia tobacco to Hamburg; Mediterranean produce to the Netherlands; European manufactures to Africa and America. According to the official valuations their re-exports in that year were equal in value to their exports of all English goods other than textiles; and those re-exports constituted only a proportion of the foreign goods which they sold abroad. For, since goods re-shipped from London had to pay subsidy both inwards and outwards and in addition to suffer the delay of twice navigating the often wind-locked Thames, it was normally more convenient to trade directly between foreign countries without touching England. And so to these re-exports there was added a body of invisible exports for which the evidence is fragmentary but of which the importance is unmistakable. In both the Baltic and the Far East, Londoners bought local wares in one port to sell in another. London capital found its way into the African slave trade and into the commerce of the Caribbean. But, as in the case of visible exports, it was above all in Spain and the Mediterranean that the city merchants found their opportunity. To those regions they shipped directly the fish of Newfoundland; the hides, wax and fur of Russia; the corn, timber and hemp of the Baltic; the varied products of Germany and the Low Countries. And English ships were busily engaged in trade between different Mediterranean countries.

The significance of that trade in foreign commodities should not be underrated. Although its volume must remain a matter for conjecture, it may have contributed substantially to the wealth of the London merchant classes. It certainly provided the foundation for two of the most characteristic developments of the middle and later years of the century. On the one hand, it gave the London merchants their interest in colonial expansion and shaped their attitude to colonial policy. In the seventeenth century, as in the nineteenth, the merchant looked upon colonies less as markets in which it might one day be possible to make substantial sales than as sources from which primary commodities might be speedily obtained for resale elsewhere. From that point of view, the desirable colonial policy was obvious. It was the policy of confining sales of colonial produce to English merchants; the policy that was to be enshrined in the 'enumerated commodity' clauses of the Navigation Acts. On the other hand, it was this trade in foreign produce which supplied a major cause of Anglo-Dutch rivalry. To contemporary observers, at least in this country, few nations differed more widely than England and Holland. The latter was poor to the extent of lacking not only articles for export but also the basic commodities for subsistence. The former, to eyes dazzled with national pride, was rich in both manufactured goods and raw materials. But to the historian, disabused of the idea that the fish of the North Sea belonged peculiarly to this country and that self-sufficiency is conducive to success in foreign trade, the similarity between the two countries is more striking than the differences. Each occupied a geographical position admirably suited for maritime expansion; each produced only a narrow range of commodities that could be exported in any considerable quantity; each sought to solve the dilemma by carrying and trading in the produce of other places. Even during the early seventeenth century, colonial policy and Anglo-Dutch rivalry were taking shape under the pressure of those circumstances. The later years of the century saw little more than the intensification of trends already apparent before the Civil War.

8

The Sixteenth and Seventeenth Centuries: The Dark Ages in English Economic History?

Traditionally, an inaugural lecture should be used by the new occupant of a University Chair to expatiate upon the nature, methods and significance of the subject which he professes. But those are matters which my predecessors at the London School of Economics have so illuminated, both by precept and by example, that I am forced to choose a more modest theme. My purpose is merely to offer some comments upon the present state of the study of modern economic history in this country and, in particular, to draw attention to a tendency which has recently developed for modern economic history to be split, somewhere in the eighteenth century, not merely into two periods but almost into two separate subjects.

Despite the convention that modern economic history begins with the sixteenth century, it has, of course, long been realised that some sort of dividing line was to be found somewhere or other in the eighteenth. But, until recently, historians working on either side of that line tended to plough similar furrows. Not only did they ask similar questions; to a surprising and even suspicious extent they arrived at similar answers. On either side of the line one could find the small land-owner always disappearing and the middle classes always rising; capitalism always growing; trade always expanding; the standards of living of the working classes always falling. And but two decades ago, almost perfect equilibrium was obtained; for it was discovered that the sixteenth and early seventeenth centuries had produced an industrial revolution to balance the more notorious revolution of the eighteenth and nineteenth. So great was the emphasis on the continuity of English economic life and on the basic similarities between the various centuries that at times one was led to doubt whether anything happened in the eighteenth century at all.

In recent years, as I see it, the trend has been in the opposite direction. The emphasis on continuity has been seriously weakened. But it has been weakened, less by changes in historical interpretation, than by changes in historical method. A generation ago, the main requirement of an economic historian was that he should be able to read, since most of his sources were literary. The archetype of the learned monograph consisted of a thin rivulet of text meandering through

[1] A shortened version of an Inaugural Lecture given at the London School of Economics and Political Science, University of London, on 6th March, 1956, Professor R. H. Tawney in the chair.

wide and lush meadows of footnotes. Though much derided, there was much to be said for that type of work. The brevity of his text made it difficult for an author to obscure his argument ; the copious quotations in his footnotes were often more entertaining than anything the author himself could contrive. Today, that type of monograph has gone. To some extent it has been the victim of economic progress, for it is one of the eternal verities of history that as societies become wealthy they are no longer able to afford pleasures that were well within their reach when they were poor. But, very largely, it has been the victim of a change in fashion. Today the first requirement of an economic historian is that he should be able to count, for his materials are largely statistical. The archetype of our modern fashion is one in which a stream, often a less than limpid stream, of text tumbles from table to table and swirls round graph after graph. In his inaugural lecture my predecessor asked that a greater use should be made of statistics in the writing of economic history. The Almighty has answered his prayer, not with a shower, but with a deluge.

So far as an amateur in these matters can tell, the application of statistical methods to the study of the English economy in the eighteenth and nineteenth centuries has yielded highly valuable results. It has enormously increased the precision of our ideas about that period ; it has in some measure increased the accuracy of those ideas. But, like most improvements, it has not been made without cost. The economic history of the eighteenth and nineteenth century is in some danger of becoming a specialized subject in the sense that only those with a peculiar mental equipment will be able to understand it. It is already becoming a specialized subject in the sense that, since quantitative methods can be applied only to such phenomena as are by their nature measurable, the economic historian is tending to contract his field of interest. In this respect it is perhaps relevant to notice the number of proposals that have recently been made for the development of social history; a discipline which seems to be designed, at least in part, to take over the field from which the economic historian is retreating. But the most serious cost of these new developments has, perhaps, been the break in the continuity of historical study between the sixteenth and seventeenth centuries on the one hand and the eighteenth and nineteenth centuries on the other. So long as literary sources are being used, historians in either of those periods can deal with very similar questions—and tend to get very similar answers. For literary sources often have their origin in the complaints of the disgruntled or of social reformers, and the literature of economic and social protest shows an almost monotonous uniformity throughout the ages. To take but one example, the lament that " artificers and labourers . . . waste most part of the day and do not deserve their wages, sometimes in late coming to their work and early departing therefrom, long sitting at their breakfast and their dinner . . . and long time at sleeping in the afternoon " might, so far as its substance is concerned, have been made in any of the last five centuries. Only the cadence of its phrasing suggests that it comes, as indeed it does, from the early sixteenth.

But once statistical sources have to be used the historian of the early modern period rapidly gets out of step. Not, to be sure, because of any objection to quantitative methods as such. In fact, the application of statistical techniques to the study of the early period has sometimes been taken almost to extremes. Thus, if I am correctly informed, the history of the Papacy has recently been re-written on the basis of two statistical indices—one of managerial efficiency and the other of religious zeal. It would appear that the index of managerial efficiency stood at a respectable 60 in both the sixteenth and seventeenth centuries, but that the index of religious zeal fell from a low 35 in the sixteenth to an even lower 25 in the seventeenth. It would, however, be dishonest for the historian to claim the credit for that particular application. Like so much that is bold and imaginative in the interpretation of the past, it is the work of an economist. Professed historians have worked at a lower level ; but they have worked assiduously and by now have accumulated a not inconsiderable volume of statistical data. Unfortunately, those data are more impressive in their volume than in either their quality or their range. They are largely confined to the fields of prices, government revenue and foreign trade; and even in those fields they are highly suspect. Having collected his figures, the historian is too often in the position of not knowing whether it is better to use them or to explain them away. Nor, in that quandary, does he often get much help from his literary sources ; for contemporaries wrote in an even greater statistical void than does the modern historian. Admittedly, the seventeenth century saw the birth of Political Arithmetic—" the art of reasoning by figures upon things relating to government ". But the figures even of Petty, the father of that art, were seldom more than guesses. And although it may have been mere coincidence that Petty's guesses were usually " very grateful to those who governed ", it was certainly no accident that the guesses of other people were normally highly favourable to themselves. One example of the wildness of contemporary guesses may perhaps suffice. In 1694 a committee in the House of Lords was debating a bill to allow, for the duration of the war, the importation of Italian raw and thrown silk via the Netherlands. Counsel for the London Silkthrowers, arguing for the importation of thrown silk, asserted that the throwers numbered nearly 200,000. Counsel for the London Weavers, arguing for the importation of raw silk, challenged that figure and the committee adjourned for a more exact total to be produced. When it reassembled it was presented, not with one total, but with two. The Beadle of the Silkthrowers claimed that there were 80,000 workers in the industry ; one of the Company's Assistants thought there were only 30,000. It is, perhaps, not surprising that the Lords were among the advocates of improved statistics at the end of the seventeenth century.

To the teacher and student, at least, this tendency for modern economic history to split virtually into two subjects, by asking different questions and using different methods, is a matter of some moment. Those undergraduates who, selecting economic history as their special subject, direct their attention mainly to the eighteenth and nineteenth centuries complain—and complain bitterly—that there is no precision in what they read or what they are told about the sixteenth and seventeenth. Those whose interests lie mainly in the earlier modern period complain that the history of the nineteenth century is full of every sort of figure except the human. Since quantitative data are also lacking for the Middle Ages, it might seem that all my argument amounts to is that, in this respect as in many others, the Middle Ages really lasted until the Glorious Revolution and that the problem might be solved simply by altering the periods into which history is conveniently divided. But this as a solution—if solution it be—is one which historians as a whole will not accept. If the student of the sixteenth and seventeenth centuries is deficient in the statistical techniques now being applied to the nineteenth, he is almost equally deficient in those more esoteric methods by which the truth about the Middle Ages is discovered. The position has been recently put, quite bluntly, by Professor Heaton in a passage which, too long to be quoted in full, may be summarised as follows: the great growth of population, production, trade, migration and capital investment of the eleventh to the thirteenth centuries is well established. The stagnation and recession in population and enterprise from about 1350 to at least 1450 is supported by much gloomy evidence. After at latest 1750 the emphasis is on the abnormal growth of population. The central problem becomes how to feed and clothe generations of children outnumbering by far those of any earlier times. Some countries failed to solve it, with consequent starvation, disease, falling living standards, revolution and emigration. The British solved it because sufficient landlords, farmers, manufacturers, merchants and others had the wit and resource to devise new instruments of production, evolve new methods of organising and administering production, and dig out unprecedented quantities of capital for fixed plant and operating expenses. But what of the period between 1450 and 1750? " In many respects this early modern period is the Dark Ages of economic history ".

Although this problem presents itself in its most acute form to those historians who are mainly concerned with such measurable things as the population, output, and the national income, it is not peculiar to them. If one may judge by the very interesting discussions which have arisen out of Maurice Dobb's *Studies in the Development of Capitalism*, the sixteenth and early seventeenth centuries are a period of some difficulty for the Marxists also. It is part of the Marxist creed that feudalism was overthrown by capitalism. But it is also generally accepted by Marxist historians that whereas feudalism was in an advanced state of disintegration by the end of the fourteenth century, the capitalist period cannot be said to open until considerably later.

Indeed, at a conference of British Marxist historians held in 1947, it was agreed that " the Tudor and Stuart state was essentially an executive instrument of the feudal class more highly organised than ever before. . . . Only after the Revolution of 1640–1649 does the state in England begin to be subordinated to the capitalists. . . . The revolution of 1640 replaced the rule of one class by another." Thus the Marxist is faced by the problem of finding for the sixteenth and seventeenth centuries an interpretation which, while permitting feudalism to disintegrate in the later Middle Ages as the evidence requires, will nevertheless preserve it to be slain in the seventeenth century as theory demands. One suggestion, that of Mr. Sweezy, is to call the system which prevailed in the fifteenth and sixteenth centuries " pre-capitalist commodity production " to indicate that it was the growth of commodity production which first undermined feudalism and then, somewhat later, after that work of undermining had been substantially completed, prepared the ground for capitalism. But it seems that any such suggestion, however reasonable it may superficially appear, leads only into the " Pokrovsky-bog of merchant capitalism " and will not serve for a revolutionary view of historical development. The alternative method —that of keeping feudalism alive by subtly changing its definition— has the demerit of keeping it alive too long. The problem, it would seem, is still unresolved.

Hence the historians of Tudor and Stuart England at present stand indicted by their fellows. Their labours, it would seem, have been outside the main field of historical enquiry. Whoever seeks to trace the development of the English economy through the ages, whether he is primarily interested in such matters as population, output and national income, or whether his main concern is with class structure, finds that he loses the thread of his story at some time in the fifteenth century and picks it up again only some two hundred years later. Between, to repeat the accusation of Professor Heaton, come the dark ages of economic history. That is an indictment which demands an answer.

One thing is clear enough. There can be no reasonable doubt that the sixteenth and seventeenth centuries saw an increase in the output of English agriculture and industry. The England of the early Tudors was rich in unused physical resources—idle land, unexploited woodlands, unworked minerals. By the end of the seventeenth century these resources were being used to a far greater degree ; more land was being cultivated; woodlands were being either carefully managed to provide fuel or grubbed up to make room for corn and pasture; the growth of mineral output had been spectacular in the case of coal and substantial in the case of iron, lead, and salt. Nor was expansion confined to primary production. There was a marked widening of the range of England's secondary industries with the introduction of new forms of woollen textiles and the development of the cotton and silk manufactures, glassmaking, papermaking, brassmaking, sugar refining and of other trades hitherto practised, if at all, only on an insignificant scale. And in the country's economic relationships with the outer world, although change was gradual, its cumulative effects were profound. At the beginning of the sixteenth century England was still mainly an exporter of wool and unfinished cloth to north-western Europe. By the end of the seventeenth she was not only exporting a wide range of woollen fabrics to all of Europe, the Near and Far East, Africa and America ; in addition she was sending both men and capital across the Atlantic and, with the aid of a vastly expanded mercantile marine, carrying on a substantial re-export trade in Asiatic and American produce. The problem is to relate that undoubted expansion to the demographic changes which accompanied it. From the taxation records which have survived it seems reasonably certain that the population of England approximately doubled between the late fourteenth and late seventeenth centuries; and although the evidence for the intervening years is inconclusive, it seems likely that most of that growth occurred after 1500. A growth of population in a country with abundant unused resources is likely to be accompanied by an expansion of output. The problem of the historian of Tudor and Stuart England is to decide whether the expansion so induced was also accompanied by progress; i.e. by an increase in income per head.

In the absence of statistical data, no direct approach to that problem is possible. Moreover, for a number of reasons, the most obvious of the indirect methods of approach do not yield conclusive answers. It might seem an elementary matter to compare the conditions which obtained at the beginning of a period with those obtaining at its end; but such a comparison is made difficult by the changes which occurred in the nature of historical records during the sixteenth and seventeenth centuries. In the early years of the sixteenth century whole categories of records which the medievalists find invaluable begin to peter out or disappear completely, partly as a result of the Reformation, partly as a result of the new administrative methods introduced by the Tudors. After the middle of that century there emerges another body of materials extraordinarily rich but significantly different from that which preceded it. Then, after the Restoration, those materials peter out in turn with the decline in the powers of the Privy Council and their place is taken by a new pamphlet literature and by the tax records which eventually develop into the statistical sources used by my more up-to-date colleagues. At first sight, it is true, the economy in 1700 looks very different from what it had been in 1500. But it does so partly because the most easily available records illumine different facets of it.

Something, one might suppose, could be deduced from changing habits of consumption. And it is clear that by the end of the seventeenth century the upper classes, and the more prosperous farmers and tradesmen, enjoyed a wider range of goods and services than had their ancestors of two hundred years before. But changing patterns of consumption do not necessarily mean that the incomes of consumers have increased. It was a constant complaint of the times that the new habits meant a decline in " hospitality " and at least one pamphleteer attributed the sluggishness of agricultural prices in the late seventeenth century to the fact that gentlemen paid for their new-fangled pleasures by going without their suppers and demanded that, in the public interest, all gentlemen should have suppers prepared for them whether they partook of them or not. Moreover, there is abundant evidence that some of the gentry paid for their new standard of living by dissipating their capital. Finally, there is the problem of the poor. Even at the beginning of the sixteenth century the lot of the poor had been hard. " Poor labourers, carters, ironsmiths, carpenters and ploughmen ", wrote Sir Thomas More, " by so great and continual toil as drawing and bearing beasts be scant able to sustain . . . get so hard and poor a living and live so wretched and miserable a life that the state and condition of the labouring beasts may seem much better and wealthier. . . . These silly poor wretches be presently tormented with barren and unfruitful labour, and the remembrance of their poor, indigent and beggarly old age killeth them up. For their daily wages is so little that it will not suffice for the same day, much less it yieldeth any overplus that may daily be laid up for the relief of old age." The little we know of the movement of real wage rates suggests that the lot of the poor was to deteriorate still further; and both the history of the Poor Law and the calculations of such men as King and Davenant suggest that by the end of the seventeenth century the poor may have constituted a larger proportion of the population than at the beginning of the sixteenth. The inequality with which the national income was distributed makes it dangerous to deduce changes in that income from changes in the consumption habits of the wealthier classes.

Nor is the detailed history of agricultural and industrial production as helpful as might be hoped. By the end of the seventeenth century, it is true, writers extolled the virtues of machinery as saving labour and increasing output per head. But labour-saving devices played an insignificant part in the economic changes with which we are concerned; and when they appeared they were bitterly opposed. From Starkey to Davenant all were agreed that the country's major economic problem lay in the under-employment of its labour force. Partly that underemployment was due to the seasonal fluctuations in agriculture, mining and transport; partly to the fact that many men were producing for local markets too small to keep them continuously occupied; partly to the high leisure preference which the inhabitants of poor countries so often possess. When the rewards for toil were meagre, the temptation to toil no more than was necessary for a bare subsistence was great. Whatever the relative importance of those different causes, the path of wisdom seemed to contemporaries to lie less in the provision of equipment to save labour than in the provision of more working capital to set that labour on work, in the creation of new markets to absorb its output, and in the provision of a legislative and economic environment in which the costs of voluntary leisure should be painfully high. The purpose of the inventions of the sixteenth and seventeenth centuries was less to save labour than to bring the forces of nature under greater control. In so far as national income per head changed during that period, it is more likely to have changed because of changes in the level of employment than for any other reason. And of all economic phenomena, the level of employment is one of the most difficult for the historian to assess.

Consequently, as is so often the case, the historian is driven back on to the coherency theory of truth. When the direct evidence relating to his problem is so scanty, can he construct a consistent and plausible argument from such material as he has? It is in the light of that question that recent work on the economic history of the sixteenth and seventeenth centuries must be surveyed. Most of the recent studies in that field deal either with overseas trade, or with local history, or with the relationship between religion and economic life, or with the fortunes of the landed gentry. To what extent can materials collected on topics so diverse be used to illuminate the problem of economic growth?

The relevance of foreign trade to that problem is obvious enough. It is the one field in which statistics are reasonably abundant, and despite their many imperfections there can be little doubt that foreign trade and shipping grew rather more rapidly than population; and with them grew employment in the exporting industries, the mercantile marine, and in the increasing number of trades dependent upon imported raw materials. But foreign trade accounted for only a small fraction of the national output; most production was for home consumption and it is in this field that the crux of our problem lies. Fortunately, it is above all on this field that the local historians for the most part cast their light. One of the difficulties which beset the student of the sixteenth and seventeenth centuries is the fact that most of his material is narrowly local. Not only is that obviously true of records which relate to a particular manor, or parish, or town, or county, or business; it has constantly to be remembered that most of the general statements about the economy as a whole were made by men whose knowledge was essentially local. It is not until the very end of the seventeenth century that much effort was made by the government, or by economic interests, or by writers to bring together similar information for different parts of the country so as to afford a conspectus of the whole. It was not until the eighteenth that those efforts were crowned with spectacular success in the work of Defoe. For the period with which we are concerned the historian is constantly puzzled to know whether the progress or decay which he finds in any specific place is purely local, and to decide whether a process which appears to be continuous is in fact so or merely appears so because it occurs in different parts of the country at different times. In such matters only detailed work in local history can resolve his difficulties and in that sphere much detailed work remains to be done. But even from the work that has been done so far, two developments of major importance emerge. One is the growth of London from a city with a population of some fifty or sixty thousands to one with a population of half a million; a growth based partly on foreign trade, partly on manufacturing, partly on the provision of financial and professional services, partly on its role as the country's political and social centre. The other is the economic development of the hitherto backward west and north. That development was reflected in the growth of the textile industries of Devon, Lancashire and the West Riding, of the metallurgical and leather industries of the Severn Valley and the Black Country, of the potteries of Staffordshire and of coal, glass, and salt production on Tyneside; it was reflected also in the rise to commercial importance of Bristol and Liverpool with their easy access to Ireland, Africa and, above all, America. Nor, it seems, was that growth restricted to industry and overseas trade for, at least in the West, there was much land over which cultivation could be extended once the industrial areas provided a market for foodstuffs and once the introduction of artificial grasses facilitated the reclamation of hitherto barren land. By the end of the seventeenth century, if contemporaries are to be believed, those regions were characterised by cheap food because of agricultural improvements, by low wages because of cheap food, and by low poor rates because of the industrial demand for labour.

Those developments, taking place on opposite sides of the country, had one effect in common. They greatly stimulated internal trade. London did so primarily by virtue of the large market which its population offered to provincial producers. It was fashionable to bewail the growth of the capital as draining the life-blood of the country, and it may be that in some measure that growth did, in fact, depress industrial and mercantile activity elsewhere in southern and eastern England. In overseas trade the Southern and Eastern ports found it difficult to compete with London ; and there may be some substance in the argument that the metropolitan demand for food raised prices and wages in nearby industrial areas. At least, it is noticeable that by the later seventeenth century the major industries in the Home Counties were those such as spinning, knitting, lacemaking and straw-plaiting that depended on female rather than on male labour. But the benefits which flowed from the city's expansion were too obvious to be missed by more perceptive commentators. " It may be well worth the enquiry of thinking men ", wrote Davenant, " what truth there is in this common and received notion that the growth of London is pernicious to England; that the kingdom is like a rickety body with a head too big for the other members. For some people who have thought much on this subject are inclined to believe that the growth of the city is advantageous to the nation". Among those who thought thus was Houghton. " Let us," he wrote, " consider what the consequences will be of making London as big again. . . . In likelihood

we should spend twice as many coals, which would double the shipping
to Newcastle and that double the trade and people at Newcastle. . . .
Whatsoever is said here for Newcastle will likewise serve for Norfolk
for stuffs, stockings or fish ; for Suffolk and Cambridgeshire for
butter; for the counties about London for most sorts of food ; for
the West for serges, tin, etc. ; for Cheshire for cheese; for Derby and
Yorkshire for lead, alum and several other ; and in short, for all
counties and places in them; for I believe there is no county or place
in England but directly supplies London, or at one hand or other
supplies them that do supply it."   In its turn the development of the
North and West stimulated internal trade, not only because of the
demand which the growing industrial population created for foodstuffs,
but also because the industries upon which it was based were all
producing for more than a local market.

This development of inland trade, it may be argued, was one of the
most significant features of economic life under the Tudors and Stuarts.
But it is difficult to speak of it with precision for, since most of it
passed overland, it has left no statistical record.   Fortunately, it is the
habit of men to bewail their blessings and in some measure its story
can be reconstructed from the complaints to which it gave rise.   Under
the Tudors the villain most frequently consigned to eternal damnation
was " that caterpillar which cometh between the bark and the tree "—
the middleman in primary produce.   By the early seventeenth century
he had come to be accepted as a necessary evil and criticism was being
directed at shopkeepers who sold goods which they had not produced;
but by the end of that century even they had acquired the respectability
of a vested interest demanding protection from intruders.   " The
inland or home trade of England ", it was asserted in a slightly later
broadside on that theme, " is an ancient establishment of business,
form'd from the beginning in the mere nature and consequence of
things, from the situation of places, the growth of materials, and other
conveniences of the manufactures.   This method of trade consists
not in the bare producing or manufacturing the first principles of our
trade, such as the wool, leather, metals and minerals, in which our
country abounds, but in the buying and selling, carrying and re-carrying
the goods from place to place for sale.   This is very significantly called
the circulation of trade, by which every part of the island is fully supply'd
with what they respectively want.   Trade going on in this happy
progress, has for many ages increased to a mighty degree, so that
manufactures of one kind or another are carried on in every county,
shops are open'd in every corner, and in the most remote parts well
furnished with goods of all needful kinds, as well of our own produce
as of foreign importations.   The shops, with the wholesale dealers
and manufacturers who supply them are infinitely numerous, and
being generally kept by the most substantial people, are the support
of the whole trade of the kingdom ; these may be said to pay the
landed men their rent, the government their taxes, the parishes their

assessments, and the poor their allowances; they bear all the burthens and chargeable offices in the towns and parishes where they dwell." Such men, it was argued, clearly deserved and needed to be nourished and defended. " For now, to the infinite and unexpressible loss and discouragement of all these fair traders, they find this beautiful constitution of trade broken in upon and invaded by the frauds and arts of the hawkers and pedlars, and private clandestine traders, who, upon pretence of selling cheaper than the shops, insinuate themselves into the opinion of the buyers, which pretence also is a delusion in fact (except where smuggling, or dealing in prohibited goods, and other unlawful practices, may enable them to do so). On this occasion the fair trader, as well by wholesale as retale, as also the woollen and silk manufacturers of this kingdom, humbly represent; first that these people travelling or rather wandering from place to place, and having no legal abode, thereby avoid all the several payments and assessments which the fair tradesmen, who are house-keepers and settled inhabitants, are subjected to. Secondly, that by carrying their packs from house to house they invert the order of trade, supplant the fair dealer, and forestall the markets : and thus the scheme of our inland trade is broken, and the manufactures know no regular motion. The carriers are intercepted, and must in time cease to travel, for want of double carriage; or the foreign goods (which the shop-keepers must have) will come heavily charged with the said double carriage: the inns and houses of entertainment on the road (which are now, beyond comparison, the best in the world) will sink, and the whole commerce feel a sensible and terrible decay." And by the end of the seventeenth century the growth of inland trade was inspiring more important demands than that for the taxation or suppression of hawkers and pedlars, for it was the major cause of a spate of projects for improving harbours, roads and rivers.

The significance of this needs no elaboration. The growth of internal and foreign trade meant that an increasing amount of production was for more than local markets, and Adam Smith's explanation of how larger markets lead to the division of labour and the efficiency which specialisation engenders has long been an integral part of economic doctrine. Moreover, it would seem that production for a large market permitted more regular employment than production for a small, so that the changes which increased efficiency may well have served also to raise the general level of employment.

The changes which, during the same period, took place in the relationships between religion and economic life have inspired a literature to which justice cannot be done in any brief summary; but the nature of these changes can at least be crudely indicated by the contrast between two well-known prayers. The first is the Prayer for Landlords officially published in 1553 and then abandoned by the Anglican Church for ever:

" The earth O Lord is thine, and all that is contained therein; we heartily pray thee to send thy Holy Spirit into the hearts of them that possess the grounds, pastures, and dwelling places of the earth that they, remembering themselves to be Thy tenants, may not rack and stretch out the rents of their houses and lands, nor yet take unreasonable fines and incomes after the manner of covetous worldlings, but so let them out to others that the inhabitants thereof may both be able to pay the rents, and also honestly to live, to nourish their families, and to relieve the poor.

Give them grace also to consider that they are but strangers and pilgrims in this world, having here no dwelling place but seeking one to come. That they, remembering the short continuance of their life, may be content with that that is sufficient, and not join house to house, nor couple land to land to the impoverishment of others, but so behave themselves in letting out their tenements, lands and pastures that after this life they may be received into everlasting dwelling places."

The other is to be found among the papers of a financier who was considered shady even by the unexacting standards of the early eighteenth century in which he lived.

" O Lord, thou knowest I have mine estates in the City of London and likewise that I have lately purchased an estate in fee simple in the County of Essex. I beseech Thee to preserve the two counties of Middlesex and Essex from fire and earth-quake. And as I have a mortgage in Hertfordshire, I beg Thee likewise to have an eye of compassion on that county. For the rest of the counties; Thou mayest deal with them as Thou art pleased."

Whatever the reasons for it, that transformation of Divine Grace from an instrument for perpetuating the uneconomic allocation of resources into a protection for economic enterprise and business foresight was among the intellectual achievements of the age. The influence of public opinion upon individual action is, admittedly, one of the imponderables in history. But it is surely not fanciful to suggest that, for men whose skins are not abnormally thick, the incentive to acquire wealth is strengthened by the belief that its possessor will deserve well of the Almighty and obtain social acceptance by all right-minded people.

Nor were such factors the only ones operating to create a social climate favourable to the entrepreneur. " To what purpose," wrote Weston, " do soldiers, scholars, lawyers, merchants and men of all occupations and trades toil and labour with great affection but to get money, and with that money when they have gotten it to buy land ? " It is by now a commonplace of the textbooks that, between the middle of the sixteenth century and the closing years of the seventeenth, sales by impecunious gentry and an even more impecunious Crown made land more easily available to moneyed men than ever before. And if land by itself was not a sufficient passport to social bliss, gentility was not out of reach. At first sight it is true, the status-system of the sixteenth and seventeenth centuries does not seem highly favourable to the rising man. As I understand it that system, at least in its cruder manifestations, was essentially biological. It was based upon a colour bar; though the relevant colour was that of the blood rather than of the skin. A man's status depended less on his own distinction than on the possession of an ancestor who had been distinguished before him. And the more remote that ancestor, and hence presumably the less of his blood which flowed through an Elizabethan's veins, the higher the status of that Elizabethan was. One of the most pathetic stories of the sixteenth century is that, I think, of the efforts of Lord Burleigh— a man of distinction by any rational criteria—to prove his descent from a Welsh princeling who probably never existed and who, if he did exist, was probably hardly distinguishable from the sheep of his native hills.

The advantages of a colour bar to those on the sunny side of it are too obvious to need exposition. But, as modern experience shows, the operation of such a bar raises certain philosophical problems. For the proposition that socially valuable qualities are the monopoly of a biological group is not one that is easily reconciled with experience. It was this dilemma which inspired, no doubt, the remark to be found in that curious work *The Blazon of Gentry* : " Jesus Christ was a gentleman, as to His flesh, by the part of His mother . . . and if He had esteemed the vain glory of this world (whereof He often said His Kingdom was not) might have borne coat-armour. The Apostles also were gentlemen of blood . . . but through the tract of time and persecution of wars, poverty oppressed the kindred and they were constrained to servile works." It was that dilemma which, solved in some countries only by revolution, was so magnificently dealt with in England by the College of Heralds. That College was set up to prevent men of low birth from passing as gentlemen. If contemporaries are to be believed, its labours produced exactly the opposite effect. To quote the well-known words of Sir Thomas Smith, Elizabethan ambassador and secretary of state, " as for gentlemen, they be made good cheape in England. For whosoever studieth the lawes of the realme, who studieth in the universities, who professeth liberall sciences, and to be shorte, who can live idly and without manuall labour, and will beare the port, charge and countenaunce of a gentleman, he . . . shall be taken for a gentleman : . . . (and if need be) a king of Heraulds shal also give him for mony, armes newly made and invented, the title whereof shall pretende to have beene found by the sayd Herauld in perusing and viewing of olde registers, where his auncestors in times past had bin recorded to beare the same : Or if he will do it more truely and of better faith, he will write that for the merittes of that man, and certaine qualities which he doth see in him, and for sundrie noble actes which he hath perfourmed, he by the authoritie which he hath as king of Heraldes and armes, giveth to him and his heries these and these armes, which being done I thinke he may be called a squire, for he beareth ever after those armes." Nor was that written in terms of disapproval. Posing the question whether that manner of making gentlemen is to be allowed or no, Smith came to the conclusion that " it is not amisse ".

Thus it is arguable that economic development in Tudor and Stuart England was more than the simple result of population growth. Quite apart from such external factors as the rise of Antwerp and the influx of American silver, the social climate was becoming more favourable to business men and, braced by that climate, business men seized their opportunities to build up a volume of internal and overseas trade that brought with it at least some of the benefits of specialisation and possibly raised the general level of employment. For that reason it is possible to think of this period in terms of economic progress as distinct from mere economic expansion. Yet a caveat must at once be entered. Even when all allowances have been made for the changes in the nature of the records, it is difficult to resist the conclusion that such progress as occurred was a feature of the seventeenth century rather than of the sixteenth—and of the later seventeenth century rather than of the earlier. The growth of London, of the extra-European and entrepot trades, and of western and northern industry were Stuart rather than Tudor phenomena. Although the new attitude to business enterprise was being reflected in the House of Commons at the end of Elizabeth's reign, for another generation it was to be denied full expression by the policies pursued by the privy council. Admittedly, the land market was brisk from the middle of the sixteenth century, but the most prominent purchasers in it seem to have been professional rather than business men. Partly, no doubt, that was because government service and the law did not permit the ploughing back of profits. But partly it seems to have been the result of a relatively under-developed economy in which the professions offered higher rewards than more mundane business. If, in the early seventeenth century, one wishes to find competition at its most fierce it is to be found, I suggest, not in trade or industry but in the conflict of jurisdictions between the Courts. That conflict is part of the constitutional history of England, and I would not insult my legal colleagues by implying that the lawyers who fought it were inspired by any motives other than the desire to protect the liberties of Englishmen. But the economic historian cannot but notice that, in their case, the financial rewards of civic virtue were considerable. Today, it may be, the stories of the large earnings to be made in the law are purely figments of envious imagination. In the seventeenth century they seem to have been better founded.

This distinction between the earlier and later parts of the period can obtain some support from other evidence. It is, for example, suggested by what we know of the movement of prices and wages. Admittedly, our data are but fragmentary and were influenced by changes in the supply of money. But a feature of the later sixteenth and early seventeenth centuries seems to have been a rapid rise in rents and agricultural prices combined with a much slower rise in wages and industrial prices. Such a combination suggests an economy in which agriculture was not expanding sufficiently to provide men with all the food, the farms and the employment that they needed and in which industrial development was too slow to make up for the deficiencies of agriculture. Nor is that suggestion implausible. Commercial statistics suggest that under Elizabeth foreign trade grew but little and that the later years of James's reign saw a series of major depressions. Coal-mining apart, there is little evidence of rapid industrial expansion before the second quarter of the seventeenth century. The main form of agricultural improvement was the enclosure of open fields and commons—it was estimated that two acres of enclosed land were worth three in the open fields or seven on the commons—but that was not always easy. In the more densely populated areas common rights were highly prized and were defended by their owners with great bitterness and, perhaps, with less obscurantism than the improvers alleged. The less densely populated areas, in which the institutional obstacles to enclosure may have been less, were often remote from the main centres of consumption and cursed with large areas of marshy or relatively infertile soil. It needed the greater urban and industrial markets of the seventeenth century, cheaper capital, and better methods of drainage and land reclamation to spread agricultural improvement throughout the country. Nor were the Fates always kind ; there is some evidence that bad harvests were particularly frequent in the late sixteenth and early seventeenth centuries and that the efforts of men were in some measure frustrated by the vagaries of the weather. Today it is unfashionable to think of Elizabethan England as a country in which population pressure was gradually reducing many to poverty and possibly diminishing the national income per head; but that was a view which some contemporaries held. The argument of overpopulation was repeatedly used by the advocates of American colonisation; there is no reason to doubt their sincerity; it is even possible that they were right. One reason why the middle and later years of the seventeenth century present a rather brighter picture may be that population growth was temporarily checked by emigration and bubonic plague, to be resumed only when agricultural, industrial and commercial expansion were more fully in their stride.

Thus it is possible for the historian of Tudor and Stuart England to give at least a tentative reply to the indictment of Professor Heaton; although he cannot measure the changes which occurred during that period he can at least suggest the directions in which affairs were moving. To the Marxist he has scarcely any reply at all. The most striking thing about the social analyses made by Wilson at the end of the sixteenth century and King at the end of the seventeenth was that their categories, unlike those used by Colquhoun at the end of the eighteenth, were essentially medieval—landowner and merchant ; clergyman and lawyer; petty trader and handicraftsman; seaman and labourer. Despite the contemporary murmurings about " monied men " neither of those authors—and neither of them was a fool—saw any need for any separate category of industrial or financial capitalists. Nor, perhaps, is that surprising. Most of the entrepreneurs who brought about the economic changes were small men readily included in the category of prosperous artisans or tradesmen. Those who provided the considerable fixed equipment in the mining, metallurgical or shipping industries were easily thought of as landowners or merchants, for that in fact is what they were. The effect of the economic changes of the sixteenth and seventeenth centuries was less to create new categories of men than to offer the existing categories new opportunities and to inspire them with a new spirit.

It is important, however, that an economic historian should not even seem to accept the suggestion that he is concerned solely with the story of change. If his interests were so confined the sixteenth and seventeenth centuries would indeed be an unrewarding field, for the economic changes which they saw were not great. A historian's function is, surely, to discover how men have behaved in the various environments within which they have lived. In that respect the historian of the Tudor and Stuart economies may perhaps claim some modest success. Whether his discoveries and conclusions are of interest and value to workers in other branches of social study is, of course, for them to say. But perhaps a historian may be permitted two comments. One is inspired by a remark recently made at dinner by one of my most distinguished colleagues in this University. It was, if my memory serves me, " Despite what Professor Fisher thinks, I say that history should be based on facts. If it is not based on facts it is sociology ". And, in my experience, the economic historian working in the sixteenth and seventeenth centuries finds it particularly easy to hold sympathetic converse with sociologists. Whether or not it is because they have a similar attitude to facts, they share an interest in similar problems. I suspect that, if a social history of the eighteenth and nineteenth centuries ever develops, it will cover many of the topics with which the economic history of the earlier period now deals.

My final comment is inspired, like so many of my views on this subject, by the work of Professor Tawney. Just consider some of the more obvious features of the Tudor and Stuart economy. It was one in which the methods of production were simple and the units of production were small; in which middlemen and usurers were both hated and indispensable; in which agricultural progress was seriously impeded by the perpetuation of communal rights over land. The chronic underemployment of labour was one of its basic problems and, despite moral exhortations, among the mass of the people the propensity to save was low. Consider the comments made by the rector of Bodsworth on two of his parishioners in 1551. " These men earn twenty shillings a year each. Their masters with whom they dwell find them all manner of tools, so they spend nothing in getting their wages save find themselves in clothes. Either of them might save at the year end clearly five shillings and eightpence." And what was their reply ? It was that they could not save a penny. Moreover, if contemporaries are to be believed, both the incentive to work and the propensity to save were being undermined by that crude form of social services known as the Elizabethan Poor Law. It was an economy heavily dependent on foreign sources for improved industrial and agricultural methods, and to some extent for capital, but in which foreign labour and business men were met with bitter hostility. In it ambitious young men often preferred careers in the professions and government service to those in business, and fortunes made in business were too readily converted into land. It was an economy in which monetary stability was periodically threatened and sometimes upset by unwise policies on the part of the government, and in which an embryo money market had its efficiency impaired by a glut of government paper that it could not digest. Men increasingly pinned their hopes on industrialisation and economic nationalism to absorb its growing population; but industrialisation was slow to come and the blessings of economic nationalism proved to be mixed. Such an economy may have little in common with our own; but at least some of its characteristics are still to be found in countries so different from ours that we call them underdeveloped. I would suggest—and in this I am fortified by the example of Professor Tawney's classic study of *Land and Labour in China*—that an understanding of the economy of Tudor and Stuart England is not the worst equipment for a study of the economically less developed parts of the modern world. In the last resort, perhaps the darkness of the sixteenth and seventeenth centuries depends upon the angle from which they are approached and upon the questions that are asked about them.

9

Tawney's Century

'THE century which separates the Dissolution of the Monasteries from the Great Rebellion may almost be defined... as "Tawney's century".'[1] So wrote Professor Trevor-Roper, and many will think his definition a happy one. Yet it is doubtful whether all will accept his reason for offering it—i.e. that Tawney has reinterpreted that century in terms of a rising gentry drawing their strength from new agricultural techniques and a declining aristocracy weakened by economic conservatism and fashionable extravagance—or share his fear that such an interpretation is in danger of becoming a new orthodoxy. Unanimity is scarcely a characteristic of those whose work owes most to Tawney's influence, and Tawney himself has made the appropriate comment upon the fragility of historical orthodoxies—'all flesh is grass and historians wither quicker than most.' His influence has been exercised through more varied channels and at a more profound level. A great teacher has the gift of attracting men of sufficient calibre to be able critically to test his suggestions in the light of the empirical evidence which they unearth, to modify where necessary the views which he originally inspired, and to carry investigations beyond the point at which he himself left them. He shapes the course of scholarship not only through his own, inevitably provisional, conclusions but also—and perhaps mainly—through his capacity to suggest the questions that are most worthwhile exploring. It is by operating through both these channels that Tawney has made the pre-Civil War period his own. Much of what has recently been written about that period is Tawney modified and amplified in the light of further research. And even those who reject his views most vigorously find themselves answering, rather than ignoring, the questions which he has raised. In the last

[1] H. R. Trevor-Roper, *The Gentry, 1540-1640*. (1953), p. 1.

resort, his influence lies in his flair for suggesting to the twentieth century what of interest is to be found in the sixteenth and seventeenth and, as Burkhardt pointed out, what any age finds interesting in its past is the very marrow of history.

The reasons why the twentieth century should be interested in the economic history of the sixteenth and seventeenth are no doubt various, but one is suggested by Sir Theodore Gregory's shrewd description of that part of the world which it is now fashionable to call underdeveloped:[1]

> 'There may be a fringe of plantation-cultivation and some large-scale industrial and mining enterprise, but there is also a mass of peasant cultivators... and an indigenous industry organised not on the basis of power-driven machinery but on the basis of the human hand. Finance is provided by the "money-lender" not by a commercial bank; life flows in a traditional pattern. Birth rates are high and so is mortality, production *per capita* is low and the struggle for existence is hard... It is a familiar pattern and the danger is of over-simplification. There is the temptation to suppose that because the technical way of life in many parts of the world is traditional, therefore the populations who live that life are simple, unsophisticated souls, unaffected by the economic calculus, unaware of the pull of the more or less, the greater or the smaller gain. Nothing could well be more mistaken. I venture to think... that it is not in those parts of the world... that self interest and the profit motive are tempered by considerations of the public good.'

Those words might well constitute a description of the England of which Tawney is the great expositor, for the late sixteenth and early seventeenth centuries constitute perhaps the last period in English history in which economic appetites were remarkably vigorous but in which economic expansion was still slow.

Of the vigour of economic appetites under the later Tudors and early Stuarts there can be little doubt. Both contemporary comment and contemporary behaviour testify to it, and Weber's attempt to

[1] Sir Theodore Gregory, 'The Problems of the Under-developed World', *Lloyds Bank Review*, Oct. 1948 pp. 39-40.

identify a capitalist ethic distinct from the simple desire for economic gain appears increasingly unconvincing as more about individual capitalists becomes known. The slowness of economic growth must, in the absence of statistics, be more open to question. Clearly, it was not an age of stagnation. The growth of population was undoubtedly accompanied by some expansion of the national income. As a result of the developments in foreign trade and of the growth of London there was a widening of the range as well as an increase in the volume of the goods and services available for consumption. Yet the steep and prolonged rise in agricultural prices may reasonably be inter-preted to mean that agricultural production was slow to expand. For what they are worth, the Customs figures suggest that for much of the period exports were sluggish. The persistence of high interest rates may well mean that the rate of capital accumulation was slow. The lag of wages behind prices, the contemporary concern about paupe-rism, and the mounting fear of over-population all suggest that the growing labour force was absorbed into employment only with difficulty; and it is perhaps significant that the second quarter of the seventeenth century, when the upward swing of agricultural prices began to flatten out and real wage rates began to rise, was also a time when disease and emigration were probably combining to check the rate of population growth. With respect to such an economy, the task of the historian is less that of demonstrating the expansive force of economic ambition than that of examining the impediments which contained it, less that of proclaiming its successes than that of re-cording the strains and stresses to which it gave rise.

In primary production, the obstacles to expansion lay mainly in the field of supply and arose largely from the limitations of contem-porary techniques. In fishing, it is true, men seem to have found it easier to catch herrings than to sell them; but elsewhere the difficulty lay in raising output rather than in disposing of it. The story of mining was one of a growing struggle with the problems of drainage and ventilation as deposits near the surface became exhausted. That of agriculture was largely one of the increasing difficulties with which men wrested an adequate supply of commodities from the soil. At first sight, that difficulty may seem surprising since the labour force was growing and land was, by modern standards, still plentiful. But much of that land was infertile; much was waterlogged; many areas were still thinly peopled; yields were generally low; and the demands upon the soil were many. For in the sixteenth and seventeenth centuries, as in the Middle Ages, men looked to the land not only for their food but also for their drink, for their fuel, and for such basic industrial materials as timber, wool, hides, skins and tallow. It was called upon to provide, not only the horses which maintained the internal system of transport, but also the fodder by which those horses were themselves maintained. And much land was still required to satisfy the appetite of the king and upper classes for the chase. Under such circumstances economic and demographic expansion tended to place upon the land a strain that, in later ages and under different circumstances, they were to place upon the balance of payments. In the course of time, the combined pressure of these competing uses was to be relieved in a variety of ways. For both political and economic reasons the hunting rights of the king and his subjects were to be curtailed. The pressure of the demand for fuel was to be eased by the substitution of coal for wood, by the concentration of the major fuel-using industries in those regions where fuel was most abundant, and by the importation of iron smelted abroad. The pressure of the demand for timber was to be eased by the greater use of brick in building and by the growth of substantial imports from Scandinavia and the Baltic. Improvements in water transport were to bring with them economies in horse power. English pastures were to be supplemented by those of Ireland, Wales and Scotland, which sent increasing quantities of wool and livestock into the English market. And as the pressure of these competing claims was eased, the efficiency of land use was to be raised by the introduction of turnips and the artificial grasses to raise the fertility of the lighter soils and to improve the country's grasslands. But those developments belonged to the seventeenth century rather than to the sixteenth, and to the later years of that century rather than to the earlier. It was not until the later years of Charles II that the flow of produce from the land was to become so great as to inflict upon men the horrors of plenty. Bacon looked back on the reign of Elizabeth as a critical period during which

England had become dangerously dependent on foreign grain, and both the course of prices and the literary evidence suggest that, despite land reclamation and the increased use of lime, marl and leys, the pressure upon the land continued to mount at least until the reign of Charles I.

Given these competing demands upon land, it was inevitable that the question of land use should become a major issue. Should men be allowed to change the use of their land—and in particular to convert arable to pasture—as considerations of profit prompted them? Should the forest rights of the king and the hunting grounds of his greater subjects, compatible though they were with both rough grazing and the production of wood and timber, be swept away to permit an extension of arable and improved pasture? Above all, should rights of common grazing—a relatively inefficient form of land use—be preserved in the interests of social stability or be suppressed in the interests of productivity? In large measure, no doubt, those questions were resolved by the forces of the market. Men converted their land from arable to pasture, or from pasture to arable, as prices dictated. More than one landowner converted his chase or his park into farms. Enclosure—i.e. the suppression of common grazing rights—by agreement was a feature of the age. But as the pressure upon land mounted, the question of its use became increasingly a political one. Despite growing criticism in the Commons and the ranks of the landlords, the Crown clung to the Tudor policy of forbidding the conversion of arable to pasture save where that conversion ministered to the improvement of arable farming itself. The Crown clung to its forest rights, partly for reasons of prestige and partly, perhaps, because the surrender value of those rights tended to increase with time. Although enclosure by agreement was legal, the difficulties of obtaining agreement were sometimes such as to produce demands that agreement should be dispensed with. As one Jacobean, probably an M.P., argued, 'the difficultys attending inclosures lye only in the preposterous wills of perverse men who may, and will not, understand reason nor entertain a benefit offered them; and it is therefore not fit that matters of publick good should rest on the consultation and determination as such as afore resolve wilfully to withstand it, not knowing truly what they oppose.'[1] But the political climate was not yet favourable to enclosure by compulsion.

In secondary production, by contrast, the obstacles to expansion seem to have lain in the field of demand rather than in that of supply. Technical difficulties, it is true, existed. As in mining and agriculture, men's impotence in the face of wind and weather tended to make employment irregular. Changes in their relative scarcities raised the problems of substituting coal for wood as an industrial fuel and long wool for short in the manufacture of textiles. In some industries English methods were poor by comparison with those of the Continent, and skilled immigrants were required to repair the deficiency. But these problems were either solved or remained comparatively unimportant in the century before the Civil War. Both the course of prices and the literary evidence suggest that, although secondary producers may have found it difficult actually to reduce their costs, they did not find it difficult to increase their output at current prices. In most industries, the main factor of production was labour and labour was both plentiful and cheap. It was easy enough to set more men and women on work; the problem, as many a poor law officer found, was to dispose of their output. The situation was, in short, one that is often found in countries in which the agricultural sector is large but agricultural productivity is low. High food prices meant that the industrial worker had little to spare for the purchase of manufactured goods, but the low output which made those prices high also limited the purchasing power of many agriculturalists. The labourer and cottager, irregularly employed and miserably paid, were poor customers. The small husbandmen, most of whose petty surpluses might be swallowed up in rent, were little better. Prosperity was largely confined to the landlords and more substantial farmers, and although their purchases of manufactured goods were no doubt considerable they were hardly enough to ensure a high level of industrial output. Much of their wealth went on personal services; much on building; much on luxuries and imports. Industrial activity was, moreover, further discouraged by the fact that the bulk of the population lived scattered in small communities with the result that

[1] J. St. John *Observations on the Land Revenue of the Crown* (1787), Appendix III.

much production was for local markets too small to encourage any high degree of specialisation. One of the most striking features that emerges from the probate inventories of the time is the extent to which the more prosperous artisans tended to diversify their interests instead of ploughing back their profits into their basic activity.

The effects of that situation on thought and policy are obvious enough. On the one hand, there was a series of attempts to check the production of industrial goods—or at least to restrict the number of industrial workers. The commercial crisis of 1551 was followed by a series of measures designed to prevent any repetition of the mushrooming of textile production that had characterised the preceding boom. Although it is possible that the Statute of Artificers was primarily designed to ensure an adequate supply of cheap agricultural labour—in a letter to Sir Thomas Smith, Cecil described it as 'a very good law agreed upon for indifferent allowance of servants' wages in husbandry'[1]—in its final form it placed serious restrictions on the flow of labour into industry. And although there is no evidence that the government, either central or local, took positive steps to enforce those restrictions, Mrs. Gay Davies has shown that common informers were sufficiently active to make them of some significance. Moreover, in the late sixteenth and early seventeenth centuries, many of the corporate towns reconstructed their gild systems and tightened up their bye-laws in an effort to ensure full employment for their citizens by suppressing the enterprise of those who did not share their freedom. On the other hand, men increasingly looked to the manipulation of foreign trade to solve the problems of industry. The curtailment of manufactured imports would create and stimulate the production of native substitutes for them; new markets overseas could make good the deficiencies of the market at home. Unfortunately, the circumstances of the time tended to favour the growth of imports rather than that of exports.

From the later middle ages until the eighteenth century, England's major export consisted of woollen textiles; no other English product —and certainly no other English manufacture—was in great demand abroad. In the late fifteenth and early sixteenth centuries Eng-

[1] Conyers Read, *Mr. Secretary Cecil and Queen Elizabeth*, (1959), p. 274.

land had enjoyed important competitive advantages in the production of the heavier fabrics suitable for the climate of north, central and eastern Europe and exports of those fabrics had risen substantially, with the consequence that more labour had found employment in the textile industry and that more land had been put down to grass. By the middle of the sixteenth century, however, that rise was virtually over. During the next hundred years such exports, for a complex variety of reasons admirably discussed by Dr. Supple, were to fluctuate around a trend that rose scarcely at all and by the reign of Charles I was undoubtedly falling.[1] By that reign, it is true, the trade in heavy woollens was being significantly and increasingly supplemented by a trade in the lighter and cheaper fabrics known as the new draperies. But under the early Stuarts those draperies were still very new, and for most of the century before the Civil War English industry can have received but little direct stimulus from expanding exports. Admittedly, that century was a time of great mercantile activity and saw the creation of great mercantile fortunes. But the aim and effect of much of that activity was less to increase the volume of English trade than to transfer that trade to English hands. Under the later Tudors, tariff changes and the cancellation of the privileges of the Hansards gave native merchants a predominant position in the shipment of goods from England. Under the early Stuarts, and to some extent even before, those goods were increasingly being shipped, not to some cross-channel entrepot, but to more distant regions whither they had previously been taken by Continental middlemen, and imports were more frequently being obtained in or near their countries of origin. By the reign of Charles I, moreover, a re-export trade in Asiatic and colonial produce was beginning to appear and Englishmen were carrying goods between foreign ports without ever bringing them to England itself. Thus commercial expansion took the form, not only of a slowly increasing export of native commodities, but also of a rapidly increasing export of commercial and shipping services. This export of services enriched the merchants, added to the national income, and led to a growth of imports. But

[1] B. E. Supple, *Commercial Crisis and Change in England, 1600-1642*, (1959). pp. 136-49.

its effects on industry were essentially indirect and ambivalent. Greater imports of raw materials such as wool, silk and cotton no doubt gave some stimulus to English manufactures: but greater imports of consumer goods must have had a contrary effect.

Modern experience suggests that economies in which the competition between alternative uses for land is keen and in which industry is sluggish are likely to see the development of two phenomena. There is likely to be a vigorous struggle for the occupancy and ownership of land; and ambitious young men are likely to seek in the professions the wealth that is not abundantly available in the business world. Tudor and Stuart England was characterised by both. 'Do not', wrote Winstanley, 'all strive to enjoy the Land? The Gentry strive for Land, the Clergy strive for Land, the Common people strive for Land; and Buying and selling is an Art whereby people endeavour to cheat one another of the Land.'[1] At the bottom of the social ladder there was a growing competition for agricultural holdings, a competition that was reflected in a steep rise of rents and entry fines. In the middle of the sixteenth century it had been usual to attribute that rise to the avarice of landlords, but by that century's end the more percipient observers saw that it had its roots in the struggle of tenant against tenant. Even from remote Pembrokeshire it was reported that whereas 'in tymes past... fewe sought leases for most commonly the Landlord rather made suite for a good tenante to take his lande then the tenant to the Landlord... and as for fynes yt was not a thinge knowne among them a hundred yeares past... nowe the poore tenants that lyved well in that golden world ys taughte to singe unto his Lord a newe songe... the worlde ys so altered with ye poore tenants that he standeth so in bodylie feare of his greedy neighbour, that ii or iii yeares eare his lease end he must bowe to his Lord for a newe Lease and must pinche yt out many yeares before to heape money together.'[2] Nor was that struggle surprising. It was the result, partly of the growth in population, but partly of the state of agricultural technique. A man's ability to profit from the rise in agricultural

[1] Quoted in Christopher Hill, *Puritanism and Revolution*, (1958), p. 153.
[2] G. Owen, *The Description of Pembrokeshire*, Cymmrodorian Society Record Series, (1892–7), Part I, p. 190.

prices obviously depended on his having a worthwhile surplus for sale; and since the limited range of knowledge at his disposal made if difficult to obtain that surplus by more intensive cultivation there was an obvious temptation to seek it by enlarging his farm. In practice, no doubt, the tendency thus to create larger farms was kept in check. But it was often kept in check by competing offers from desperate smallholders driven to offer rents greater than their agricultural output really justified.

Further up the social scale, there was a parallel competition for estates. 'For what purpose', wrote Sir Richard Weston, 'do soldiers, scholars, lawyers, merchants and men of all occupations and trades toil and labour with great affection but to get money, and with that money when they have gotten it but to purchase land?' Such men competed to purchase, not only manors, but also freeholds, copyholds and even long leaseholds. For, as an investment, land offered the attraction of relative safety combined with the prospect of a rising income. And, as a consumer-good, an estate, with the amenities and status that accompanied it, was among the most seductive that the age could offer.

The history of the professions in the sixteenth and seventeenth centuries has yet to be written, but at least its main outlines are becoming clear. As C. S. Lewis has pointed out, those centuries saw education move up the social scale. Grammar schools multiplied and the more successful among them significantly changed their social complexion. The universities not only expanded but were gradually converted into congeries of boarding schools for the sons of gentlemen. Increasingly, the Inns of Court served as finishing schools for men who had no intention of devoting themselves to the law. That growing demand for education may, in part, have reflected a growing demand for culture. But contemporary comment leaves no room for doubt but that education was looked upon mainly as an avenue leading, through the professions, to influence and affluence. For that reason, some were to argue that it should be denied to the sons of the lower orders and Bacon was to warn of the dangers of educating more persons than the market could absorb.

Both the vigorous demand for land and the enthusiasm for a

professional career may legitimately be held to reflect the relative unattractiveness of the alternative employments for capital and skill. In that sense, they appear as results of the slowness of economic growth. Yet in economic affairs cause and effect are not always clearly distinct, and the diversion of so many resources into those two channels may also be seen as one reason why that growth was, in fact, so slow. With respect to the demand for land the case is clear enough. The purchase of an estate did not necessarily mean any increase in the amount of real capital invested in agriculture; a rising rent roll might well represent the results of inflation and hard bargaining rather than of any growth in real output; the briskness of the land market was partly the result of a process whereby the savings of the professional and mercantile classes were used to finance the expenditure on consumption of those from whom they bought. It is difficult to believe that, in an age when capital accumulation was slow and the rate of interest was high, such was, from the point of view of the community, the most beneficial use to which savings could be put. Those contemporaries who attributed the growing commercial supremacy of the Dutch partly to the fact that, whereas English mercantile fortunes were often transmuted into land, the fortunes of the Dutch were retained in trade, did so with some justice.

With respect to the professions, the case is perhaps more tenuous. Professional services are an integral part of the national income; their growth in volume and quality no doubt made England richer; it would be ludicrous to dismiss the works of Shakespeare as products of the mis-allocation of economic resources. Yet two points may, perhaps, be made. The first is that, if contemporaries are to be believed, there was not always a close relationship between rewards obtained and the services rendered, and some men achieved wealth without adding much to the public welfare. The second is that, whatever was to be the case in later periods, in Tudor and Stuart England success in the professions depended on qualities very similar to those required for success in business. On the acquisitiveness and business capacity of lawyers it is needless to comment, for they were long to remain a feature of English life. According to at least one contemporary, medical men showed similar qualities; and the fact

that Barbon, Petty and Hugh Chamberlayne, three of the biggest
speculators of the later seventeenth century, were all doctors certainly
suggests some affinity between medicine and money-making. As the
Church became poorer, financial success within it came often to
depend upon the discreet purchase of benefices, the operation of those
benefices by means of dependent wage labour supplied by an ecclesiastical proletariat, and the astute exploitation of any real estate that such
benefices carried with them. Many public offices, it is clear, were treated less as contractual obligations than as a species of property that
could be bought, leased and mortgaged and that yielded its fruits in
the form of fees and perquisites which it was the incumbents' responsibility to maximise. Even University teaching, sometimes regarded ᴉ˹ the last resort of the unwordly, showed some of the same
characteristics. 'I am credibly informed', wrote Burleigh, 'that thorowe
the great stipendes of tutors and the little paines they doe take in the
instructinge and well governinge of their puples, not onely the poorer
sorte are not able to maintaine their children at the universitie; and
the ritcher be so corrupte with libertie and remissness so that the tutor
is more afrayed to displease his puple thorowe the desire of great
gaine, the which he haithe by his tutorage, then the puple is of his
tutor.'[1] The professions, it would seem, were absorbing talents that
the business world might well have used.

The vigorous demand for land and the scramble for professional
employment are, it has been suggested, found in many under-
developed economies. But in Tudor and Stuart England they were
encouraged, not only by the nature of the economy, but also by the
contemporary system of public finance. As John Aylmer pointed out
to his fellow-countrymen, that system was essentially one of light
taxation.[2]

'Now compare them (i.e. the Germans) with thee: and thou shalt
see howe happye thou arte. They eate hearbes: and thou Beefe

[1] J. B. Mullinger, *The University of Cambridge*, (1884), Vol. II, p. 398.
[2] Quoted in Geo. Orwell and Reginald Reynolds, *British Pamphleteers*, (1958), Vol. I, p. 31.

and Mutton. Thei rotes: and thou butter, chese and egges. Thei drinck commonly water: and thou good ale and beare. Thei go from the market with a sallet: and thou with good fleshe fill thy wallet. They lightlye never see anye sea fish: and thou has they belly full of it. They paye till theire bones rattle in their skin: and thou layest up for thy sonne and heir. Thou are twise or thrise in thy lifetime called uppon to healpe thy Countrye with a sub-sidie or contribution: and they daily pay and never cease. Thou livest like a Lorde, and they like dogges... Oh if thou knewest thou Englishe man in what welth thou livest and in how plentifull a Countrye: Thou wouldst vii times of the day fall flat on thy face before God, and geve him thanks, that thou wart born an English man, and not a french pezant, nor an Italyan, nor Almane.'

The attractions of light taxation are never difficult to perceive. But when it is accompanied by heavy government expenditure such attractions are apt to be delusive, since the alternative methods of financing that expenditure may well prove more burdensome. Such, it may be argued, was the position that obtained by the end of the sixteenth century. By that time the Crown was relying to a significant extent on the sale of privileges, which tended to restrict economic activity; on the creation and sale of offices, which drew more labour and enterprise into the performance of unnecessary professional duties; and upon land sales that tended to absorb the country's savings. There can be little doubt that one reason for the attractiveness of land as an investment was that royal sales kept its price lower than it would otherwise have been. It may well be significant that, as the sale of royal lands declined, the rate of interest tended to fall and men turned more of their attention to land drainage, land reclamation, and colonisation.

If it be granted that, in the century before the Civil War, circum-stances raised the questions of land use, land ownership, land occu-pancy, foreign trade, public office and public finance to the status of major issues, it is easy enough to see why the century may aptly be described as Tawney's. For each of these questions has been illuminated both by his own writings and by the work of those whom he has taught. Nor is that all. History is concerned, not only with men's behaviour, but also with their beliefs; and men's changing beliefs with respect to individual ambition, business enterprise, and economic innovation provide economic history with one of its most important themes. After the Restoration, those forces were to be increasingly sanctified by both theory and experience. But before that happy event neither theory nor experience offered them much support. The view that the golden age lay in the past, that men were living in a senile universe, that all change was the equivalent of biological decay was repeatedly advanced in the later sixteenth century and was expounded at length by Goodman in the reign of James I. Nor do Hakewill's attacks on that argument seem to have had much immediate effect. And Goodman found no difficulty in supporting his pessimism with appeals to contemporary economic experience. For at a time of rising food prices, low wages and growing pauperism it was easier to demonstrate that many men were becoming rich by methods which made others poor than to show that there was any increase in total wealth. Under such circumstance, the economic appetites inevitably became objects of suspicion and controversy, and the most perceptive accounts of contemporary attitudes to them are still those contained in the famous introduction to Wilson's *Discourse on Usury* and in *Religion and the Rise of Capitalism*. In the history of social thought, as well as in the history of economic practice, Tawney has made the late sixteenth and early seventeenth centuries his own.

10

Influenza and Inflation in Tudor England

Early in the seventeenth century George Hakewill took up the task of refuting those arguments in favour of cosmic degeneration that were being so persuasively re-stated by Geoffrey Goodman. To him, the proposition that the whole universe was in a state of inevitable and irreversible decay was not only offensive to the honour of the Creator but also inimical both to sound morality and to social and economic endeavour. So he wrote:

> My third reason for the penning and publishing of this discourse is that the contrary opinion thereunto seems not a little to rebate and blunt the edge of men's virtuous endeavours. For being once thoroughly persuaded in themselves that, by a fatal kind of necessity and course of times, they are cast unto those straites that notwithstanding all their striving and industry it is impossible that they should rise to the pitch of their noble and renowned predecessors, they begin to yield to the times and necessity, being resolved that their endeavours are all in vain and that they strive against the stream ... Besides the same opinion serves to make them more careless both in regard of their present fortunes and in providing for posterity. For when they consider how many thousand yeares nature hath beene, as it were, in a fever *Hectique*, daylie consuming and wasting away by degrees, they inferre that in reason she cannot hold out long and therefore it were to as little purpose to plant trees or to erect lasting buildings ... as to provide new apparrell for a sicke man.

With the contention that men were inferior to the ancients in strength, size or longevity Hakewill dealt expeditiously and at least to this own satisfaction. Women and fish proved more difficult, and the arguments relating to them could be answered only with the aid of sin and the Dutch:

> The greatest of Physitians and the founder of that Science affirms that women neither lose their hair nor grow diseased in their feet. But now we see they are both bald and gowty, not because their nature is changed but the course of their life. They have forfeited the privilege of their sex by their own viciousness, and having together with their modesty put off their womanhood, they are deservedly plagued with men's diseases.

> But it is said that though the waters decay not yet the fish ... at leastwise in regard of their number, are much decayed ... the Seas being grown fruitless and barren, as is portended, in regard of former ages and that so it appears on record in our haven towns. But if such a thing be (Which I can neither affirm nor deny, having not searched into it myself) themselves who make the objection shape a sufficient answar thereto, by telling us it may be so by an extraordinary judgment of God (as he dealt with the Egyptians) in the death of our

fish for the abuse of our flesh-pots, or by the intrusion of the Hollander, who carried from our coast such store as we might better load ourselves with . . . And no doubt but were our coasts spared for some space of years it would again afford as great plenty as ever.

It was only when he turned to agriculture that Hakewill regained confidence and carried conviction:

> But that which further persuadeth me that neither the goodness of the soyle, nor the seasonableness of the weather, nor the industry of the husbandman is now inferior to that of former ages is this, that both his fine and rent being raised, the apparell and education of his children more chargeable, and the rates of publique payments more burdensome, yet he fares better and lays up more money in his purse than usually in those times he did. Besides it is certain that if we compare time with time the famines of former ages were more grievous than ours . . . touching famine verily we and our age have seen nothing . . . It will be said, if the plenty of corn and victuals be as great as in former ages, how comes it to pass that their prices are so much inhanced? But if . . . together with the inhancing of prices we likewise take into our considerations the inhancing of coin, it will appear that the prices of things are not so much inhanced as is supposed . . . Whereunto may be added the plenty of coin and multitude of men . . . Either of which asunder, but much more both together, must needs be a means of raising the prices of all things.[1]

In economic matters Hakewill was but an amateur; his fleeting reference to capital accumulation was too specific to sound impressive and his reference to currency debasement was made in unfashionable terms. Yet to his explanation of Tudor price movements historians have been able to add remarkably little, though they have added that little at remarkable expense. For the broad upswing of prices his explanation still stands, and recent attempts to be more precise about specific parts of that upswing have as yet been fruitful only in exciting speculations. The purpose of this note is to suggest a possibility that future speculators may be willing to admit into their calculations.

Of the many ways in which Tudor price data may legitimately be arranged, two are demonstrated in the following tables:

Table 1. *Percentage Increases in the Decennial Means of Grain Prices.*[2]

Period	Wheat (T.R.)	Wheat (B)	Barley
1490/9–1540/9	91	91	45
1540/9–1560/9	41	70	45
1560/9–1630/9	239	133	160

[1] Geo. Hakewill: *An Apologie or Declaration of the Power and Providence of God in the Government of the World.* (2nd ed. 1630) pp. 21–2, 134, 145, 147–8.

[2] The percentages of wheat (B), and barley are calculated from decennial means prepared by Lord Beveridge for the International Price History and contained in boxes T1 and T2 of the Beveridge Price History MSS at the London School of Economics. The percentages of wheat (T.R.) are calculated from data collected by Thorold Rogers and are included to remind readers of a minor but irritating difficulty. Both the Beveridge and the Thorold Rogers data show rises in wheat prices of approximately

Table 2. *Median Daily Wages Rates of Building Workers in Cambridge, Canterbury, Dover and Eton.*[1]

Period	Carpenters	Labourers
1500–4	6d	4d
1540–4	7d– 8d	5d
1560–4	12d	8d
1630–4	12d–20d	10d–14d

Those tables suggest at least two important similarities between the first half of the sixteenth century and the years 1570–1639, each of which periods is known to have been one of monetary inflation. In each of them cereal prices rose at a rate that, although high enough to impress (and perhaps to over-impress) historians by its cumulative result, was too low to evoke much response from contemporaries. Tudor and Stuart Englishmen were alive to the agonies and dangers of harvest failures. But few of them spent much time looking back over their shoulders at the prices which their fathers had enjoyed, and a long upward drift of those prices at a compounded rate of little more than one per cent – or even less – per annum was insufficient to silence for long the farmer's traditional complaint that when crops do not fail corn is too cheap. In 1593 the restrictions on the conversion of arable land to pasture were eased although grain prices were as high as they had been thirty years earlier when those restrictions had been imposed.[2] And Sir Simonds D'Ewes' classic exposition of the horrors of plenty relates to a year – 1620/1 – when wheat was at a level that would have been considered high at any time before the mid-nineties.[3] Secondly, in each of these periods money wages were markedly less buoyant than grain prices, and real wage rates may reasonably be presumed to have fallen. Yet, the extent to which that fall may be attributed to similar causes in each period is still uncertain, for wages and grain prices may diverge for a variety of reasons that lack even the convenience of being mutually exclusive. For the later years it is easy enough to accept the view that population growth was keeping wages down and forcing food prices up, since there is some supporting evidence that population was growing. But whether that process was of any significance in the first half of the sixteenth century we are

the same magnitude between the end of the fifteenth century and the eve of the Civil War. But the two series approach the same destination by different routes and, in particular, diverge significantly during the early years of Elizabeth's reign. Consequently, some arguments based on the relative movements of the prices of different commodities founder if one set of wheat prices is substituted for the other. Fortunately the argument developed in this note is not among them.

[1] Calculated from tables contained in box W2 of the Beveridge Price Hist. MSS. The Oxford wage figures used by my colleagues Professor Phelps Brown and Miss Sheila Hopkins in their study of wages during this period rise rather more slowly than those given here, for carpenters were still earning only 6d in the early 40s & only 10d in the 60s. But the differences are not of a kind to invalidate the argument of this note.

[2] 35 Eliz. c. 7.

[3] 'The rates of all sorts of corn were so extremely low as it made the very prices of land fall from twenty years' purchase to sixteen or seventeen ... all farmers generally murmured at this plenty and cheapness; and the poorer sort that would have been glad but a few years before of the coarse rye-bread did now, usually, traverse the markets to find out the finer wheats, as if nothing else would serve their use or please their palates'. *The Autobiography and Correspondence of Sir Simonds D'Ewes*, (ed. J. O. Halliwell 1845), Vol. I, p. 180.

as yet too ignorant to say. Sticky wage rates are not, by themselves, conclusive evidence of population growth, and according to the author of the *Supplication of the Poor Commons* the labour market at this time was glutted because rising rents forced many farmers to employ their own children instead of educating them and employing others.[1] With respect to each period it must always be borne in mind that, in terms of grain, England was not a self-contained economy. The great stream of Baltic corn passed southwards along her coast; the great staple for grain lay just across the North Sea at Amsterdam; to that stream and staple England sometimes contributed, from them she sometimes drew. Of the volume of her overseas trade in grain we know but little, for the customs records are fragmentary and it was a matter of common knowledge – or at least of common belief – that much grain was smuggled out. Yet two points may, perhaps, legitimately be made. The customs figures collected by Gras suggest that, as was to be expected, the bulk of grain exports went out through the ports of eastern England.[2] According to a report to Salisbury in 1604, shipments from eastern ports quickly raised prices as far inland as Warwickshire.[3] And since most of the price series used by Beveridge and Rogers come from the eastern half of England, it may well be that their indices were significantly affected by exports. The second point is that both Gras's figures and contemporary comments suggest that exports were more substantial in the later period, when European prices were rising, than they had been in the earlier sixteenth century when those prices had been stable. In particular, they suggest that exports were particularly buoyant in the 'seventies and early 'eighties. It was during these years that Harrison published his well-known explanation of how high prices could co-exist with physical plenty:

> Albeit that there be much more ground eared now almost in every place than hath been of late years, yet such a price of corn continueth in each town and market without any just cause (except it be that landlords do get licence to carry corn out of the land only to keep up prices for their own private gain and ruin of the commonwealth) that the artificer and poor labouring man is not able to reach unto it.[4]

And it was probably during these years that the farmers of Norfolk spelled out the need for exports to keep grain prices up and the consequences that were likely to follow if exports were curtailed:

> First a great nomber of fermours who have in thes late yeares hyrid landes both of noblemen, gentil, and others shalbe utterly undon seing thei shall not be able to paie ther rentes and defraie ther other charges yf the prices of corne be overthrowen.
> Secondly, as the high prices of corne are known to have been a great occasion of increase of tilledge, so the pluckinge downe of the price cannot but worke a

[1] J. Strype, *Ecclesiastical Memorials*, (Oxford, 1822), I, pp. 616–17.
[2] N. S. B. Gras, *The Evolution of the English Corn Market*, Cambridge, (1915), Appendix C.
[3] *H. M. C. Salisbury*, XVI, pp. 464–5.
[4] *Elizabethan England* (ed. F. J. Furnivall), p. 96.

decaye of tilledge. And herby manie mischiefes will ensue, for a multitude of your highness subjectes will therbie be unsett on worke and being idle will fall to comytt many evil partes and offences against your Lawes, for which many of them are like to be brought to their ende.[1]

Since grain prices began to rise in the 'seventies, long before there was any concrete evidence of renewed monetary inflation, it is tempting to believe that they did so as a response to the growth of both English and European population; in fact, since grain was normally bought for specie, grain exports may have done something to renew monetary inflation. And that the export-induced buoyancy of grain prices was neither unobserved by, nor objectionable to, a Parliament consisting predominantly of landowners is made clear by the fact that the maximum price at which wheat might be exported without licence was raised from 6s. 8d. a quarter in 1555 to 10s. in 1563, 20s. in 1593, 26s.8d. in 1604 and 32s. in 1624.[2] It seems likely that in this matter Parliament, like the farmers of Norfolk, drew less on economic theory than upon their own experience and that, at a time when continental prices were rising, exports did act in some measure as a ratchet to prevent the increased production of corn from significantly reducing the prices by which it had been inspired. By contrast, there was another factor that was probably much more important in the early period than it was to be in the later. In the early sixteenth century the prices that rose most rapidly seem to have been those of meat, while those of wool were inflated by the prosperity of the export trade in cloth. There may therefore have been some substance in the contemporary argument that, by encouraging the conversion of arable land to pasture and the overstocking of the commons, the prices of livestock products drew those of cereals up after them. For the later period neither the relative price movements, nor contemporary comment, suggest that any similar sequence was operating.

But although, on close examination, the similarities between the early sixteenth century and the years 1570–1639 may not be very great, it is clear that those periods resembled each other far more than either resembled the two decades that separated them. The grain prices collected by Thorold Rogers and Beveridge all soared between the middle 'forties and early 'fifties under the impact of currency manipulation, but then fluctuated around a fairly stable trend until the early 'seventies. The series differ in detail; but they all suggest two decades during which the great upswing in grain prices had been temporarily halted. By contrast wage rates were far more buoyant than they had been earlier, or were to be later, and in Cambridge (though not Oxford), Canterbury, Eton and Dover they continued to rise until by the 'sixties they were double what they had been at the end of the fifteenth century. Thus two periods in which cereal prices rose while real wages fell were separated by an interval in which cereal prices remained virtually stable while real wages made some recovery. It is the existence of this interval that calls for an explanation. Were it simply that the rise in grain prices was halted the ex-

[1] *Tudor Economic Documents* (ed. R. H. Tawney & E. Power), I p. 162.
[2] D. G. Barnes, *A History of the English Corn Laws from 1660–1846* (London, 1930) p. 3.

planation might not be far to seek. During the 'fifties and 'sixties the Mint was relatively inactive save during the deflationary recoinage of 1561, so that the pressure from monetary inflation was also temporarily eased. And the sluggishness of foreign trade may, by depressing wool prices, have induced some reconversion of pasture to arable. Yet neither of those circumstances provides any explanation of the buoyancy of wages.

For both the check to food prices and the rise in wages, Mr Brenner has suggested a demographic explanation. For he writes:

> By the middle of the sixteenth century food prices had risen to an extent that incomes no longer permitted early marriages and the survival of large families. The rate of population growth abated and for nearly three decades food prices no longer rose sharply in excess of industrial prices, rents almost stagnated, and both nominal and real wages rose again.[1]

But he quotes no contemporary evidence of changing marriage or birth rates. Nor is his argument inherently probable. In order to affect the supply of labour in the late 'fifties, Mr Brenner's Malthusian checks would presumably have to have started operating at latest by the early 'forties; and in the early 'forties real wages were substantially higher than they were to be at the end of the sixteenth century when they do not seem to have had any depressing effect on the labour supply. The purpose of this note is to suggest that, although the explanation was probably demographic, it is more likely to be found in an epidemic to which the Tudor Englishman could offer less effective resistance than he could to an epidemic of chastity. Nor is there any difficulty in finding one to fit that role, for it has long been known that the catastrophic harvests of 1555 and 1556 were followed by one of the major influenza epidemics in English history.

The story as told in the contemporary chronicles was summarised by Strype in a passage that will bear repeating.

> What diseases and sicknesses every where prevailed! the like whereof had never been known before, both for the lasting and mortality of them: which being hot burning fevers, and other strange diseases, began in the great dearth 1556, and increased more and more the two following years. In the summer 1557, they raged horribly throughout the realm, and killed an exceeding great number of all sorts of men, but especially gentlemen, and men of great wealth. So many husbandmen and labourers also died, and were sick, that in harvest time, in divers places, men would have given one acre of corn to reap and carry in another. In some places corn stood and shed on the ground for lack of workmen. In the latter end of the year, quartan agues were so common among men, women, and young children also, that few houses escaped: and these agues were not only common, but to most persons very dangerous, especially such as had been sick of the burning fevers before. In 1558, in the summer, about August, the same fevers raged again in such manner, as never plague or pestilence, I think, saith my author, killed a greater number. If the people of the realm had been divided into four parts, certainly three parts of thos four should have been

---

[1] 'The Inflation of Prices in England, 1551-1650', (*Econ. Hist. Rev.*, Second Series, XV, 1962, p. 284).

found sick. And hereby so great a scarcity of harvestmen, that those which remained took twelve pence for that which was wont to be done for three pence. In some shires no gentleman almost escaped, but either himself, or his wife, or both, were dangerously sick, and very many died: so that divers places were left void of ancient justices and men of worship to govern the country. Many that kept twenty or thirty in their houses, had not three or four able to help the residue that were sick. In most men's houses, the master, dame, and servants, were all sick, in such sort, that one could not help another. The winter following also, the quartan agues continued in like manner, or more vehemently than they had done last year. At this time also died many priests, that a great number of parish churches, in divers places of the realm, were unserved, and on curates could be gotten for money.[1]

That epidemic, or rather series of epidemics, obviously fits into the chronology of price movements neatly enough, for it was in the late 'fifties that the upward movement of grain prices hesitated while wages continued to rise. Yet the literary evidence is not by itself sufficient for the historian's purpose. Contemporaries were impressed by the large numbers who fell sick (Harrison said a quarter of the population), by the fact that even the well-to-do were unable to evade it, and by the satisfactory ecclesiastical consequences of removing a substantial number of Catholic clergy. Haddon even believed that both Mary and Pole were influenza victims. Yet contemporaries leave unanswered the question of how lethal and widespread the epidemic actually was.[2] Some two hundred years ago Thomas Short tried to answer that question from parish registers, but the registers that he found were few and their geographical distribution is unknown.[3] A more definite answer is suggested by the statistics of wills proved in various consistory courts. Admittedly, the relation between the number of wills proved and the number of actual deaths may normally be slight, for wills are not made by a random sample of the population and over a long period their totals are affected both by changes in testamentary habits and by the better registration of the proceedings arising from them. But in the short run a large rise, followed by a similar or larger fall, in the number of wills proved is as good a measure of an epidemic as one is likely to find. Hence the relevant figures for a number of courts are set out in Table 3.

And a similar rise and fall is reflected in the figures for the enormous diocese of Lincoln although the cases for that diocese are indexed in such a way as to make precise tabulation impossible.[4] Such figures clearly suggest that the

---

[1] *Op. cit.*, III, part II, pp. 156–7.

[2] In 1561 Sir Thomas Smith produced his 'Dialogue on the Queen's Marriage' in the course of which a character was made to assert that, possibly because of God's disapproval of Mary's behaviour' in the last two years of her reign so many of her subjects were made away, what with the executions of sword and fire, and what by sickness, that the third part of men in England was consumed' (Strype, *op. cit.*, vol. III, part II, p. 147). But, given the licence that orators and poets normally claim, that remark cannot be read to mean more than that the losses were substantial.

[3] C. Creighton, *A History of Epidemics in Great Britain*, (Cambridge, 1891), I, p. 405.

[4] These figures have been compiled from ..ne indexes of wills published for York by the Yorkshire Archaeological Society, for Norwich by the Norfolk Record Society, and for Lichfield, Lincoln, Leicester, Gloucester, Worcester and the Prerogative Court of Canterbury by the British Record Society.

Table 3. *Average Number of Wills proved annually in*

Quinquennium	Canterbury	York	Lichfield	Norwich	Leicester	Worcester & Gloucester
1551–5	412	486	412	175	51	236
1556–60	714	1,250	1,018	459	199	903
1561–5	379	494	367	133	89	259
1566–70	400	567	293	121	107	298

epidemic was both widespread and highly lethal. How lethal it is impossible to say, but in a confessedly speculative note some reflections on this point may perhaps be allowed. According to Gregory King the normal birth and death rates at this time were about 35 and 31 per thousand respectively.[1] Table 3 suggests that for a quinquennium, death rates averaged about 150 per cent above the normal. A death rate of some 77 per thousand would, if combined for five years with a birth rate of 35, reduce the population by almost twenty per cent and might reduce the wage-earning population by an even greater proportion since the ranks of the wage-earners would be thinned not only by death but also by movement to replenish the diminished number of husbandmen and employers. Such reasoning obviously contains too many assumptions to permit of any firm conclusion that the number of wage-earners fell by a fifth. But, since a considerably smaller fall than a fifth would be enough to affect wage rates, it demonstrates that no wildly improbable demographic implications lie hid in the proposition that one effect of the famines and epidemics of the 'fifties was to give a temporary buoyancy to wage rates.

That the buoyancy was only temporary is made clear by Table 2. To some extent epidemics anticipate deaths that would have occurred in the near future and the small number of wills proved during the 'sixties suggests that during that decade the death rate may have been low; the steady growth in the number of wills proved that began in the 'seventies is likely to have been partly caused by a growing population; and the fluctuations in that number suggest that, although the influence of the epidemics is clearly observable in the 'eighties and 'nineties, it was not on the same scale as in the reign of Mary. And by the 'nineties Lambard could treat the growth of population as a matter of common knowledge:

> That the number of our people is multiplied it is both demonstrable to the eye and evident in reason, considering on the one side that nowadays not only young folks of all sorts but churchmen also of each degree do marry and multiply at liberty, which was wont not to be, and on the other side we have not, God be thanked, been touched with any extreme mortality, either by sword or sickness, that might abate the overgrown number of us.[2]

---

[1] *Natural and Political Observations and Conclusions upon the State and Condition of England* (1696), reprinted in *Two Tracts by Gregory King*, ed. G. E. Barnett (Johns Hopkins, 1936), p. 25.

[2] Conyers Read (ed.), *William Lambarde and Local Government*, (Cornell, 1962), p. 182.

But the fact that the fall in population was only temporary does not deprive it of all interest. For one thing, as this note has argued, it provides a possible explanation of a marked kink in Tudor price curves. For another, it offers a possible explanation of the rather puzzling collection of statutes passed in 1563. They include the famous Statute of Artificers (that not only provided for the fixing of maximum wages rate but allowed men to be conscripted for labour in harvest), an act for the better relief of the poor, another for raising the price at which corn might be exported, and another for making more effective the ban on the conversion of arable land to pasture.[1] It has never been easy to reconcile these statutes with each other or with the commercial depression that obtained when they were under discussion. The fixing of maximum wages might have been a deflationary measure consequent upon the recoinage of 1561, but why was it accompanied by an act designed to raise the price of corn? Increased provision for the relief of the poor might be required because of the unemployment associated with a depression, but in that case why did action have to be taken to check the rise in wages? The urge to convert arable land to pasture is traditionally associated with high wool prices; why did it have to be guarded against when wool prices were low? Perhaps no reconciliation between these measures is to be expected, for much of Tudor economic legislation took the form of private members' bills and different members might well manage to recruit support for incompatible measures. Yet a sudden fall in the population would provide a reconciliation of a sort. A decline in the number of adults would not only make labour scarce and wages high but would also leave a larger number of dependents to be cared for by means of poor relief; the fall in the number of adults would depress the price of corn as well as raise the price of labour; and dearer labour might well encourage a switch from arable to pasture despite the sluggishness of wool and textile prices. At least, no student of the period ought to be surprised or shocked by the suggestion that the famous Statute of Apprentices is as likely to have been the result of an epidemic of influenza as of a sudden outbreak of the intellectual malady known as 'mercantilism'.

Finally, the proposition that there was a temporary but sizeable drop in the population in the middle of the sixteenth century would seem to have more interesting general implications. The demographic history of the sixteenth and seventeenth centuries is a subject for which our evidence is slender but about which assumptions, whether implicit or explicit, must inevitably be made. It is generally believed that the population of England approximately doubled between the end of the fourteenth and the end of the seventeenth century. Few, if any, can believe that it grew at a uniform and constant rate between those dates. Little is known of the periods in which that growth was slowed down or reversed. Medieval historians seem generally reluctant to assume that much growth took place before the second half of the fifteenth century; it can be argued with some degree of plausibility that growth was less vigorous in the middle than at either the beginning or the end of the seventeenth century. But what of the years from the later fifteenth century to the reign of Charles I?

[1] 5 Eliz. c. 4, c. 3, c. 5 and c. 2.

That growth was uniform and continuous for a century and a half is unlikely. That it started slowly and then accelerated appears sometimes to be assumed, although no obvious reason for that acceleration presents itself. The data in this note suggests that there may have in fact been two periods of growth separated by one of temporary recession. In that case one might expect to find signs of population pressure appearing, diminishing and then re-appearing with greater vigour. Nor is it impossible to find some data that appear to support such a sequence. Rents seem to have risen more vigorously before 1550 and after 1570 than they did in between those years. The literature of distress produced by the 'forties was separated from that of the 'eighties and 'nineties by Harrison's eupeptic account of English life in the 'sixties or early 'seventies. The case would obviously be stronger if there were matching evidence from the behaviour of those who most obviously benefited from the growth of population – the landlords and larger farmers. But any such evidence that might have existed was masked by the intrusion of politics. Both the fifteen-forties and the last decade and a half of the century – each a time when the level of rents and prices suggests that landlords and farmers may have been enjoying the effects of population pressure – were periods of heavy military expenditure that was met largely by direct taxation and the sale of Crown lands. It was upon the landlords and farmers that much of that taxation fell and to them that many of the Crown lands were sold. It may be that the fruits of population pressure made it easier for them to meet the royal needs, but it would be illegitimate to deduce simply from their ability do to so the fact that they were enjoying such fruits. When Elizabeth's military expenditure came to an end the prosperity of landlords and some farmers was clearly revealed in rural re-building, in the growth of London, and in the development of a crisis in the balance of payments. Both rural re-building and the growth of London began before 1604, but it seems likely that they both accelerated as the demands of the government fell off. The trade statistics are too fragmentary to support any conclusive argument, yet they point to an interesting possibility. During the last decade of the sixteenth and the first decade of the seventeenth century there was a slow expansion of exports; in its earlier stages it seems to have resulted in an influx of bullion and an inflation of the currency; in its later, to an inflow of commodities that by 1610 had brought the Mint to a standstill. It is tempting to believe that this change not only coincided with, but in part arose from, the diversion of farming and landlord profits from the purchase of Crown lands and the payment of taxes to private consumption. But for a similar diversion in the middle of the century it would be idle to look, for the high level of government expenditure continued until the late 'fifties. Thus this argument must end on a speculative note. Yet perhaps this is as it should be. For many years Professor Postan has been urging his colleagues to speculate more; it is perhaps fitting that at least one article in a number of the Review dedicated to him should follow that advice.

11

The Growth of London

Since it is the current fashion among historians to dress up their guesses with statistics, perhaps this essay too had better start with some figures. We do not know the exact population of London in the early seventeenth century. A census of 1631, it is true, showed 130,000 residents in the City proper, but that census might be unreliable, and, in any case, by this time men already talked and thought of a greater London, a London that stretched westward as far as Long Acre and Westminster, that included Clerkenwell in the north and Southwark across the river, that pushed long fingers of ribbon development along the roads to Shoreditch, to Bethnal Green, to Limehouse, to Rotherhithe and to Bermondsey. By the time of the Civil War the population of this area may have reached a quarter of a million. Already one Englishman in twenty may have been a Londoner.

By contrast, it is doubtful whether any provincial city had more than 20,000 inhabitants, and reasonably certain that only four or five had as many as 10,000. Thus, London differed from other towns not so much in degree as in kind. It was unique by virtue of its size as well as by virtue of its wealth. And to many historians that simple fact alone helps to explain much of what happened under the early Stuarts. They have observed the impact on English agriculture of the City's demand for food and the impact on English mining of its demand for fuel. They have rejoiced at the good fortune whereby London was able to maintain a commercial theatre when Shakespeare and his fellows were available to write for it.

But before going further with an attempt to consider the possible relations between what contemporaries thought of as this monstrous growth and the social tensions of the time, it is well to begin with a word of warning. It is important to remember that civil war is apt to produce situations and to breed emotions that the historian cannot safely read back into the pre-war period. Early in the Civil War, when the membership of both Lords and Commons was split, and before Cromwell's New Model Army had come into being, it was tempting to see the conflict very largely as one of London against the crown and the provinces. Thus it is easy to understand how a parliamentary pamphleteer could attempt to inspire enthusiasm by telling of the cavalier's prejudice against the City, how they had already shared the various properties out amongst themselves and resolved to murder their creditors 'so they say, "We shall be both out of debt and have money to boot." ' And it is equally easy to see that a Royalist could declare:

> If [posterity] shall ask who would have pulled the crown from the King's head, taken the government off the hinges, dissolved Monarchy, enslaved the laws, and ruined their country; say, twas the proud, unthankful, schismatical, rebellious, bloody City of London.[1]

But the pre-war evidence shows a much less melodramatic state of affairs. Although it is true that provincial merchants complained of the arrogance and success of their London competitors, and the provincial preachers thought of Londoners as peculiarly addicted to sin, in general the links between the capital and the country were close and their relationships were both amicable and mutually profitable. And although both James and Charles tried to check the growth of London, in this they were only continuing a policy that Elizabeth had begun at the request of the Lord Mayor and aldermen.

In fact, if social conflict means anything more than the tension and friction to be found in all human communities, it is difficult to find signs of it in early Stuart London. But of normal tension and friction there was plenty, for these are the accompaniments of change, and the growth of London was perhaps the greatest change

[1] *Somers Tracts* (1810), iv. 598.

that was happening at this time. Since London was the largest of English towns, it threw up on a large scale the social difficulties that elsewhere were still only just visible. And since it was the only really large town, it created problems peculiar to itself. Let us take those two categories in turn.

Any seventeenth-century corporate town, including the City of London itself, can crudely but conveniently be thought of as being divided into three social groups. At the bottom of the pyramid was the mass of wage-earners who provided the physical labour that an unmechanized community required. They were generally poor, and for the most part unskilled, and even those who had learned a trade were forbidden to practise it since they had not been admitted into the freedom of the town. Above them was a thinner layer of trades-men and skilled artisans who, as free citizens, were entitled to set up business on their own, but whose scale of operations was usually extremely modest. And at the top was a small elite of wealthier business and professional men who monopolized the civic govern-ment.

In any town constructed in this way, there were three issues which could create a ferment. The first was the need to prevent the number of the labouring poor from exceeding the local demand for their labour. The larger the town the more difficult this was; and in the case of London the problem reached crisis dimensions. For the capital was the obvious Mecca for the ambitious and the footloose; it was the obvious market in which the out-of-work labourer could hope to get casual employment; it was by far the most promising milieu for the thief, the prostitute and the professional beggar. Moreover, as contemporaries complained, the influx of these people was en-couraged by some London property-owners.

> The desire of Profit greatly increaseth Buildings and so much the more for that this great concourse of all sorts of people drawing near unto the City, every man seeketh out places, high-ways, lanes and covert corners to build upon, if it be but sheds, cottages and small tenements for people to lodge in, which have not any means either to live or to employ themselves about any other manner of thing, than either to beg, or steal, by which

means of idleness it comes to pass that in some one parish there are above two thousand people which do live without any man's knowledge how, not using any manner of art or trade. This sort of covetous builders exact greater rents, and do daily increase them, insomuch that a poor handicraftsman is not able by his painful labour to pay the rent of a small tenement and feed his family. These builders neither regard the good of the commonwealth, the preservation of the health of the City, the maintenance of honest tradesmen, neither do they regard of what base condition soever their tenants are, or what lewd and wicked practices soever they use so as their exacted rents be duly paid, the which for the most part they receive either weekly or monthly.[2]

And while some created slums in this way by throwing up flimsy cottages for letting at inflated rents to immigrants, others did so by converting barns and stables into dwellings or by subdividing large but decayed houses into a multiplicity of tenements. So from the fifteen-eighties onwards the City authorities had repeatedly pointed out the dangers of the situation. A particularly detailed account of them is set out in a privy council order of 1632.

This day was read again the petition presented by the Lord Mayor, Aldermen and Commons of the City of London in which they remonstrate that the freedom of London which was heretofore of very great esteem is grown to be of little worth by reason of the extraordinary enlargement of the suburbs where great numbers of trades and handicraftsmen do enjoy without charge equal benefit with the freemen of the City of London. And that the city on every side is much pestered with great multitudes of newly erected tenements which of late times have been and now are in building which daily draw multitudes of people especially of the meaner sort and many loose persons . . . and by occasion of these new erected buildings the markets in London are forestalled and the prices of all victuals raised, the pipes that convey water to the citizens are built upon, and it is not to be doubted that from these new buildings when the streets

[2] Quoted in N. G. Brett-James, *The Growth of Stuart London* (1936), pp. 98–9.

shall be paved much gravel, sand and soil will be conveyed into the river and navigation both eastwards and westwards thereby prejudiced. And likewise an apparent danger may grow to the City and suburbs in case of infection in regards that the City is encompassed with new erected tenements, the suburbs being now grown far bigger than the city.[3]

Consequently, from 1580 onwards there was a long stream of royal proclamations on the matter. These forbade the subdividing of old houses into tenements, and the erection of new dwellings without licence. They laid down specifications to which builders were to conform, and they established what a later generation would have called a Green Belt around the City. It is obvious that such measures did not stop the growth of London's population, and in so far as they discouraged building they may well have intensified those problems of overcrowding, high rents and public health that they were designed to solve.

And at the other end of the social scale, the mere size of London also made serious a tension that was comparatively unimportant elsewhere. Traditionally, the urban artisan producing consumer goods for a local market, sold direct to his customers without the aid of any middleman, and in most provincial towns this was still the normal procedure. But in some of London's more fashionable trades the functions of the retailer were becoming separated from those of the actual producer. This was not surprising in itself. Not only do large markets normally encourage specialization and the division of labour, but in a large city there are good reasons why retailing should be concentrated along the main thoroughfares while actual production is carried on in the back streets or even in the suburbs. Yet the separation inevitably led to fears that the few and relatively wealthy shopkeepers would exploit the more numerous and much poorer artisans. And when those artisans came to depend for the supply of their raw materials on the same shopkeepers that distributed their products, their fears were increased. And the agitation of the small London master craftsman against the growing subjection to capitalist middlemen is one of the most prominent themes of

[3] Public Record Office, Privy Council Register, 29 Nov., 1632.

London history under the early Stuarts. A typical expression of his views can be found in the complaints of the leather-dressers (the glovers, pointmakers and white tawyers) against the leather-sellers.

> For whereas in all other trades, though the shopkeepers grow-ing rich do make the workmen their underlings, yet they suffer them according to their increase of ability to become like them-selves, and in the meantime to exercise the favour and privilege of their company and society; and though in some trades the shopkeepers sell to the workmen their materials, yet they take them again from them wrought and manufactured at reasonable rates, as Goldsmiths, Skinners, Silkmen and divers others. But the Leathersellers who pretend themselves to be of the same trade with the Glovers, Pointmakers and White Tawyers if they once put their griping hands betwixt the Grower or the Merchant and any of the said Trades they never part with the commodities they buy till they sell them at their own pitched rates without either regard or care whether the workmen be able to make his money thereof or no.[4]

The traditional instrument for the protection of an artisan's interest was, of course, his gild. But by the early seventeenth cen-tury the control of virtually every City gild had passed out of the hands of its artisan members. As a result, the early Stuarts received a long series of demands, either for the reform of the existing gilds or for the separate organization of the artisans. And, in fact, new gilds of small masters were numerous and were found, for example, among the felt-makers, the glovers, the skinners, the pinmakers and many others. But organization by itself solved little, for the bargain-ing power of the shopkeepers and middlemen still remained pre-dominant. Hence some of these gilds developed what may be thought of as a bastard form of co-operation. A common fund was set up for the purchase of raw materials and for the repurchase of finished products from members. But since the members of the gild were poor, the necessary capital had to be obtained from outside. The Pinmakers Company, for example, got their finance from the

[4] Quoted in G. Unwin, *Industrial Organization in the Sixteenth and Seven-teenth Centuries* (1904), p. 129.

government for they were able to negotiate a contract with the king. Usually, however, a new gild could only get its stock or capital from a private capitalist—and often from the very same man who had been instrumental in getting them a charter—and thus the artisans bound themselves to a single monopolist in place of the hated shopkeepers. Their last stage was seldom more prosperous than the first, and this struggle of the artisans against control by men wealthier than themselves is perhaps the nearest approach to a real social conflict that seventeenth century London could show.

But from the point of view of the Lord Mayor and aldermen another issue was more immediately important. They, like the magistrates of every other corporate town, were concerned to maintain the value of the City's privileges by restricting production and distribution to those who had been admitted to the City's freedom. Yet, even more than the magistrates of provincial towns, they found that policy difficult to enforce. It was not easy to suppress interlopers in the crowded wards of the City. If suppressed in the City, they easily moved into the prosperous suburbs, where the City had no jurisdiction. When Charles offered to extend the City's jurisdiction over the suburbs the Lord Mayor and aldermen refused to add to their responsibilities. And when, as a result, Charles created a separate corporation for Westminster and the other suburbs, it looked as though the privileged position of London's citizens might well be eroded.

Despite the size of London, it would be possible to treat all these issues as simply matters of local history were it not for the fact that they were all in some measure tied to one of the main themes of the time—the crown's chronic lack of money. James and Charles no doubt banned the erection of new buildings in good faith, but they enforced the ban not by pulling down new buildings but by taxing those who erected them—a procedure that pleased neither the City authorities who had asked for their destruction, nor the builders who paid the taxes, nor the tenants who had to rent them. The new gilds of small masters may have been designed in the interests of their members, but they tended to work to the profit of the businessman who purchased a charter and privileges on their behalf. And the new corporation of Westminster and the suburbs was also expected to raise money for the crown. For those reasons, all these local issues got drawn into the general disagreement between king and parliament.

But of course there were developments in London to which there were really no provincial equivalents. The Tudor and Stuart monarchy depended for its stability partly on a strict censorship of the written word and the suppression of popular discussion about affairs of state. In the small communities of provincial England those restrictions were enforced with some success; but as London grew larger not all the powers of the Star Chamber could effectively quell the pamphleteering and the gossip of the capital. The Earl of Clarendon, reflecting upon the reigns of James I and Charles I put this point trenchantly.

> There cannot be a better instance of the unruly and mutinous spirit of the city of London, which was the sink of all the ill humour of the kingdom, than the triumphant entry which some persons at that time made into London, who had been before seen upon pillories, and stigmatized as libellous and infamous offenders; of which classis of men scarce any age can afford the like.[5]

Nor did those ill humours remain in that sink, for the gossip and rumours of London were circulated to the provincial gentry by assiduous letter writers and whispered in taverns by the carters and carriers who handled inland trade. Moreover, to the exciting political and social gossip of the taverns there were added the less exciting but potentially more dangerous sermons of the radical clergy. Londoners could afford the best preachers; Londoners got the best preachers; and most of the best preachers were Puritans.

Even more important was the fact that London owed its expansion partly to a change in the habits of the country gentry. Members of that class had long been visiting the capital on legal and other business. But in the early seventeenth century their visits seem to have become longer and more frequent, although it was still the custom for them to stay in hotels and lodgings rather than to

[5] Edward Hyde, Earl of Clarendon, *History of the Rebellion and Civil Wars* (1839), i. 323-4.

possess town houses of their own. Lawsuits were the curse of the age and few gentlemen could avoid them. London was the great market both for the purchase of land and for the negotiation of marriages. Above all, it was the one place in England that could offer real relief from the intolerable tedium of country life. And, with the increasing use of the coach, men no longer found it so easy to leave their wives at home. The enthusiasm with which their wives accompanied them led to James's famous and ungallant outburst against:

> Those swarms of gentry who, through the instigation of their wives and to new model and fashion their daughters (who, if they were unmarried marred their reputations, and if married lost them), neglect their country hospitality and are a burden to the city and a general nuisance to the kingdom.[6]

For the matter was serious. The essentially patriarchal system of Stuart England depended on the willingness of landlords to reside in the provinces where they could act both as employers and as representatives of the state. Landlords who spent much or all of their time in London served neither purpose. Nor was this all. When parliament was in abeyance, visits to London provided great opportunities for the opposition leaders to keep in touch with each other. And if the Venetian ambassador is to be trusted, Charles was both aware of those opportunities and alarmed by them. Consequently, it is not surprising to find that measures to prevent the growth of London in general were increasingly supplemented by others to discourage the gentry in particular. Some of those measures could be indirect, as one gossip-writer explained to his client.

> We have very plausible things done of late. To encourage Gentlemen to live more willingly in the country all Game Fowl— as Pheasants, Partridges, Ducks and Hares—are by proclamation forbidden to be dressed or eaten in any Inns, and Butchers forbidden to be Graziers.[7]

Normally, however, a more direct approach was preferred; the gentry were ordered out of town by proclamation and laggards

[6] I. Disraeli, *Curiosities of Literature* (1834), vi. 175.
[7] W. Knowler, *The Earl of Stafford's Letters and Dispatches* (1739), i. 176.

risked prosecution in the Star Chamber. How far provincial life benefited we don't know; but it can hardly have pleased either the gentry who were treated like schoolboys or the London catering and entertaining industries that depended on their custom.

Finally, it must not be forgotten that London was the financial centre of the economy and that the Stuarts were dependent on the City for loans in a twofold sense—they depended on the citizens to provide the money and on the Lord Mayors and aldermen to collect that money for them, since no banking system yet existed. His ability to borrow from the City had enabled James to dispense with Parliament for nearly ten years. It was Charles' inability to continue borrowing that forced him to call Parliament in 1640. And under James, Londoners had not only lent generously to the crown but they had largely financed the settlement of Ireland on the crown's behalf. One of the major mistakes of the Stuarts was to destroy their credit with the City. And this is how Clarendon put the matter: as London was rich

> . . . it was looked upon too much of late time as a com-mon stock not easy to be exhausted, and as a body not to be grieved by ordinary acts of injustice; and therefore it was not only a resort, in all cases of necessity, for the sudden borrowing great sums of money . . . but it was thought reasonable, upon any specious pretences, to revoke the security that was at any time given for money so borrowed. So . . . a grant made by the King in the beginning of his reign (in consideration of great. sums of money) of good quantities of land in Ireland and the city of Londonderry there, was avoided by a suit in the star chamber; all the lands, after a vast expense in building and planting, re-sumed into the king's hands, and a fine of fifty thousand pounds imposed upon the city. Which sentence . . . made a general im-pression in the minds of the citizens of all conditions, much to the disadvantage of the court; and though the king afterwards remitted to them the benefit of that sentence, they imputed that to the power of the parliament, and rather remembered how it had been taken from them, than by whom it was restored.[8]

[8] Clarendon, ii. 142–3.

Thus, if no great social conflicts appear in the history of London at this time, there was plenty of friction. And that friction was important. As I see it, the famous Civil War was the result less of a major social conflict than of the break-down of a clumsy political machine in the hands of a remarkably inefficient operator. But the difficulties of Charles I were increased by changes that were making England more difficult to govern, and the growth of London was among the most important of those changes. And when the machine did break down the influence of London was vital. It was fear of the London crowd that on occasion drove the House of Lords to agree with the House of Commons; it was the City authorities who protected the five members of the Commons whom Charles tried to arrest for treason. And it was the City militia that prevented Charles from opening the war with a knockout blow. That was why some were to attribute all the political evils of the time to London.

12

London as an 'Engine of Economic Growth'

THE concepts of centre and periphery do not easily fit the economy of a country except, perhaps, in a metaphorical sense. For economies progress from a state of self-sufficiency to one of regional specialisation, and regional specialisation creates a pattern that is essentially policentric. Different activities develop around different centres that are linked to each other by a web of communications and trade. One may easily speak of textile centres, of mining centres, of commercial centres. But it is with less confidence that one can speak of a centre to the economy as a whole; and especially when the economy in question is largely agricultural, for agriculture is essentially a dispersed activity that defies centralisation. Yet it can be argued that, in the seventeenth century, London was in an important sense the economic centre of England.

The arguments for seeing it as such are basically two. The first, and minor, may be dealt with briefly. It lies in the fact that, when one looks for emerging areas of specialisation in Tudor and Stuart England, London is prominent under a variety of headings. It was the largest centre of population in the country; at the beginning of the sixteenth century it was probably five times as large as the largest provincial town; at the end of the seventeenth century it was fifteen times as large. Consequently it was the most important single market for consumer goods and, in an age when most consumer goods industries were carried on in close proximity to the consumer, it was the largest centre of such industries. It was the country's largest port, and as a result its chief commercial and financial centre. As the country's largest town, and as the centre of government, it was the obvious location for ambitious professional men. The centralization of the English political and legal systems meant that only in London were the rewards of government service or legal practice of much substance. Then, as now, it was the most profitable location for doctors, especially as many were content to diagnose and prescribe for an illness by correspondence. As the one town in which commercial publishing and printing were allowed, it naturally attracted the professional writer. And although ecclesiastical posts in London do not seem to have been exceptionally remunerative, ambitious bishops and clergymen were likely to spend considerable time there in search of preferment, if not for more spiritual reasons. As the largest town – and moreover one in which the Court normally resided – it offered a wider range of urban amenities than any other place in England and thereby attracted the gentleman bored with the intolerable tedium of country life: an attraction that was intensified by the possibility, when in London, of dabbling in politics, obtaining favours from those in power, borrowing money, buying or selling land, arranging marriages for his children, and generally meeting men of his own social class from other regions.

In all these respects London both influenced and was influenced by developments in the provinces, and the main difference between the sixteenth and seventeenth centuries was one of degree. London was already the centre of commercial and professional life in the early sixteenth century, but it was only in the 1580s that the development of the theatre, the conversion of large houses into taverns, and the complaints of contemporaries began to suggest that London was becoming important as a centre of social intercourse; and its population seems to have grown more substantially after 1600 than before. Consequently, on the principle that, when carried beyond a certain point, differences of degree become differences of kind, it might well be argued that, whereas during the sixteenth century London was highly influential, in the seventeenth century it took on the role of the country's economic centre.

But the major argument for attributing to it that role is more substantial. It can be appreciated only if the nature of the English economy at that time is borne in mind. That economy was, above all else, small. Not only was its total population small – about a tenth of that of modern England – but the great majority of that population lived in small communities and worked on small farms or in small workshops by methods that yielded only a small output per head. The fact that most men lived in small communities meant that a large proportion of them still had some access to land and could produce at least some of their own foodstuffs; and to that extent there persisted a strong subsistence element in the economy. The fact that communities were small, and that most goods were produced in or near the place at which they were consumed, meant that much commercial production was for small local markets. The fact that output per head was low meant that the national income was small, not only in its total volume, but also in the range of goods and services that composed it. Experience suggests that few economies of that nature contain within themselves self-generating tendencies to change. They can remain stable for centuries. For neither subsistence production nor production for small local markets encourages either a growth in investment or the division of labour – the twin engines of economic growth. And the availability of only a narrow range of consumer goods and services is notoriously a great disincentive to effort, and an encouragement to what in the sixteenth and seventeenth centuries was denounced as laziness, but is now more politely described as leisure preference.

In such an economy, substantial change is likely to come about only as a result of one or both of two factors. A growth in population will increase the demand for basic necessities and, by enlarging the markets for them, stimulate both investment and the division of labour. A growth in non-local trade will not only widen markets, and thereby stimulate investment and specialisation, but will provide an additional stimulus to effort by widening the range of goods available. Both of these factors were at work in Tudor and Stuart England, and it was with respect to them that the role of London changed in such a way as to justify the concept of the capital as the centre of the economy.

Anything said about population change in the sixteenth and seventeenth centuries must of necessity be largely speculative, for the scanty data afford hints rather than firm conclusions. Yet two propositions seem reasonably secure. In the sixteenth century the growth of population was fairly general throughout the country, and although the rate of growth was highest in London the greatest volume of growth took place in the provinces. A reasonable guess migth be that, whereas the population of England and Wales increased by something like a million, that of London may not have increased by more than one hundred and fifty thousand. Thus the major impetus to increased agricultural and industrial production came from provincial rather than from London demand, especially as London was in some measure fed on imported grain. In the seventeenth century, however, there were signs of a new demographic pattern. In many parts of the provinces the growth of population seems to have slowed down;

substantial growth seems to have been confined to three areas. One was Tyneside, where the coal industry was expanding largely in response to London demand. Another was in the West Midlands, where the metal industries were flourishing. But the most pronounced growth occurred in and around London. The reasons for these changes are still obscure. In some areas the age of marriage seems to have risen and the birth rate to have fallen. There is some evidence of a major epidemic in the 1640s. But one factor was undoubtedly the massive migration to London that both increased the population of the capital and depressed that of the provinces. And whatever the reasons for that migration may have been, its result was that, in the seventeenth century, the dynamic effects of population growth on the economy as a whole were increasingly mediated through London.

A comparable change may be discerned in the case of foreign trade, the most obvious form of that non-local trade that provides a stimulus to simple economies. In purely quantitative terms, it appears that London's proportion of total overseas trade may have declined slightly in the seventeenth century. But what is important is a change that occurred in the nature of English trade. Economists draw a useful distinction between trade expansion that is primarily export-led and expansion that is primarily import-led. In the first case trade expands because, as in modern Germany, of the efficiency of the export industries and their ability to undersell competitors abroad. In such circumstances the dynamic factor is obviously to be found in the exporting industry; merchants may add an additional dynamic factor by opening new markets; but on the other hand their role may be the largely passive one of moving a larger quantity of goods along established channels. In the case of sixteenth-century England, it is clear that trade expansion was primarily export-led. Trade was buoyant in the first half of the century when the superiority of the English cloth industry was marked. It became sluggish in the second half of the century, and by the end of the century there were increasing complaints about the difficulties of competing with the reviving textile industries on the Continent. This was the standard explanation of commercial difficulties from the 1590s until the 1630s. It was this competition that made the increase of export taxes by king and Merchant Adventures so burdensome in the early seventeenth century. It was this competition that inspired so much legislation and so many projects designed to prevent the export of English and Irish wool and English fuller's earth to foreign rivals and to improve the quality of English textiles. The rise in exports was, of course, accompanied by a rise in imports. But it was not always easy to find returns that could profitably be sold in England, and in consequence there was an influx of bullion that contributed to the rise in prices. In this process, the role of the London merchants seems to have been largely passive. Their efforts to find new markets were more spectacular than fruitful, and for the most part they performed the passive role of moving increasing quantities of goods into the Netherlands for distribution throughout Europe by foreigners. Thus in overseas trade, as in demographic change, the dynamic factor during the sixteenth century has to be sought in the provinces rather than in London.

But in seventeenth-century England, as in the England of today, trade expansion became increasingly import-led. Trade grew, less because of the competitive efficiency of English industry, than because of the English demand for foreign goods. For to the demand for such traditional imports as linens, expensive silks and wines – a demand that grew with the population – there was added a vigorous market for the fruits, the cheap silks, the cheap spices, the cheap sugar, and such new commodities as tobacco and calicoes that flowed in gradually mounting quantities from Spain, the Mediterranean, Africa, America and the East and West Indies. That appetite for imports was a dominant feature of English trade throughout the seventeenth century and goes far to explain why, in that century, Englishmen were so often concerned with the problem of the balance of payments — for later experience has shown that import-led trade expansion and balance of payments problems often go together.

Moreover, the timing of the first balance-of-payments scare in seventeenth-century England may suggest one reason why English trade was becoming import-led rather than export-led. That scare came at the beginning of the second decade of the century – just before the notorious Cockaigne experiment – and it is tempting to see it as a delayed result of that big switch in agricultural incomes in favour of landlords and larger farmers that had taken place since the 1580s. It is reasonable to suppose the beneficiaries of that redistribution of income had a more than average propensity to consume imports – contemporary comment certainly suggests as much – and the delayed response to that redistribution may well be accounted for by the fact that it was those beneficiaries of income redistribution who largely met the cost of the Irish and Spanish wars through the payment of subsidies and the purchase of royal lands. It is easy to believe that, once the demands of wartime finance were ended, they indulged in an import spree. But if the change in the nature of English trade from export-led to import-led was started by a redistribution of the national income in favour of those with a greater propensity to consume imports, it was perpetuated by the gradual cheapening of such imports as spices and sugar and the introduction of new imports such as tobacco and calicoes – to name only the most obvious.

This change from export-led to import-led commercial expansion had one obvious implication: it meant that the dynamic element in trade expansion had shifted from the manufacturer to the merchant. Export-led growth depended on the competitive efficiency of the manufacturer; import-led growth depended on the enterprise of the merchant who scoured the world in search of desirable commodities to meet the English appetite for foreign wares. And a shift of the dynamic element from manufacturer to merchant meant, in seventeenth-century England, a shift from the provinces to London. And this new role of London was reinforced by two further circumstances. Imports, of course, had to be paid for. But they were paid for only in part by an increased export of English manufactures, despite the versatility of the provincial textile industries in producing new draperies for new markets. In large part, they were paid for by re-exports; and re-exporting was essentially the function of London merchants. Moreover when, as is usually the case, the rising tide of imports led to a movement for import substitution, that movement took an interesting turn. On paper, there were plenty of schemes for establishing in England the production of substitutes for imported manufactured goods. Some of the notorious monopolies granted by the early Stuarts were designed to that end. But most of these schemes remained on paper; most of the monopoly projects failed. The truth of the matter was that, textiles apart, most imports were of commodities that could not be produced in England. In textiles, there was some success in developing a silk industry on the basis of raw silk imported from the Levant – a development that took place mainly in London. But little success was achieved in the case of linen, for a linen industry would have required for its growth a large mass of cheap female labour that was already well employed in the woollen industry. And it was impossible for English workers to compete with the low-wage labour of India in the production of cottons. For the most part, import substitution took a different form. It took the form of substituting English colonies for foreign countries as sources of supply. Above all, it took the form of substituting the services of English ships and merchants for those of foreigners. The great import-substitution measures of the seventeenth century were not protective duties but the Navigation Acts. The competitor to be eliminated was not England's great industrial rival, which was France, but her commercial rival – the Netherlands. To re-phrase the matter in modern jargon, it was in the realm of invis-ible rather than in the realm of visible import that substitution occurred. And it is well known that in the financing of colonies and in the provision of shipping and mercantile services London played a major role. Once more, the dynamic factor is found in London rather than in the provinces.

Moreover, these demographic and commercial changes both promoted and were further stimulated by one of the major developments that took place in pre-industrial England – the creation of a system of communication that linked London to all parts of the provinces. The physical manifestations of that system were a rapidly growing fleet of coastal vessels that plied between London and all provincial ports; a growing fleet of barges on the Thames and its tributaries such as the Lea; a spreading network of carriers, who with their pack-horses or carts linked every town in England to the capital with a regular schedule of ser-vices; and a rash of shopkeepers in every town and important village linked by these carriers and these vessels to wholesalers in London. This distributive system not only brought produce to be consumed in or exported from London, and not only distributed London's imports throughout the country, but also brought wares from one part of England to be shipped onwards to other parts and provided channels along which news and people moved with ease. It was in the seventeenth century that London became the centre of England in the sense of being at the centre of a regular system of communications; a fact that was confirmed in the later seventeenth century by the establishment of a general post office based on the capital.

Thus, it can be argued that in the course of the sixteenth and seventeenth centuries the role of London in the English economy changed significantly. In the sixteenth century London was important as being the largest town with the largest mercantile com-munity and offering the widest range of urban amenities – but it was in no real sense the economic centre of the country. In the seven-teenth century it became the centre of the economy – not only or even mainly because it became larger and its range of urban ameni-ties became wider – but because the two dynamic factors conducing to change became increasingly channelled through it. The problem is to consider what can usefully be said about the pattern of relationships that consequently emerged between London and the rest of England. At a very high level of generalization, certain obvious comments suggest themselves. It is clear that the development of London was made possible or at least stimulated by some of the major changes that were occurring in English provincial life. Obviously the congregation of half a million people in a single urban community was made possible only by the increase in agricultural production and productivity that occurred in the England of the time. The migration of labour to the capital owed much to the nature of the English agrarian system. For in that system the effects of population pressure tended to be, not the sub-division of holdings into dwarf allotments that held men on the land, but the creation of a landless class that was usually able and often willing to move. In the sixteenth century they seem to have moved mainly to the remaining areas of woodlands and marsh where land, or at least the use of commons, was still available. But in the seventeenth century, as the forests dwindled and the marshlands were drained, they moved more and more towards London. At a rather higher social level the system of primogeniture, which often cast the younger sons of the gentry on to the world to shape their own fortunes, often sent them running in search of careers in either trade or the professions. The ability of the more prosperous landowners to make frequent visits to London obviously owed something to the rising rents that swelled their incomes after the 1580s. And it may have owed something to the development of the coach which, by making it more difficult for them to leave their wives at home, operated to make their visits both longer and more expensive. Clearly, London's commercial expansion was heavily dependent both on the capacity of provincial industry to supply it with exports and on the capacity of provincial consumers to take off its imports; in both respects the general expansion of the Tudor and Stuart economy made the growth of London possible.

Looking in the other direction, it is easy to accept the verdict of seventeenth-century writers that the London market was a major stimulus to production and regional specialisation in the provinces. What is more speculative is the effect on provincial life of the wider range of goods and services, whether imported or locally produced, that London had to offer. This wider range of goods and services must have raised the standard of living of those who were able to enjoy them, for it is a commonplace that beyond a certain very low level of consumption rising standards mean that a greater variety of goods rather than a greater volume of goods is consumed. What is less certain is the effect of the availability of this wider range of goods and services on productivity in England as a whole. It is tempting to believe that it did something, and possibly something very substantial, to reduce that leisure preference that is so serious an obstacle to economic expansion in simple economies. To test any such proposition empirically is impossible. But certainly Hume, Adam Smith and the classical economists – men who knew from first hand an economy not greatly dissimilar to that of Tudor and Stuart England – attached enormous importance to this effect of commercial growth. And modern growth economists have used very much the same arguments under the title of the demonstration effect of foreign commodities in under-developed economies.

In this respect it may be pertinent to ask who it was that consumed imported goods and was thereby open to their pressure to increase productivity. One class clearly was that of the landowners and it was a commonplace of contemporary satirists that some landlords, to meet their expenses in London, demanded greater rents from their tenants; and the need to pay these greater rents may well have led tenants to increase their output where possible. But had the consumption of imports and city-made goods been confined to the upper classes it is doubtful whether much weight could reasonably be attached to them as a spur to production. The significant feature of some of the most rapidly growing imports was that they penetrated a considerable way down the social scale. Tobacco seems to have been consumed by all classes except the very poor. Currants were so widely consumed that the Venetian ambassador was able to report somewhat mysteriously to the Doge and Senate that there was a season in England when it was so dishonourable for a man not to be able to consume currants that he would hang himself in shame if such a tragedy occurred. Cheap silks and cheap sugar were both enjoyed by the middle ranks of the population, and one of the standard objections to cheap Indian calicoes was that they made it impossible for a man to distinguish between his wife and his serving girl, a situation that causes embarrassment in all ages. The penetration of imported goods down the social scale is perhaps best illustrated by a comment made by Defoe in the reign of Queen Anne. One of the many objections to that lady was that she had many relations, with the result that deaths among them repeatedly plunged the English Court into mourning. One consequence was that the London Mercers were left with a stock of coloured ribbons and silks that they could not sell, and with a demand for black ribbons and silk that they found it difficult to supply. Explaining why the repercussions of the death of some minor German aristocrat were so profound, Defoe pointed out that by aristocratic convention every member of the court was bound to wear black on such an occasion, that every lady in or near London wore black in the hope of persuading her neighbours that she was connected with the court, and that every shop girl wore black in the hope of persuading the world that she was a lady. The truth of that explanation is, of course, irrelevant; the point is that Defoe's readers would accept the proposition that the shop girls were consumers of imported goods. And observations that point to a similar conclusion could be multiplied with ease.

Some years ago Professor Nef argued that in the seventeenth century the economic histories of France and England parted company. France, he asserted, remained true to the habits of civilised society by concentrating its resources on the production of articles of grace and beauty. England sank to a lower cultural level by diverting those forces to the production of cheap commodities in mass demand; he poured scorn on an economy that devoted so much labour and capital to the digging of coal. His point might have been made more effectively, although perhaps less dramatically, had he observed that much of England's import trade was aimed at the middle and lower classes. Nor is this fact perhaps very surprising. The calculations of the national income made by Gregory King at the end of the seventeenth century are no doubt unreliable in detail, but the interesting thing about them is that he places only about a quarter of the population on a level of extreme poverty. To the remaining three-quarters of the population, he attributes an income that leaves some margin over the basic needs for subsistence and therefore a margin from which imported and London-made goods might be purchased. And the buoyancy of what may be called the popular market for imported goods owed something to the fact that, in England, not only was taxation normally light but the upper classes were not able to claim exemption from it. Given this considerable penetration of society by imports and London-made goods, it is not difficult to believe that they were having some effect in diminishing men's leisure preference and so stimulating economic growth.

At a rather lower level of generalization, it is perhaps possible to make half-a-dozen points without sinking into details of local history that would be inappropriate here. Something can reasonably be said of the multitudinous complaints that were made at the time about London's development. On examination these complaints fall into three main groups of which one may be quickly dismissed, since it dealt essentially with problems of urbanization within London rather than with any relationship between the City and the provinces. The second group of complaints were really variants on the general theme of opportunity cost. The availability of goods and services in London and from London meant a change in men's patterns of expenditure that adversely affected the provinces.

If landlords went to the capital, employment, hospitality and charity in the provinces declined; if workers went to the capital, agricultural rents declined; if London merchants brought in East India calicoes, the provincial textile industry declined. Arguments of that type were abundant and not always ill-founded.

Finally, there was a third group of complaints based on the theme that Londoners used their economic power and political influence unjustly to exploit their provincial fellows. That theme found its most vigorous expression with respect to London's dominating position in England's trade in the late sixteenth and early seventeenth centuries. The reasons for London's dominating position were, of course, largely geographical: lying on a navigable river sixty miles inland and with easy overland access to all parts of the country, it was the obvious place for the collection of exports and the distribution of imports, especially when the main market to be served was that of the Netherlands. A merchant in a provincial port could draw only on the products of his hinterland for his exports and sell his imports only to the inhabitants of that hinterland. A merchant in London could draw exports from all parts of the country and distribute his imports as widely. As was said in the late seventeenth century, by comparison with London an out-port was a prison. Yet there seems to have been some substance in the argument that for a time the merchants of London used their predominance which these advantages gave them, first to obtain excessive privileges from the Crown, and then to use those privileges to exploit the producers and consumers of provincial England. Certainly it is difficult to refute that accusation with respect to the Merchant Adventurers of London during the reigns of Elizabeth and James, for it is clear that they then expanded their fortunes less by finding new markets for English cloth and cheaper supplies of English imports, than by squeezing both provincial and foreign merchants out of the profitable trade with the Netherlands. And it is easy to believe that having excluded foreign merchants so largely from that trade, they used their oligopolist position both to depress the price of English cloth at home and to raise the price of the imported goods that they placed on the English market. To that extent, at least, there was some justification for the argument that London was parasitic on England. But it was a justification strictly limited in time for it did not apply to most of the sixteenth century, when foreign merchants were still active in English trade, and it did not apply to most of the seventeenth century, when the weaknesses of the English cloth industry and the development of trade with other parts of the world had greatly reduced the Merchants Adventurers' capacity for either good or evil.

Another topic that permits of some general remarks is the effect of London's growth on the economic geography of the country. For reasons of transport, London's demand for such bulky commodities as grain, hay and wood fuel, and for such perishable commodities as fruit and vegetables, was met for the most part from the counties adjacent to it; and for the same reason the same area provided it with most of its meat supply. The result was to intensify the agricultural nature of south-eastern England and to push the major industrial areas away from the capital even before that process was completed by the use of steam power. In the sixteenth and early seventeenth centuries there were considerable textile industries in Kent, Surrey, Hampshire and Berkshire and a flourishing iron industry in the Weald. By the end of the seventeenth century those textile industries had virtually disappeared and the Wealden iron industry was languishing. One reason given by contemporaries was that the London demand for food kept food prices high; in consequence wages in the area from which London drew its food were high; and so industry was lost to areas where both food and labour were cheaper. Unfortunately the price and wage data that have survived do not enable us to test that argument, although it is clear that from the 1590s wages in London itself rose increasingly above their level in the more distant parts of the country. And whether or not the wage argument was valid, it is clear that entrepreneurs within sixty or eighty miles of the capital found agriculture more profitable than industry. The textile areas of Kent turned to the fattening of cattle; the textile towns of Reading and Newbury turned to the processing of and trading in grain for the metropolitan market. In the Weald it was found more profitable to root up coppices and convert the land to pasture than to continue it under wood for the supply of the iron industry.

London's demand for food and fuel was not, of course, confined to the neighbouring counties. But elsewhere it was less intense and more selective. Dairy produce came from Cheshire and Suffolk, coal from Newcastle; store cattle for fattening in the south-east came not only from the north and west but in increasing numbers from Scotland and Ireland.

For the most part, London's own industries were able to overcome the handicap of high wages. Many of them – such as building and tailoring – were by their nature best carried on, or necessarily carried on, in close proximity to the consumer. Luxury trades, in which labour formed only a small proportion of costs, were best carried on in the capital that formed their largest market. Some, such as tanning and sugar-refining, remained tied to the capital because of the availability of their raw material. Others, like silk-weaving, were carried on largely by alien immigrants who found the capital more congenial and more hospitable than small country towns. But there can be discerned some movement of industry from London to the provinces, the most notable examples being the movement of the hosiery industry to Nottingham, of the shoemaking industry to Northampton, of the silk-throwing industry to north Essex. And it is possible to discern a significant division between London and the provinces in the matter of industry; Londoners added the finishing touches to many wares, but the initial stages of production were carried on in the provinces where labour was cheaper and water power more abundant. Clothes were made in London not only for Londoners but for the provincial upper classes; but cloth was made in the provinces. London had a large cutlery industry, but it used blades forged in Sheffield or the West Midlands. And as Professor Barker has recently shown, the flourishing London clock and watchmaking industry was based on the assembly of parts made in Lancashire.

There is, however, only a limited profit in thus discussing London and the provinces, for a major feature in the English scene was the fact that Londoners and provincials did not crystallize as completely separate groups of people. One of the most obvious characteristics of the English gentry was that they tended to retain their provincial homes and take lodgings or houses in London rather than shift from the countryside permanently to the city. At any time in the seventeenth century many Londoners were first-generation immigrants to the city; many who were permanently domiciled in the city retained some property or at least family connections in the countryside; and a significant part of the city's population consisted of people visiting it for purposes of education or business or pleasure for a period that, although it might last for some years, was not intended to be permanent. It was this situation that made the influence of London so pervasive.

A final point that may be worth making is that the pattern of relationships that appeared so clearly in the seventeenth century proved not to be permanent. In the course of the eighteenth century population growth became less confined to the city and consequently the increase in the demand for agricultural produce became more diffused, especially with the growth of subsidised exports. Also in the course of that century foreign trade became once more export-led rather than import-led, so that the dynamic factor shifts once more to the manufacturing areas. And the improved network of communications could be used by provincial merchants and by provincial manufacturers to distribute goods other than through the capital. And as one observes this modification in the pattern, one is inevitably reminded of the theory of international trade that depicted international trade as 'an engine of economic growth' by virtue of the fact that, although in the earlier stages of development industrialized countries stimulated mainly primary production in other parts of the world, in the course of time the latter producers by a process of import substitution tended to become industrialized themselves. There is, perhaps, sufficient similarity between that model and what happened in seventeenth-century England to justify the title of this paper.

Index

Spanish Company 102, 126
speculators 160
squirearchy 108, 110, 111
—, *see also* gentry, landed
Staplers 98, 102
—, *see also* wool
Star Chamber 78, 118, 180, 182
starchmakers' company 45-6, 47
Starkey, Thomas 137
State Papers, England 34, 123
Strype, John 168-9
Stuarts *see* Charles I; James I
Stumpe, William 85
subsistence 186-7, 194
Summerson, Sir John 116
sumptuary legislation 51, 84
Supple, B.E. 33-4, 156
Sweezy, P.M. 135

Tawney, R.H. 4-5, 16-17, 18-19, 20, 23, 25, 27, 32, 36, 91, 108, 146, 147, 149-50, 162
'Tawney's century' 17, 149, 161-2
taxation 60, 117, 120, 140, 160-1, 172, 194
—, advantages of light 161
—, *see also* crown finances
technological change 44, 124, 126, 137-8, 147, 154
—, *see also* economic growth; economic systems, change in
tenure *see* landlords; primogeniture
textile production 84, 93, 96, 97, 124, 126, 139, 154, 155, 188, 190, 196
—, embryo factory system 86
—, regulation of 50, 51, 52-3, 55-9
—, textile centres 48-9
—, *see also* calicoes; cloth trade; New Draperies; New Drapery at Hatfield; silk; trade, and textiles; wool
theatre *see* London, theatre
Thirty Years War 121, 123
Thompson, E.P. 4-5
thought *see* economic thought; political thought; religion, religious thought
tobacco 189, 190, 193
Tout, T.F. 107
towns, contrasted with country 47, 49-50, 98
—, corporate 175
—, and extra-urban jurisdiction 49-50, 56-7, 179
—, gild regulation in 43-4, 47, 48, 155 *see also* companies; gilds
—, industry in 47
—, London/provincial towns compared 173
—, problems in 106, 117-18

—, provincial town markets 73
—, regulations in 98, 155
—, settlement laws of 51
—, as social product 105
—, social structure 175
—, society in 116-17
—, suburbs 47, 48, 69-70, 73, 79, 179
—, trade in 71, 75-6
—, *see also* London
trade 10, 106
—, coastal 65-6, 71, 72, 74, 78
—, foreign 82, 93, 138, 145, 155-6, 188, 195, 198
—, inland 140, 141, 191, 198
—, overland 78 n.8, 79
—, statistics 68 n.5, 82, 84, 119, 138, 145, 151, 172
—, terms of 87, 90
—, textiles 123, 188
—, *see also* exports; grain trade; imports; London, food trade and export trade; merchants; re-exports; slave trade; towns, trade in; wool, trade
transport 72, 74, 75, 78, 79, 106, 114, 137, 141, 152, 181, 196
—, carters and carriers 180, 191
—, *see also* London, transport
Trevor-Roper, H.R. 149
Tudors *see* Henry VIII; Mary I
turnips 152

underdevelopment 7, 16-20, 147, 150, 160, 193
—, *see also* development economics; economic backwardness; economic systems; 'pre-industrial'
underemployment 137, 146
—, *see also* leisure preference
unemployment 51, 97, 99, 102, 127, 137, 171
—, *see also* employment; poor law
Universities 158, 160
—, *see also* Cambridge University; London, University; Oxford University
Unwin, George 13, 81, 100 n.2
usury laws 87, 91 n.2
—, *see also* interest, rates of

Veblen, Thorstein 7, 14
Venice, ambassador to England 95, 181, 193
—, State Papers 113, 123

wage rates 137, 139, 144-5, 146, 151, 155, 165-6, 168, 169, 171, 196
—, wage-earners 170, 175